JUST KIDS

JUST KIDS

YOUTH ACTIVISM AND RHETORICAL AGENCY

Risa Applegarth

THE OHIO STATE UNIVERSITY PRESS
COLUMBUS

Library of Congress Cataloging-in-Publication Data
Names: Applegarth, Risa, author.
Title: Just kids : youth activism and rhetorical agency / Risa Applegarth.
Description: Columbus : The Ohio State University Press, [2024] | Includes bibliographical
    references and index. | Summary: "Analyzes case studies around youth-led activism on
    issues such as war and peace, immigrant rights, and gun reform to show how children
    and teens push back against public discourse that treats them as symbols rather than
    as effective organizers, speakers, writers, and demonstrators"—Provided by publisher.
Identifiers: L CCN 2 023043721 | I SBN 9 780814215319 (hardback) | I SBN 0 814215319
    (hardback) | ISBN 9780814283325 (ebook) | ISBN 0814283322 (ebook)
Subjects: LCSH: Youth movements—Case studies. | Activism—Case studies. | Social
    change—Case studies. | Rhetoric—Social aspects.
Classification: LCC HM831 .A497 2024
LC record available at https://lccn.loc.gov/2023043721

Other identifiers: ISBN 9780814258996 (paperback) | ISBN 0814258999 (paperback)

Cover design by Brad Norr
Text design by Juliet Williams
Type set in Adobe Minion Pro

For Harriet Loyd, Winnie Loyd, and Arthur Applegarth

CONTENTS

ACKNOWLEDGMENTS

To the extent that this book sheds light on the rhetorical practices of young activists and advocates for social change, it does so entirely due to the generosity of many people, especially the research participants who took time to meet with me for in-person and video interviews across several years—who spoke to me after getting off work, between classes, over summer break, on snow days, in the midst of everything else happening in their lives. To these participants: I am so grateful for the work you have done, the work you're still doing, and the care with which you shared that work with me.

I owe gratitude to many people whose personal, intellectual, or institutional support has enabled this research. First among them is Matt Loyd, who generously supports me from start to finish and makes it look easy the whole while. I don't remember when you first told me about the Children's Peace Statue project, but I couldn't have imagined this book would eventually be the outcome. Thank you for sharing that story and so much else with me since then.

Many talented librarians and archivists enabled this research, including the incomparable Jenny Dale at UNCG's Jackson Library. Marilee Schmit Nason, curator at the Anderson-Abruzzo Albuquerque International Balloon Museum, shared generously of her time and expertise. Camy Condon not only trusted me with her incredible personal archive related to the Children's Peace

Statue, but she gave me a glimpse of what a formidable force for good she's been in so many people's lives.

This book would not exist if not for the encouragement and insight I had the good fortune to receive from Tara Cyphers at The Ohio State University Press. Across conversations, coffees, and emails over the years, you've offered me just what I needed, just when I needed it. I don't know quite how people manage to write books without you cheering them on—I'm glad I didn't have to try. I am grateful as well to the two readers who pushed my thinking further through their insightful responses to the manuscript.

Several friends, writing partners, and writing groups sustained, inspired, and accountability-ed me to move this project from idea to its current form. Shevaun Watson and Jen Borda invited me to join their writing group in 2018, when my doubt was deep; their encouragement buoyed me month by month across the next several difficult years and kept me striving to create pages worthy of their brilliance. To my long-standing writing partners and extraordinary friends Sarah Hallenbeck, Lindsay Rose Russell, Erin Branch, and Heather Branstetter: we lost so much when we lost Chelsea Redeker Milbourne in 2020, but your presence (and hers) is indelible in my writing and thinking. Here at UNCG I have benefited from writing group exchanges with Jen Feather, Jennifer Keith, Amy Vines, Heather Brook Adams, and Jenn Park; the piercing attention of these smart readers has improved this project and deepened my appreciation for writing in community.

The numerous forms of institutional support I have received from UNCG enabled me to move this research forward at several crucial junctures, including a Friedlaender Award from the English Department, a Faculty First Award from the Provost's Office, a transcription grant from the Humanities Network and Consortium, a subvention grant from the Office of Sponsored Research, and a Linda Arnold Carlisle Research Grant from the Program in Women's, Gender, and Sexuality Studies. The support I've received from friends and colleagues here has been vital and sustaining; thank you especially to Xhenet Aliu, Danielle Bouchard, Claudia Cabello-Hutt, Sarah Jane Cervenak, Tony Cuda, Paul Cloninger, Noel Cox, Alyson Everhart, Jen Feather, Holly Goddard Jones, Jennifer Keith, Lisa Levenstein, Cybelle McFadden, Christian Moraru, Nancy Myers, Derek Palacio, Anne Parsons, Emilia Phillips, Scott Romine, Maria Sánchez, Gia Coturri Sorenson, Anne Wallace, Karen Weyler, Jennifer Whitaker, Bonnie Yarbrough, and Steve Yarbrough. To Heather Adams I owe boundless gratitude for a collaborative partnership that stretches across so many realms—intellectual, administrative, pedagogical, personal. You inspire me as a teacher, push me as a writer and researcher, buoy me as a colleague and friend. May our cup always overflow; may we never see the end of our perpetual agenda.

It is a pleasure to be indebted to colleagues and friends throughout the profession who spur my thinking with their good questions and delight me by entertaining my silly ones: Jacob Babb, Dylan Dryer, Jess Enoch, Michael Faris, David Gold, Sarah Hallenbeck, Jordynn Jack, Melanie Kill, Kt Leuschen, Heather Lindenman, Paul Lynch, Andrea McCrary, Becca Richards, Courtney Rivard, Lindsay Rose Russell, Angie Rousaville, Carl Schlachte, Wendy Sharer, Michelle Smith, Amy Wan, Scott Wible, and Courtney Adams Wooten.

My marvelous friends and family have provided a supportive community beyond what any one person deserves. I'm thankful for the love of the whole tremendous Fritzel, Layton, Muich, and Campbell clans. I am bountifully loved, supported, and entertained by Joy Sparks, matriarch and card sharp; Chenoa Sowa, the bossy big sister everyone should have; Dakota Applegarth, the little brother who can still transform a summer afternoon into a long adventure; Robert Sowa, generous and goofy in equal (abundant) measure; and Avery Sowa, the kindest and most thoughtful kid-turned-grown-up I've ever known. In addition to the marvelous family I began with, I have also had the incredible fortune to be welcomed warmly into the loving and fun-loving family of my in-laws. Dick, Mary, Thomas, Andrew, and Katie: as parents, siblings, and friends, you all are unbeatable. From the earliest days of Hervey family gatherings in Amarillo and meeting Mary Louise in Albuquerque, I've been treated—and I've felt—as though I belonged with you all; thank you. I'm especially grateful to Roger and Leta Loyd, our nearby North Carolina family for almost two decades and certainly the most serious Duke fans I have deeply loved. An extra measure of gratitude is due to Dick Loyd for his beautiful photographs of the Children's Peace Statue.

Claudia Brown, you didn't get to see this, but you would have *really* loved it.

Dear friends near and far have sustained me as the ideas for this project developed. To Leslie Eager I am so grateful for the (approximately) one million meals, books, movies, walks, and conversations we've enjoyed—including during our perilous wintertime writing retreat—and all the ones still ahead. Autumn Eakin, Lisa Del Monte, Kelly Ross, Tom Guthrie, Kate Guthrie, Diane Aycock, Teague Lyons, Ginger Moored, Heather Adams, Cris Nuñez, Sarah Estow, Jen Feather, Audra Abt, Amy Vines, and Martijn Van Hasselt: you are the best. Underlying every moment and behind everything else is my love and gratitude for Matthew, Harriet, Winnie, and Arthur: our life together is a gift. Any writing I do needs to matter as much as baking, hiking, painting, and playing with you all. Thanks for your patience; now let's go outside.

Activism, Agency, and the Temporality of Childhood

"That resolution will not pass the Senate," Dianne Feinstein said, interrupting the prepared speech of a sixteen-year-old visiting her San Francisco office in February 2019, "and you can take that back to whoever sent you here." The late senator was meeting with a group of young people—ranging in age from eleven to twenty-four and affiliated with the Sunrise Movement, the Bay Area Earth Guardians, and Youth Vs. Apocalypse—who were asking her to vote in favor of the Green New Deal resolution, introduced a few weeks earlier by New York Representative Alexandria Ocasio-Cortez and Massachusetts Senator Edward Markey. But the meeting had quickly devolved, with Senator Feinstein "lecturing" and "condescending" to the group and both parties interrupting each other in frustration.[1] When the Sunrise Movement released video of the contentious encounter, it quickly went viral, generating headlines, press releases, interviews, even a *Saturday Night Live* sketch in which an aggravated Feinstein, portrayed by Cecily Strong, repeatedly asks for a "do-over" as she lashes out and then registers how her caustic dismissal of idealistic children might appear to her audience.

---

1. Lisa Friedman, "Dianne Feinstein Lectures Children Who Want Green New Deal," *New York Times*, February 22, 2019, https://www.nytimes.com/2019/02/22/climate/feinstein-sunrise-green-new-deal.html; and Peter Wade, "Sen. Dianne Feinstein Condescends to Kid Activists Touting Green New Deal," *Rolling Stone*, February 23, 2019, https://www.rollingstone.com/politics/politics-news/feinstein-green-new-deal-activists-799240/.

What does such a scene indicate about the rhetorical power of young activists, about their relationships with their audiences, and about the persuasive tactics they employ to accomplish their ends? This book begins from such scenes, in which public and media attention rests upon children, teens, and other youth as they engage in acts of petition, protest, organizing, and public address. In some ways, such scenes are (or are made into) spectacles. Media coverage emphasized this: the *New York Times* led with the headline "Dianne Feinstein Lectures Children"; *Rolling Stone* announced, "Dianne Feinstein Condescends to Kid Activists"; and *USA Today* reported "Dianne Feinstein Criticized for Arguing with Kids."[2] These headlines exploit the surprising juxtaposition of a senior US senator—and a Democrat, ostensibly sympathetic with the activists' cause—responding with sarcasm and impatience during a public encounter with young people and generate clicks from the apparent generational contrast between Feinstein's age and the youthfulness of those confronting her.

Despite its treatment as media spectacle, the encounter between youth climate activists and Senator Feinstein also suggests the tensions between *symbolic power, rhetorical savvy,* and *material constraint* that motivate the inquiries in this book. Media framing of youth activism often relies upon a familiar understanding of young people as potent symbols, representing at various times *hope* or *naivete, innocence* or *exploitation,* either the pure intentions or the utter selfishness of the young. Although such polarities suggest the variability of contemporary associations with children and teenagers, they share a fundamental orientation toward young people as figures who represent either promising or fearful futures. The tendency to treat children as symbols rather than rhetors appears not only in news coverage but also within the encounter itself, as when Senator Feinstein retorts that the children can "take that back to whoever sent you here and tell them." This expression voices the charge, often levied at young people, that their words and actions are not their own, that they are not speaking but being manipulated by other agents who, by staging the encounter, are exploiting children's symbolic power. As sociologist Jessica Taft has argued, this is a common assumption—"that children who are involved in social movements or who engage in political speech are merely pawns of adult activists," victims of "brainwashing," whose claims can be "dismissed as mimicry."[3] The encounter between young activists and Senator Feinstein, in other words, reflects the reality that childhood is a potent rhetorical

2. Hayes, "'I Know What I'm Doing,'" *USA Today,* February 22, 2019, https://www.usatoday.com/story/news/politics/2019/02/22/dianne-feinstein-criticized-arguing-kids-over-green-new-deal/2956607002/.

3. Taft, *Kids Are In Charge,* 6.

construct often wielded but infrequently examined—and rarely considered from the standpoint of children. If children and young people are symbols of innocence and hope, or ciphers who mimic or are manipulated by the adults around them, in neither interpretation can they be understood as agents who act on and through their surroundings.

But this encounter can be viewed otherwise: as a demonstration of youth engaging in rhetoric, using their words and bodies to influence attitudes and induce actions. Whether their strategic rhetoric takes the form of traditional public protest, such as marching, assembling, and speechmaking, or newer forms of protest grounded in social media networks, such as directly engaging with elected officials through Twitter, young people's actions should make their agency as rhetors visible. This book contends that children and youth are not merely symbolic receptacles for the fears and hopes of adult audiences. Instead, the many young activists who are highlighted in this book act with rhetorical knowledge and purpose: they craft their speeches, time their remarks, choose their words; they share tactics and resources with supporters both online and in person; they stage events, build and maintain organizations, teach others how to hew to talking points in interviews with journalists and how to persuade reluctant organizations to become sponsors or allies. Despite a long-standing, well-established tendency of media organizations to portray young people as figures to be lauded, protected, or feared, young activists are clearly using their available means to alter the social, political, and material worlds they inhabit.[4]

In addition to foregrounding the contrast between viewing young people as potent symbols or as persuasive speakers, the confrontation between climate activists and Senator Feinstein also hints at the numerous material constraints young activists must navigate. After asking a sixteen-year-old speaker her age, Feinstein retorts, "You didn't vote for me." Material constraints bar children and teens from formal avenues of influence in many civic spaces—exclusions that necessitate creative tactics. For instance, the Dream Defenders—a group of teens and other young activists who began organizing Black youth in 2012 following Trayvon Martin's murder—occupied the Florida Capitol for thirty-one days in 2013, after George Zimmerman's acquittal, pressing legislators to repeal Florida's stand-your-ground law.[5] Through incursions into civic spaces (such as statehouses and Senate offices), young activists juxtapose their lack of voting power against the urgency of their demands. School

4. On the tendency of media to portray young people as lacking in agency, see Burman, "Between Identification and Subjectification"; Moeller, "Hierarchy of Innocence"; Raby and Sheppard, "Constructs of Childhood"; and Feldman, "Activists."

5. See "Our Story," https://DreamDefenders.org/our-story.

walkouts, likewise, convert material constraints experienced by young people into an avenue for demanding redress; required by law to be present at school, children and teens generate media coverage through their coordinated refusals to comply. Such refusals were employed widely, for instance, following the 2014 grand jury decision not to indict Darren Wilson for eighteen-year-old Mike Brown's murder and after twenty-year-old Daunte Wright was killed by Kim Potter in 2021.[6] Although adult commentators often deride young people—and Black youth in particular—for deviating from "proper procedure" or disrupting civic norms, an array of material barriers limit teens' and children's access to forms of protest. For instance, the activists I interviewed about their March For Our Lives organizing encountered numerous bureaucratic hurdles as they attempted, as fifteen- and sixteen-year-olds, to secure a city permit, rent sound equipment, purchase insurance for their events, and file paperwork to create an organization legally responsible for the funds they were receiving from community supporters. They relied heavily on the one eighteen-year-old among them to complete the numerous tasks that required the signature of a legal adult. Many of the forms of activism pursued by young people confront the legal and procedural barriers that limit their direct civic power.

In my approach to the rhetorical practices of young activists, I highlight the savviness and creativity they demonstrate in response to the widespread, unequally distributed barriers they experience to civic and political access. When and whether young people are granted a hearing depends on a host of interrelated factors, including age as well as race, sexuality, gender, dis/ability, class, language, religion, and nationality. In other words, as Barrie Thorne and other scholars in childhood studies have shown, "like gender, racial ethnicity and sexuality, age is an embodied form of difference that is both materially and discursively produced and embedded in relations of power and authority," and barriers to political power are not experienced evenly among the varied embodiments and identities of those under the legal age of adulthood.[7] In the case studies investigated in subsequent chapters, I ask: What avenues did these

6. See Elisa Crouch, "Students at Several St. Louis High Schools Walk Out in Protest," *St. Louis Post-Dispatch,* December 3, 2014, https://www.stltoday.com/news/local/education/students-at-several-st-louis-high-schools-walk-out-in-protest/article_98b9d02d-2948-5806-9d96-4afbbbdd33e6.html; Rebecca Klein, "High School Students around the Country Are Walking Out of Class for Ferguson," *Huffington Post,* December 1, 2014, https://www.huffpost.com/entry/high-school-students-protest-ferguson_n_6249802; Erin Golden, "Minnesota Students Stage Walkout to Protest Racial Injustice," *Star-Tribune,* April 19, 2021, https://www.startribune.com/minnesota-students-walk-out-of-class-to-protest-racial-injustice/600047739/; and "Hundreds Join Minneapolis Police Walkouts: 'Police Don't Care About Us,'" *The Guardian,* April 20, 2021, https://www.theguardian.com/us-news/2021/apr/19/minneapolis-st-paul-high-school-student-protest-walkout-daunte-wright-george-floyd.

7. Thorne, "Crafting the Interdisciplinary Field," 150.

collectives of young rhetors pursue when confronting an urgent, felt need for change in policy, law, or practice? For children, teens, and young people petitioning for a space to express their hope for peace, seeking protection from deportation, or requesting more restrictive laws governing the sale of deadly weapons, such requests demand exceptional rhetorical savvy, spoken as they are by individuals without official standing: nonconstituents, nonvoters, in many cases noncitizens.[8] The case studies that follow foreground the salience of age for rhetorical analysis, demonstrating that childhood is a construct that both facilitates and constrains rhetorical possibility. Age shapes encounters between interlocutors—as between Senator Feinstein and the group of activists who addressed her—and impacts how such encounters circulate to and are understood by broader audiences. Considering children, teens, and youth as strategic rhetors navigating constrained circumstances, therefore, not only confirms the significance of their activism but also invites reconsideration of their rhetorical agency. In the following pages of this introduction, I explore the connections that bring my analytical arguments and methodological commitments together, showing how these commitments led me to develop the concept of reflexive agency that I mobilize across the case study chapters. I then draw on work from childhood studies to clarify *youth* as a contingent and intersectional category of identification, connect this category to temporal dimensions of agency and reflexivity, and preview the arguments developed in each chapter.

INTERVIEW METHODS AND REFLEXIVE AGENCY

Two primary research questions orient me to the cases of youth activism that follow in this book:

1. How do young people navigate both their symbolic power and the material constraints that shape their circumstances? And how do they leverage these circumstances to achieve rhetorical (including social and political) purposes? In other words, how is age salient, both as opportunity and obstacle, in the situations young rhetors address?
2. What do the reflections of young activists (and former activists) indicate is important about their activism, on their own terms and in their own lives? In other words, how do interviews with people who are or were

---

8. This is not to suggest that being of legal voting age somehow dispenses with barriers to political power, of course, and the activism I analyze in this project both includes and exceeds a focus on citizenship; see Brandzel, *Against Citizenship*; Yam, *Inconvenient Strangers*, 18–24.

activists in their childhood, adolescence, or youth reveal how they navigate situations strategically and make sense of their own trajectories as rhetorical beings?

To address these questions, this project combines familiar forms of rhetorical analysis—attention to activists' spoken performances, staged events, media interviews, circulating texts, and so on—with qualitative interviews to enable "reflection about rhetoric's emergence, meaning, and influence."[9] In the words of researchers Amanda Nell Edgar and Andre E. Johnson, when rhetoric scholars "ask individuals to account for their own behaviors" through interviews, we "put an ear to the ground, listening for the ways local"—and individual—"histories and experiences reverberate through social movements."[10]

Seeking this "ear to the ground" perspective, I also undertook interviews because I was convinced by prior scholarship that talking *about* young people without also talking *with* them about their experiences would lead me away from my commitment to ethical research practices. Thus I sought in interviews and focus groups participants' perspectives on how their activism emerged, how it felt at the time, and how they viewed it in retrospect.[11] I expected that my interviews would yield insight into the prior schooling, writing, and speaking experiences that enabled young activists to develop the capacities they demonstrated in their work. Further, I anticipated that their perspectives would generate a clearer understanding of the emotional attachments and interpersonal networks that compelled these individuals to invest their time and energy toward activist ends.

What I found was that answering my questions led participants into complex reconsiderations of fluctuating cultural moments, gaps between what they recalled and what my archival research uncovered, and shifting relationships between their present and prior selves. Through interviews, these participants became my partners in discerning the significance of their activism over time—not only by shaping my reading of textual artifacts, archival documents, media coverage, and so on, but also because their retrospections expanded the time under consideration beyond the parameters of their most intense organizing. By asking about their preparations for the work they engaged in, their sense of successes and setbacks, and their assessment

---

9. McKinnon et al., "Articulating Text and Field," 4. See also Rai and Gottschalk Druschke, "On Being There," 2–3.

10. Edgar and Johnson, *Struggle Over Black Lives Matter*, xii.

11. The first iteration of this project received IRB approval in 2016 through UNCG IRB 16-0369. The expanded research received approval in 2018 through UNCG IRB 18-0202. See the appendices for interview and focus group questionnaires.

of what was most important about their activist work, I received responses that went straight to the heart of questions of rhetorical agency: How do we know what chains of cause and consequence precede and follow our actions? How can we say with confidence what factors led to the outcomes we experienced at the time—and if we would now diagnose our earlier rhetorical situations differently, is our later perspective more accurate or less so? Asking activists to revisit their experiences invited their ongoing formulation of their own agency and of themselves as agents. That is, although I took the agency of young activists as a given, I discovered that my participants' reflections about *what they did, why,* and *to what effect* led me into complex considerations of agency, as I witnessed participants working in the present to align (or speak to the disjuncture between) past and present selves, priorities, convictions, and actions. Thus both my analytical argument—that childhood is a construct that facilitates and constrains rhetorical possibility—and my theoretical concern—to conceptualize reflection as a site of rhetorical agency—emerge from my methodological commitment to seek young activists' perspectives directly.

My analysis of the cases of collective youth organizing that follow in this book demonstrates the first of these arguments, that childhood is a construct that impacts rhetors' strategic possibility. It is a *constraint* in Keith Grant-Davie's sense: a factor within the rhetorical landscape that rhetors must grapple with, both positively and negatively, toward the enactment of their ends. It is, in other words, a source of rhetorical potential that rhetors, young and old alike, may seek to mitigate or capitalize on. As rhetoricians Luke Winslow and Eli Mangold have argued, children's presence within an unfolding social movement activates widely shared associations with truth-telling clarity, moral obligation, and the threat of childhood's loss.[12] Such rhetorical possibilities might be minimized or amplified, as they carry both risks and opportunities for young people pursuing collective rhetorical goals. A fourteen-year-old activist might highlight her age to suggest she speaks with the clarity of an uncorrupted vision—or she might view her age as a detriment to being taken seriously as an informed speaker and choose language that downplays her youth to construct her authority in more conventional terms. The rhetorical salience of her age will vary contextually and in relation to other dimensions of her embodiment—her race, language, nationality, sexuality, dis/ability, class, religion, and more. The cases of collective organizing that follow in this book bear out this understanding of age as a rhetorically salient dimension of activism. Though their ages vary from as young as ten to as old as their

---

12. Winslow and Mangold, "Theorizing Rhetorical Children," 87–88.

midtwenties, these rhetors grapple with how to capitalize on the powerful symbolism of youth while still engaging with audiences as speakers rather than merely symbols.

Young people's rhetorical agency is strategic as well as reflexive, and each case study chapter unfolds strategic possibility as well as reflections that demonstrate how participants regard their activist work in retrospect. Each chapter analyzes the rhetorical tactics adopted by a collective, demonstrating how available means and audience uptakes are shaped by *age* as a salient dimension of their situations. I chose these cases because each is youth-led, large-scale, and sustained across multiple years. These collectives comprise scores of leaders and many thousands of variously involved participants as they attempt significant public interventions that prompt vigorous public response. The affordances and risks of childhood can be seen in the rearticulations experienced by young peace activists in chapter 1; in the racialized citizenship exclusions faced by im/migration activists in chapter 2; and in the rhetorical opening generated and exploited by the largely white teens advocating for gun reform in chapter 3. Carefully analyzing the situated, strategic work of young activists in each chapter, I explore how activists navigate constrained situations, material exclusions, and dismissal from adults, as well as how they leverage symbolic associations of childhood in pursuit of their shared goals. Demonstrating how age shapes each collective's rhetorical possibilities, I situate readers in specific tactics designed to meet a rhetorical context in which mitigating assumptions around childhood is necessary.

Such grappling with material and situational limitations and affordances, as young activists must undertake, is made easier by current understandings of agency in rhetorical studies, which have expanded both agents and forms of agency dramatically. When I assert that young people engaging in activism operate as rhetorical agents, readers outside of rhetorical studies might understand this to mean they make things happen in the world and might expect an account of what their efforts have amounted to: What laws have been passed? What policy platforms have been adopted? How has public discourse been changed by youth activism around issues such as gun violence or im/migration? Yet for readers within rhetoric, these questions miss the mark, grounded as they are in an understanding of agency as rooted in cause and effect, intentional action followed by consequence. Instead, many in rhetorical studies understand agency ecologically, involving interactions among not only rhetors and audiences but also shared discourses, material environments, technological objects, and complex networks. In rhetorical studies, agency involves us in questions that move beyond "Who convinced whom?" and "Who made this happen?"

Approaching the activism of young people from a perspective that affirms their fundamental rhetoricity, this book argues that youth exercise rhetorical agency not only through their navigation of complex constraints in pursuit of activist ends but also through their acts of retrospective reflection. Developing the concept of *reflexive agency* out of my interviews with activists, I demonstrate how activists, through metacognitive practices of reflection, articulate new linkages among the assemblages they have created, claim ownership over the significance of their work, and cultivate capacities toward undetermined, contingent futures. Rhetoric scholars Krista Ratcliffe and Kyle Jensen trace four types of agency, all of which operate "singly, relationally, and intersectionally," naming these *personal, discursive, cultural,* and *material* and reminding us that none of these forms of agency is "unlimited or unfettered."[13] Personal agency, the form with which I am most concerned here, names "the capacity and willingness of a person to act, which creates an opportunity to be heard; it is the power of people to think and act in relation to other people and things as well as other types of agencies, when addressing rhetorical problems."[14] Reflexive agency is a particular form of personal agency that emerged in my interviews as I asked activists to revisit their tactics and assessments of months or years prior. Participants articulated agency as *embodied experiences that endure,* as *rooted in perspectives that change over time,* and as *embodied capacities with unsettled future uses.* Working from these formulations, I define reflexive agency as a form of agency that constructs relations among prior, present, and future selves. Rooted in embodied experiences and inflected by temporal change, reflexive agency reaches back from present to past perspectives and practices of the self. It also reaches forward to future perspectives and practices, anticipating the self in uncertain future circumstances. Reflexive agency foregrounds the self and its capacities as unfinished, intersubjective, inescapably temporal, and engaged in perpetual becoming. In reflexive agency, rhetors renarrate their reasons and strategies, grapple with effects and consequences, and create links between prior and present selves. These are understudied but widely practiced forms of rhetorical agency that I can theorize on the basis of having solicited participants' reflections on their activism.

This formulation of reflexive agency bridges rhetorical studies and the "kinship" model of agency espoused within childhood studies by scholars such as Marah Gubar, who writes that adults and children "are akin to one another in that from the moment we are born (and even before then) we

---

13. Jensen and Ratcliffe, *Rhetorical Listening in Action,* 55–57.
14. Jensen and Ratcliffe, 55.

are immersed in multiple discourses not of our own making that influence who we are, how we think, what we do and say—and we never grow out of this compromised state."[15] In other words, children's rhetorical agency is not partial where adults' is complete, or developing where adults' is fully formed. Children's agency does not offer a definitional contrast, shoring up a binary or a too-porous boundary. Instead, agency—both its exercise and its contingencies—stretches in both directions along the line that separates adults from teens, adolescents, and children.

YOUTH AS A CONTINGENT, INTERSECTIONAL, EMBODIED CATEGORY

The rhetorical framework implied in my research questions is highly amenable to the transdisciplinary reach of scholarship in childhood studies. As scholars of childhood studies have long established, *childhood* as a category is historically contingent, imbued with meanings and contained by boundaries that vary across time and place.[16] Such scholarship underscores the myriad ways in which childhood, as cultural historians Caroline Levander and Carol Singley have argued, is "not only a biological fact but a cultural construct that encodes the complex, ever-shifting logic of a given group."[17] That is, boundaries between *child* and *adult,* and those surrounding more recently emerging concepts such as *adolescent* and *teen,* have developed in specific cultural and political contexts. Understanding *childhood* as a contingent, historically varying category—rather than one that appears naturally or aligns with universal experiences of growth and maturation—has enabled scholars across this rich interdisciplinary area to probe the specific mechanisms by which *childhood* is rendered salient, articulated to large-scale cultural projects. In the US, these projects include white supremacy, heteropatriarchy, and the production of neoliberal consumerist subjects.[18] As sociologist Jessica Taft has argued, sociohistorical approaches to childhood and adolescence emphasize that "age is not destiny" and that "what it means to be a child is context-dependent and malleable."[19]

---

15. Gubar, "Risky Business," 454.

16. Ariès, *Centuries of Childhood*; and Field and Simmons, *Global History of Black Girlhood.*

17. Levander and Singley, *American Child,* 4.

18. Raby, "Children's Participation"; Sánchez-Eppler, *Dependent States*; Webster, *Beyond the Boundaries*; Burman, "Between Identification and Subjectification"; and Stockton, *Queer Child.*

19. Taft, *Kids Are In Charge,* 5.

Key to the work of investigating *childhood* as a contingent, varying category has been articulating its production through (and its contributions to) frameworks of race, gender, and class. For instance, in Phillipe Ariès's sweeping history of the emergence of childhood, many of the characteristics now associated with childhood—as a protected stage, detached from economic production—first arose for white, aristocratic males, "the first group . . . to experience childhood as a set apart, specialized stage of life."[20] In contrast, Wilma King's groundbreaking work *Stolen Childhood* excavated the meaning of childhood for enslaved young people in the US, demonstrating that to the extent that childhood was in any way a protected status for these children, it was through the vigilant labors of their families endeavoring against outrageously inhumane circumstances to make it so.[21] In the "diverse and uneven" context of childhood in the contemporary US, Taft reminds us, "poor and working-class children and children in immigrant families tak[e] on substantial responsibilities and act[] with far more independence and autonomy than their more socially and economically privileged peers."[22] A great deal of childhood studies scholarship has shown that "the image of childhood as a time of safe, protected, and responsibility-free play is . . . a racialized and class-specific myth."[23] Robin Bernstein's work on "racial innocence," for instance, exposes the whiteness at the heart of conceptions of childhood in the US, uncovering how scripted everyday performances assigned innocence to white children and excluded Black children not only from innocence but from childhood itself.[24] These exclusions are not only inherited but perpetually reenacted in the present: in school contexts where Black youth are disciplined more harshly than white youth, in public spaces where police officers overestimate the age of Black boys beginning at age ten, and in public discourse where, as Crystal Lynn Webster puts it, "African American girls continually face disbarment from ideas of childhood and girlhood."[25] As Miriam Ticktin has argued, "innocence inserts hierarchy into the concept of suffering."[26] BIPOC youth, and Black young people in particular, are "made available for imprisonment and exploitation by the withholding of innocence."[27]

---

20. Thorne, "'Childhood,'" 20.
21. King, *Stolen Childhood*.
22. Taft, *Kids Are In Charge*, 11.
23. Taft, 11.
24. Bernstein, *Racial Innocence*, 7–8.
25. Webster, "History of Black Girls." See also Epstein, Blake, and González, *Girlhood Interrupted*, 4, 6; Blake and Epstein, *Listening*; and Shalaby, *Troublemakers*.
26. Ticktin, "World without Innocence," 587.
27. Gill-Peterson, Sheldon, and Stockton, "What Is the Now," 496. See also Meiners, *For the Children?*

While unearthing and historicizing the shifting boundaries of childhood, scholars have also articulated *temporality* as a key dimension of its manifold cultural valences. Whatever else it has been in specific cultural contexts, Julian Gill-Peterson, Rebekah Sheldon, and Kathryn Bond Stockton argue, "the child, to be sure, has been a creature of chronology."[28] Queer theorist Lee Edelman famously argued that the child, as a "repository of variously sentimentalized cultural identifications," serves as an "obligatory token of futurity," constraining political possibilities by embodying "the telos of the social order."[29] Other theorists have found children's temporal associations backward-turned, linking the past to the present by mobilizing "nostalgias that . . . are far from innocent."[30] Children serve both as idealized, hazy reminders of adults' own (scarcely remembered or entirely forgotten) past and as equally idealized portents of the (unseeable, unreachable) future.

Childhood is temporally defined as well insofar as it names a temporary status: something one is expected to grow out of, making *childhood* a key category for the regulation of capacity, sexuality, dis/ability, and consent, as numerous critiques from disability studies have shown.[31] Demarcating, governing, and surveilling the chronologies of childhood, adolescence, and maturity made the child a crucial object of study for developmental sciences that formed across the twentieth century, including psychology, education, and endocrinology.[32] These fields contributed to the constitution of childhood as "based in deferral and delay: of work, of sex, of civil rights."[33] Such "developmentalist discourses" are consequential: when they "position young people as 'becoming' rather than 'being,'" they also "define young people as incapable, partial, and deficient in contrast to an imagined vision of the capable, complete, and rational adult."[34] Such temporal linkages divest children of meaningful relationships with their own present, a present in which actual children not only signify adult investments in past and future but also act to influence the world around them. Figurations of children as *the past of adults,* as *future adults,* and as *the future of adults* all rely upon a fundamental binary that maintains children as *not adults* and, in particular, not coeval with adults but inhabiting a different time. Their agency is deferred to a later date, when they attain the status of adulthood.

---

28. Gill-Peterson, Sheldon, and Stockton, 495.

29. Edelman, *No Future,* 11–12.

30. Burman, "Between Identification and Subjectification," 297.

31. Randall, "Consent as Rhetorical Ability"; Kafer, *Feminist, Queer, Crip*; Wilkerson, "Disability"; and Rand, "PROTECTing the Figure of Innocence."

32. Gill-Peterson, "Implanting Plasticity."

33. Gill-Peterson, Sheldon, and Stockton, "What Is the Now," 496.

34. Taft, "Teenage Girls' Narratives," 29.

A further contribution of scholars working in childhood studies has been to demonstrate how binary formulations that contrast children with adults operate to stabilize the characteristics associated with adulthood. If *childhood* as a concept generates and sets boundaries around affiliated concepts—such as maturity, responsibility, culpability, and growth—it also powerfully structures the meaning of *adulthood* and the productive, self-regulating, autonomous citizen presumed to be its culmination. As Taft explains, "ideas about childhood are also always ideas about adulthood: the two categories are positioned in opposition to one another. Many of the dominant ideas about modern Western selfhood—that we are rational, free-willed, independent individuals—rely upon a binary logic in which children are *not* those things."[35] Historian Nancy Lesko likewise investigates what she calls "confident characterizations" of teenagers; these characterizations are applied in pervasive cultural scripts that assert that adolescents "come of age" through the unstoppable power of "naturally emerging" and "uncontrollable force[s]," that teens are subject to "raging hormones" that overwhelm their mental and emotional capacities, and that they are so profoundly "peer oriented" as to be "less individuated" than adults. As Lesko argues, these narratives work together to imply "that adolescents are not fully autonomous, rational, or determining, all of which are valued characteristics for successful, modern adults."[36] And sociologist Barrie Thorne notes how the "dualistic view . . . that children are innocent, malleable, vulnerable, dependent, incomplete, and in need of guidance and protection" simultaneously "frames adults as knowledgeable, autonomous, and responsible," a dualism that "is also asymmetric: adults are more powerful, children are subordinate."[37]

Ideas about childhood require the denaturalization this scholarship generates, because childhood operates as a site of power, a location where cultural logics articulate who should exercise power and who should be excluded. For instance, Jessica Taft, conducting ethnographic work on intergenerational political organizing among the Movement of Working Children in Peru, argues that children's political organizing challenges five powerful, widespread assumptions that "circulate globally" about children. These include "the binary difference assumption, or the assumption that children and adults are essentially different kinds of humans," the "natural assumption, or the assumption that childhood is a natural and universal category, with fixed traits and characteristics," the "passivity assumption, or the assumption that children are uncritical sponges who absorb the perspectives of adults," the "exclusion

35. Taft, *Kids Are In Charge*, 4.
36. Lesko, *Act Your Age!*, 3–4.
37. Thorne, "'Childhood,'" 21.

assumption, or the assumption that children should be prevented from participation in both work and politics," and the "power assumption, or the assumption that adults' power over children is just, inevitable, and/or necessary, and
should not be diminished."[38] As Taft shows, these ideas normalize young people's lack of power within families, communities, and formal political arenas.
Wendy Hesford has likewise critiqued how the figure of the child-in-peril is
mobilized in discourses that obscure the everyday, structural forms of state
violence that generate precarity and imperil children. Hesford directs critical
attention to the questions "Which children have had and continue to have
access to childhood innocence and to the protections that such designations
warrant? What norms monitor this access and thereby determine which children are recognized as rights-bearing and as deserving of a future? How do
race, gender, class, sexuality, and disability factor in these determinations and
their consequences?"[39]

The very contradictions that surround young people's experiences of
power, dependency, self-determination, and circulating cultural common-
places make childhood a vital site for considering rhetorical agency. As Hesford has argued, recognizing children as complexly agential unsettles clear
distinctions between dependency and self-sufficiency. Instead, Hesford suggests, "if we are to recognize children as political and moral subjects," we
must acknowledge that "tensions between individual capacity and vulnerability, and between protection and empowerment, are not easily resolved."[40]
These tensions are endemic to agency, not merely for young people but for
anyone positioned outside a narrowly embodied norm. Following from this
key perception, my goal in this project is to theorize from the experiences
of young people, trusting that beginning with a sustained engagement with
young people can lead outward to insights that reflect the complexity of rhetorical agency for rhetors broadly—all of whom grapple with constrained situations and bear capacities for creative rhetorical response.

Indeed, the activism that I focus on across the chapters of this project
emerges out of these contradictions, especially the tension between young
people's felt sense of constraint—which is materialized in policies, spatial pro-
hibitions, family structures, and so many other domains of exclusion from
public life—and their felt sense of power to intervene. That is, children, teens,
and other young people force a way for themselves into inhospitable public contexts, rejecting or refusing the trained incapacity that would prevent
them from acting; in this way childhood could be considered as a capacity

---

38. Taft, *Kids Are In Charge*, 4.
39. Hesford, *Violent Exceptions*, 10.
40. Hesford, *Spectacular Rhetorics*, 186–87.

rather than a liability. As I show in the cases that follow, many young people engage in activism in response to this deep contradiction. Taft argues that scholars should work against the "recurring claim that children are 'sponges' who absorb the ideas of adults around them, while adults are independent, autonomous, critical thinkers whose ideas are their own." Instead, she insists, "individuals of all ages are products of social environments *and* active subjects who interpret, navigate, and act upon those environments."[41] My task, then, is to devise ways of perceiving young people's rhetorical agency, tracing it through the artifacts they create, the events they stage, and the responses their rhetorical behaviors generate, as well as through inquiry into the sense they make of their rhetorical practices through reflection.

RHETORICAL AGENCY AS A TEMPORAL CONCERN

To study or participate in activism—to engage with social movement rhetorics as an analyst or a practitioner—is to formulate a theory of rhetorical agency. In planning, in action, and after the fact, activists labor to predict and assess impacts, to gauge audience attitudes and perceptions, and to negotiate among competing visions that may be vying for prominence.[42] Scholars of social movement and activist rhetorics are likewise called upon to account for the effects such rhetorics generate; because "social movements arise ostensibly to effect change—whether to reform unjust laws, throw off an oppressive regime, or rewrite discursive or normative practices," as Robert Cox and Christina R. Foust have argued, rhetoricians studying such movements find themselves called to account for their effectivity.[43]

If ideas about youth are deeply entwined with temporal relationships, so too is rhetorical agency a temporal concern. Studying the collective activism of young people throws into relief the extent to which both activism and agency imply temporalities—not only familiar relations of cause and effect but also cultivated urgency, prefigurative politics, collective memory, durable assemblages, augmented and diminished capacities, perspectival shifts,

---

41. Taft, *Kids Are In Charge,* 5–6.

42. See Simons, "Requirements, Problems, and Strategies"; and Cox and Foust, "Social Movement Rhetoric," 620.

43. Cox and Foust, "Social Movement Rhetoric," 621. My work prioritizes the perspectives of specific people rather than the organizational frameworks that have been the focus of traditional social movement scholarship. This follows the trajectory of social movement rhetoric toward multiplicity, dispersal, and attention to "movers" more than "movements." See RSA 15, "Whither Social Movement in Rhetorical Studies? A White Paper" (working paper, Rhetorical Society of America Summer Institute, Madison, WI, 2015).

accrued expertise, performances of spontaneity, and embodied experiences of change and continuity. Activism among young people brings temporal dimensions of rhetorical agency to the fore and highlights age as a meaningful dimension of agency, not merely as an axis of oppression.

Contemporary rhetoricians understand rhetorical agency as a relational capacity that extends "among and beyond humans," as Ratcliffe and Jensen explain, and as a distributed phenomenon, shifting among elements over time.[44] Yet even as agency exceeds the human, for speakers and writers whose rhetorical capacities are not taken for granted but called into question, *rhetoricity*—the capacity to be perceived by others as operating rhetorically—is vital. Formulated by scholars working in disability studies, rhetoricity designates the injustice experienced by many whose rhetorical agency is routinely denied. Catherine Prendergast calls *rhetoricity* the ability to be received by others as a human subject.[45] In Margaret Price's words, "to lack rhetoricity is to lack all basic freedoms and rights, including the freedom to express ourselves and the right to be listened to."[46] In contrast, many neurotypical and normatively embodied rhetors often take for granted that others will view them as agents, will register them as autonomous, will accept them as rational and volitional.[47] Marginalized rhetors who lack rhetoricity in the eyes of the audiences they address find it critically important to assert agency. An audience's readiness to assume the rhetoricity of a speaker varies by age as that intersects with other forms of embodiment, especially race, sexuality, and disability. Whether, for instance, a protestor holding a sign is five or fifteen or forty-five impacts whether that speaker is considered a prop holding up an adult's opinion, a conformist simply parroting what her friends are doing, or a rhetorical agent expressing a reasoned political opinion—and these determinations are shaped not only by age, of course, but by myriad other ways in which her visible embodiment and the substance of her expression interact.

Temporalities of Cause and Effect

The strategies, capacities, and reflections of young rhetors point to temporal dimensions of agency that are often submerged. The topos of cause and

---

44. Jensen and Ratcliffe, *Rhetorical Listening in Action*, 55. See also Hallenbeck, "Toward a Posthuman Perspective," 18; and Cooper, *Animal Who Writes*.

45. Prendergast, "On the Rhetorics," 202.

46. Price, *Mad At School*, 26–27. See also Heilker and Yergeau, "Autism and Rhetoric," 494; and Yergeau, *Authoring Autism*.

47. See Cooper, *Animal Who Writes*, 127–28.

effect represents a significant and explicitly temporal dimension of agency as that concept shows up in everyday use. Carolyn Miller argues that agency as "effectivity" has long organized the thinking of scholars in rhetoric, noting that both teaching and political organizing would be badly undermined if the idea of effectivity were fully ceded.[48] Parsing cause and effect involves fixing relations in time—what is prior, what follows after—and drawing arrows of influence. This vernacular sense of agency is often present in both public and scholarly discussions of activism. People often engage in activism because they believe (or merely hope) that engagement will be consequential: that it will matter how many people show up at a protest, that showing up expresses something meaningful even if the expression is ignored by others in power, that the action they are taking will weigh on whatever happens next. Temporal framings are also key in this everyday sense of agency as action followed by consequence because they indicate parameters for evaluation. Did the energy of the protest dissipate quickly? Did people talk about it for days or weeks or months after? Has it led to anything yet? Only twenty people came to the candidate's forum, but the media coverage afterward was positive—does that make it more successful than it seemed at the time? Temporalities of cause and effect prompt us to consider not only what impacts have followed but when and how we know whether actions have generated particular outcomes. Gauging impact is always an interpretive process, as Charlotte Hogg and Shari Stenberg argue, offering the concept of "rhetorical sway" to consider the "rhetorical endurance or lasting impact" of recent rhetorical artifacts.[49] Forms of impact such as "going viral, trending, or reaching audiences through new media platforms" should not be understood as signaling only "fleeting popularity," they explain, but as "cultural contribution[s]" that might "create[ ] dialogue or further[ ] a stalled conversation"—that is, their impacts might require different formulations of timeliness, impact, and strategy to become visible.[50]

Age, Attribution, and Embodied Agency

Agency and temporality are conjoined further insofar as agency involves—or even rests upon—embodied social location, which interacts with temporality via age and aging. That is, because agency is embodied, it changes over time, inflected inescapably by temporality. Whether in Carolyn Miller's formulation

---

48. Miller, "What Can Automation Tell Us," 143–45.

49. Hogg and Stenberg, "Gathering Women's Rhetorics," 14.

50. Hogg and Stenberg, "Gathering Women's Rhetorics," 14. See also Ingraham, *Gestures of Concern.*

of agency as "kinetic energy" that inheres between agents who attribute agency to one another, or in Carl Herndl and Adela Licona's theorization of agency as a relation rather than a possession, the attributions that constitute rhetorical agency are impacted by embodied social locations, including perceived age as that interacts with race, class, gender, sexuality, disability, language, nationality, and so on.[51] Furthermore, intersecting dimensions of social location and embodiment change over time, making temporality a significant part of the complexity of agency-as-mutual-attribution. For instance, judgments about whether someone is credible, authoritative, rational, or in possession of their faculties are strongly shaped by the interaction between ageist and ableist images, which construe some bodies as diminished or incapable. The reach of normative temporalities—of timely development, proper growth and maturation, expected benchmarks—extends into every life, inflected by race, class, sexuality, and gender expression as well as age and dis/ability. As Ellen Samuels has written, the disrupted temporalities of disability can make "crip time" feel like "time travel," frustrating a desire "to be aligned, synchronous, part of the regular order of the world."[52] The mutability of embodied social locations is particularly evident when we consider the agency of young people. Although change over time is inherent in all embodied experience, some social locations obscure this more persistently than others. Racial categories, for instance, are often characterized as fixed and permanent, even though both internal identifications and external social meanings change over time and in relation to experiences of aging.

Closely connected to embodied social location is the understanding of agency as embodied capacities that develop (and diminish) over time. Sociological life course approaches, for instance, foreground the way that both age and timing are key factors in shaping people's experiences of agency across their life, and recent work on aging in rhetoric and literacy studies has reinforced the complex ways in which literate capacities are inflected by temporality.[53] This is especially tied to age and to attitudes toward both the very young and the very old, which characterize them as having undeveloped, partial, constrained, or diminished capacities for influencing public concerns. For instance, many media responses to the encounter between Dianne Feinstein and youth climate activists relied on ageist frameworks that suggested Feinstein was, by virtue of her age, either dramatically out of touch with reality or no longer fit to govern, having outlived her usefulness.

51. Miller, "What Can Automation"; and Herndl and Licona, "Shifting Agency."

52. Samuels, "Six Ways."

53. Elder, "Time, Human Agency, and Social Change" Bowen, "Age Identity and Literacy"; Bowen, "Composing a Further Life"; and Swacha, "Older Adults as Rhetorical Agents."

This embodied dimension of agency further joins with temporality in the concept of "sense of agency" developed by rhetorician Kefaya Diab. In her phenomenological redefinition, *sense of agency* centers one's felt perception of oneself as an agent, with power and capacity to create consequences, a "movement from affect, to feeling, to knowledge" that transpires and dissipates across the duration of a lived experience. One's sense of agency is influenced by time, waxing and waning in relation to highly specific contexts (while marching with others, for instance, or when viewing a petition on a computer) and in relation to both immediate experiences in the moment and reconsideration of those experiences after the fact. As Diab explains, recounting her experience as a child engaging in a protest with her family, "being physically close to others and touching their bodies as we walked made me experience solidarity and empowerment," creating both a feeling "that passed through protestors' bodies [and kept] them moving forward" as well as the knowledge that "even if for a short while, protestors' actions affected some change in the world."[54]

Finally, if rhetorical agency is attributed, embodied, mutable, ephemeral, and felt, it is also crucial that it is (or can be) durable. Agency can be materialized and augmented by objects and organizations that extend and affirm it across time—as they do when a collective coalesces into an organization and when the organization persists beyond the involvement of specific individuals who began it.[55] This dimension of agency shows up in interviews where a great deal of energy is expended to create durability—in the form of a bronze statue, a long-lasting organization, a piece of legislation—and my analysis in the chapters that follow attends to how collectives have materialized their agency through enduring forms, even as I take additional routes to investigate the embodied and mutable agencies that operate alongside the durability of statues and institutions.

Drawing on these varied dimensions of rhetorical agency, I trace outcomes, consequences, and impacts of youth activism through the perspectives of activists themselves, developing the concept of reflexive agency. In this way, I advance the perspective articulated by political sociologists Olivier Fillieule and Erik Neveu, who argue that "movements do not simply produce repertoires and impacts on policies and politics. They also produce (or fail to produce) activists."[56] Social movements "produce lasting changes" in the self-perceptions and social relations of those who participate in them, "injecting in the social world activists with strong dispositions for collective action and the

---

54. Diab, "Rise of the Arab Spring," 262.
55. See Latour, "Technology Is Society Made Durable."
56. Fillieule and Neveu, "Activists' Trajectories," 15.

construction of claims and causes."[57] Reframing this vital insight in rhetorical terms, we might say that engaging in activism, among other possible effects, shifts activists' dispositions and relations; these alterations revise conditions of possibility. Considering activism within the lives of activists shifts the concept of durability toward what Fillieule and Neveu call the "biographical conse-quences in all spheres of life" that follow from individuals' experiences within social movement organizations and activities.[58]

Through reflection, activists remake their rhetorical agency, again and again; they forge connections among decisions, outcomes, and self-under-standings, and in doing so, they bring strategic and reflexive forms of agency together. When participants express regret for a strategic decision that had unintended consequences; when they communicate, "we tried so hard to make this happen, and I'm not sure it really matters in the long run"; when they explain that they were moving toward a particular set of actions but had to step back when the national context changed in unexpected ways; when they create a narrative to link their past activism with their present self—these are among the "biographical consequences" that follow from individu-als' experiences and reflections. Such an approach extends the insights offered by sociologists Sevasti-Melissa Nolas, Christos Varvantakis, and Vinnarasan Aruldoss, who argue that "regarding activism and childhood, or indeed activ-ism across the lifespan, it is important to attend to the rich tapestry of over-laid narratives of self as those unfold in time and across it, and from which a political self, with all its intersectionalities, emerges."[59]

This book argues that young people mitigate and leverage age as a salient dimension of the situations they address, generating strategies that do not always work. That is, like all activists, they navigate partial success, incomplete attainment of their collective goals, and experiences of failure. Constrained by symbolic associations, their tactics are especially susceptible to dismissal and rearticulation by resistant audiences: activists' efforts to disrupt fleeting cycles of media attention following mass shootings, for instance, can be recast as evi-dence of the attention-seeking nature of teens; distributed networks of climate organizers, rather than indicating a productive embrace of power-sharing, are rearticulated as demonstrating young people's inefficiency and disorga-nization. Against these limitations, I argue, young people exercise rhetorical agency both in activist strategy and in retrospective reflection, which provides a space for ongoing formulation of the import of their work. As Marilyn Coo-per argues, agents are simply "entities that act; by virtue of their action they

---

57. Fillieule and Neveu, 15.
58. Fillieule and Neveu, 15.
59. Nolas, Varvantakis, and Aruldoss, "(Im)possible Conversations," 260.

necessarily bring about changes."[60] By shifting focus away from both intention and efficacy, we dwell instead on the perpetual change that happens because of all embodied action—"including," Cooper says, "what are thought of as 'mental' actions—speaking, writing, reflecting."[61] My work in this project is to consider, in conversation with young activists themselves, how their actions, including their acts of reflection, reformulate conditions of possibility.

The case studies that follow explore both strategic agency—how activists' tactics have met the affordances and constraints of their rhetorical situations—as well as reflexive agency—how activists revisit those situations through perspectives that have changed over time. Each chapter pairs in-the-moment strategies with after-the-fact reflections and treats both as sites where young people lay claim to agency in its many forms. The collectives studied here generate rhetorical strategy out of the specific embodied experience of young people: children who have grown up performing duck-and-cover drills in their elementary school classrooms; teens and youth raised in the US without protections of citizenship, navigating exclusions that grow especially sharp at the transition out of high school; young people angered by their vulnerability to gun violence.

Chapter 1, "Agency as Embodied: Durable Activism for Peace," foregrounds *agency as embodied experience* by examining how a collective of children and teens from New Mexico formed a transnational network of supporters, using amplification and spatial linkages to augment the strength of their claim despite their lack of official standing. These young people attempted to convert their symbolic power as children into political power and worked to constitute a transnational community capable of expressing their thoughts about matters of public importance. Though the statue they designed, funded, and built was *not* ultimately granted a place in Los Alamos and instead has been relocated nomadically around northern New Mexico since 1995, the durability of the statue holds open the possibility of reformulating their activism and its impacts. My interviews with these activists some two decades later emphasize the way that embodied experiences and the physical statue itself both create ongoing rhetorical opportunities, forging new articulations of the purpose and accomplishment of their childhood activism. Even as these participants' perspectives shift, the throughlines they identify trace possibilities of resonating impact, shifting the timeline for evaluation from the immediate moment to long-term resonances.

---

60. Cooper, "Rhetorical Agency," 424.
61. Cooper, 424–25.

Chapter 2, "Agency as Perspectival: Vulnerable Undocumented Activism," develops an understanding of *agency as perspectival*—rooted experientially in context and perspective and shifting as relations shift across time and through different material, interpersonal, and political arrangements. Here I analyze the strategies of young undocumented im/migrant activists who garnered national attention beginning in 2010 through demonstrations in support of the Development, Relief, and Education for Alien Minors (DREAM) Act, which if passed could have normalized the status of hundreds of thousands of im/migrant young people. Focusing on these activists' strategic use of personal disclosure, I examine how disclosures of this sort, though risky, can operate powerfully to draw others closer to speakers' identities and experiences. Young undocumented activists throughout 2010 and beyond employed such a disclosure strategy, risking punitive consequences to challenge stigma associated with undocumented status and to make private situations of vulnerability into a matter of public concern. Alongside marches, rallies, demonstrations, and other embodied mobilizations to contest deportation and challenge anti-im/migrant legislation, the collective labors of young undocumented activists converted individuals' embodied vulnerability (to arrest, family separation, deportation, and other consequences for themselves and their families) into a source of rhetorical power. Through their retrospective sense-making as they assess impacts of their strategies, these activists articulate the value of acting despite the inescapably partial perspectives to which strategic decisions are bound.

Chapter 3, "Agency as Capacity: Disruptive Activism for Gun Reform," foregrounds *agency as embodied capacity,* a literate capacity that is future-oriented and contingent, undetermined by present successes and failures but developed through *learning-by-doing.* This chapter investigates the rhetorical strategies adopted by teen March For Our Lives (MFOL) activists, which center around disruption—of brief cycles of routine news coverage, for instance, and of expectations of decorum in youth engagement with politics. Alongside these public strategies, my interviews demonstrate how young people develop capacities through their embodied experiences with communication, organization, and reflection. By staging events, negotiating bureaucratic procedures, creating organizations capable of sustaining themselves over time, and reflecting on their individual and collective transformations, these activists generate capacities oriented toward future uses. Articulating agency in this way shifts attention away from short-term assessments of success or failure, toward longer temporalities, in which activists' capacities carry ongoing but undetermined significance.

The different location of these collectives in time—1995, 2010, 2018— brings an additional temporal dimension to reflexive agency as I develop it across this project. When I spoke with adults in 2017 who had worked to create the Children's Peace Statue more than twenty years previously, these participants—between ten and sixteen years old in 1995—recalled their activist experiences with some hesitation. They mentioned their efforts to bring the project more fully to mind in the days leading up to our interview and sometimes asked me to supply names of adult leaders and other participants they could not recall. In contrast, when I interviewed teens who had organized March For Our Lives events in their communities, in July 2018 and again in June 2020, many of these participants, who ranged in age from fifteen to eighteen, were still in the midst of intense organizing—planning large events, negotiating their relationships with allied organizations, engaging in social media campaigns, and directly lobbying state legislators. They sometimes scrolled back through their Twitter feeds to read aloud to me specific messages they had crafted, and they spoke about their activism with a dexterity born of having done, for some of them, "countless" interviews with media over the previous months. Between these poles of immediacy and distance, the participants I interviewed in 2021 who had been involved in im/migration activism in 2010 easily recalled their activism (which spanned roughly 2005 to 2019) and spoke readily about the work they had done, but they also had years of reflection to draw on as they considered their work and its impacts. Through this range of different relations to their activist experiences, my participants underscore how "overlaid narratives of the self . . . unfold in time and across it" and reveal the long tails of activism's influence within their lives, which might otherwise be obscured.[62]

Following these case studies I consider in the conclusion how reflexive agency—a perspectival, embodied capacity—can be anticipated by rhetorical scholars engaging with contemporary youth activism. Through mini case studies, I extend my three primary arguments regarding the salience of age for rhetorical possibility, the necessity of listening to children and young people, and the value of reflection as a site where rhetorical agency can be cultivated and articulated. The conclusion closes with a call for engaging with the intricacy of intergenerational communication in which neither the old nor the young are dismissed. By seeking cross-generational coalitions where participants share perspectives and build power to address rhetorical problems, we can cultivate reflexivity to help activists and scholars understand perspectival change as a rhetorical resource inflected by time but unbounded by age.

---

62. Nolas, Varvantakis, and Aruldoss, "(Im)possible Conversations," 260.

CHAPTER 1

Agency as Embodied

Durable Activism for Peace

Tension between young activists and adult opponents animated a boisterous public discussion in February 1995 in Los Alamos, New Mexico, as the County Council reconsidered their earlier decision to provide public land for the Children's Peace Statue, a statue designed and funded by children to express their collective desire for peace. Boisterous is euphemistic: some young people were shouted down while trying to speak, heckled by adults in the audience, and some were in tears when they spoke to the press after this final meeting, a culmination of several years of debate over their project. As one of the students who was shouted down while speaking recounted to me in an interview roughly twenty years later, she "just [did] not know what to do. [I felt] the same way an adult would feel, like, 'Wait, what is happening right now?'" As a fourteen-year-old, in the face of a room full of agitated adults who were shouting for her to stop speaking, she recalled, "I didn't finish; I just sort of [stuttered] and sat down." Surprised as she was by the heckling, it was only in the days afterward—as reporters contacted her to speak with her about her experience—that she realized, "Oh, what happened was pretty bad." Indeed, such a spectacular scene of intergenerational confrontation garnered national media attention; many newspapers reprinted an Associated Press story that was headlined "Los Alamos Rejects Peace Park," for instance, while the *Albuquerque Journal* reported wryly that "embarrassing a 14-year-old at a public meeting is not something that'll go into the tourism brochures anytime soon."[1] Another student who was heckled during the County Council meeting explained to reporters afterward, "I'm not normally a flustered person, but they got to me. It seemed totally out of order for them to do that to me, and it was totally unexpected."[2]

Reporters covering the contentious Los Alamos County Council meeting, and a similarly combative meeting in November 1994, identified various reasons for the council's rejection. Attempting to understand "Why Los Alamos Said No," according to one headline, required registering the fact that "70 to 80 percent of the country's existing nuclear weapons were designed" in Los Alamos, where it was feared the statue would direct blame at the community by memorializing victims of the bombings of Hiroshima and Nagasaki.[3] David Cortwright, an academic and peace activist writing for the *Bulletin of Atomic Scientists,* characterized opposition to the statue as "Los Alamos's Little War with Peace."[4] Such coverage noted that the statue's seemingly uncontroversial statement—that children around the world want a peaceful future—was refracted through the atomic history of Los Alamos and the immediate post–Cold War context of the early 1990s, when diminishing federal contracts for nuclear research created unease in a town whose economy depended heavily on such funding.

Consequently, although members of the Kids' Committee repeatedly insisted that their statue spoke of the desire of children worldwide for future peace, residents of Los Alamos voiced fears that the statue would "dishonor the memory of the men and women of the Manhattan Project."[5] As one young supporter of the statue explained to journalists, with mounting frustration, "I don't know how many times we have to say that this has nothing to do with the atomic bomb or World War II or Hiroshima. That was the inspiration, but it's grown into something entirely different."[6] One teen supporter explained that Los Alamos was chosen as an appropriate site for the statue "because it was the birthplace of the nuclear age. The research that has taken place at Los Alamos has changed the world, and the statue's message would be that adults of today would use their power to create a peaceful future for

1. Phill Casaus, "Kids' Peace Statue Stuck in Mire of Los Alamos History," *Albuquerque Journal,* February 25, 1995, D1.

2. Patrick Armijo, "Kids' Peace Statue Strikes Out Again," *Albuquerque Journal,* February 15, 1995, 6.

3. Keith Easthouse, "Why Los Alamos Said No," *Santa Fe New Mexican,* December 4, 1994, A1.

4. Cortwright, "Los Alamos's Little War."

5. Minutes of the Los Alamos County Council (LACC), February 13, 1995 (hereafter LACC 1995), 9.

6. Easthouse, "Why Los Alamos Said No."

those of tomorrow."[7] Young supporters argued that the statue had "evolved beyond World War II" and signified "hope for a peaceful future" rather than any intended critique of Los Alamos.[8]

At stake in these competing interpretations was not only the apparent message of the statue but a threatened loss of control over the meanings of Los Alamos itself. As Councilor Denise Smith explained, "As a community, we have a right to define ourselves. This [statue] would define us as the people who bear the sole responsibility for the destruction of Hiroshima, and that's not appropriate."[9] As one resident explained, she "would like Los Alamos to be remembered as having played a large part in ending the very tragic war and not as the place that built the weapon that killed many hundreds of children."[10] At earlier County Council meetings, some residents had asserted that Los Alamos National Laboratories is itself "a living peace monument" and suggested that the statue would be acceptable if it announced explicitly that "the last fifty years of peace have come [about] because of Los Alamos."[11] Another opponent expressed her resentment at "the fact that people generations away from the times, people who seem never to have heard of Pearl Harbor . . . should take it upon themselves to try to shame Los Alamos into saying—yes, we were wrong to try to win the war to do what our country asked, and you're right to come here and tell us to give land, time and money to expiate our guilt."[12] Though I do not aim to minimize the anxiety Councilor Smith and other residents articulated, I find the frustrations voiced by child and teen supporters—who had received approval for their project in 1992, when the council voted in favor of allocating land for the statue—also significant. Speaking to reporters after a contentious meeting, one teen activist explained, "I am very, very frustrated, because they can't seem to get past the past."[13]

The innocuous design of the statue might have been expected to allay such fears of blame. Selected by a panel of youth and adult judges—including "an artist, a veteran, an educator, an architect, a peacemaker, and members of the Los Alamos community"—from six thousand entries in a national competition, the statue's design (see figure 1) and final form (see figure 2) avoid reference to World War II, Hiroshima, or nuclear weapons.[14] The design, by

7. LACC, November 21, 1994 (hereafter LACC 1994), 10.

8. LACC 1995, 11.

9. Easthouse, "Why Los Alamos Said No."

10. *On Wings of Peace*, 3.

11. LACC, November 16, 1992 (hereafter LACC 1992), 5; and LACC 1994, 10.

12. LACC 1995, 9–10.

13. "Children's Plan Rejected for Peace Park at Los Alamos," Associated Press, November 23, 1994.

14. "Judging to Be Held," flyer.

FIGURE 1. Design of Children's Peace Statue (Cortwright, "Los Alamos's Little War," 5). Image courtesy of Bill Perkins.

FIGURE 2. Children's Peace Statue, adorned with strands of paper cranes, in its current location at the Anderson-Abruzzo Albuquerque International Balloon Museum. Photo courtesy of Richard Loyd.

FIGURE 3. Detail from Children's Peace Statue. Photo courtesy of Richard Loyd.

Texas eighteen-year-old Noe Martinez, depicts an open globe surrounded by a garden and originally included garden space where visitors could plant flowers to participate in creating the memorial collectively. This design was modified for a desert environment by Los Alamos landscape architect Bill Perkins, and further modified by Colorado sculptor Tim Joseph, who incorporated the design's collaborative dimension by sending cubes of wax to schools in the United States and around the world, which children molded into plants and animals and sent back to the sculptor's foundry. Joseph then cast some three thousand wax figures into bronze, which he assembled to form continents over the steel frame of the globe (see figure 3). The open steel frame, reminiscent of a molecule, subtly evokes the atomic age, while the small bronze figures, forming filigreed continents and bearing the fingerprints of the children who molded them, simultaneously suggest the fragility of the earth, the delicacy of children's care, and the durability of children's collective efforts on behalf of peace.[15] Youth supporters of the statue stated these meanings directly and repeatedly during public meetings, in press conferences, and in interviews with the media, reiterating that the statue expressed a collective desire for future peace among its international network of supporters, rather than a critique of Los Alamos or its history of nuclear development. Yet in the words of

---

15. Tracy Dingmann, "Statue Unites World's Kids," *Albuquerque Journal*, August 1, 1995, C1; and Tracy Dingmann, "Peace and Perseverance," *Albuquerque Journal*, August 6, 1995, D1 + D4.

city officials who submitted a letter to the council about their reservations, "it is difficult to believe" that criticism of Los Alamos was not the statue's goal.[16]

I open with this case because it vividly demonstrates how childhood facilitates and constrains rhetorical possibility. The confrontational scenes enacted during council meetings, and the variety of rhetorical tactics employed by opponents of the statue, underscore the vulnerability of young activists' arguments to adult rearticulations and underline the limits of adult support for young people's claims to public attention and deliberation. For instance, after the statue's inoffensive design had been finalized, opponents' concerns shifted toward control over any "wording" or plaque that might accompany the statue, although none had been proposed. One member of the Art in Public Places Board, the group that had been directed by the council to identify a location for the statue on county land, wrote a letter that was read aloud at a 1994 meeting voicing her opposition to the statue, urging the council "to make it unmistakably clear to the Kids Peace Sculpture Committee and their adult advisors as to what it will accept . . . [and] to secure the community the sole and final jurisdiction over the wording on the commemorative plaque which will be placed on the sculpture."[17] The language expresses deep anxiety in its demand for "unmistakably clear" limits, "sole and final jurisdiction" over wording. Others at the meeting likewise asked for reassurance that the statue, as a gift, could be removed at a later point if it were "misused" by peace activists.

To a certain extent, the loss of control that residents of Los Alamos feared nevertheless came to pass, because their rejection of the statue made national headlines. That rejection prompted critical editorials in distant periodicals, such as the *Boston Globe,* which wrote that nothing in the "simple vision" of "a globe surrounded by a garden" should be capable of "stir[ring] controversy." Responding to a councilor who said Los Alamos is "not ready" for the statue, the *Globe* editorial chastises, "Not ready? Not ready for innocence? Not ready for beauty, hope, or the worldwide cooperation of children? How sad that Los Alamos defines itself by one moment in history."[18] Media coverage of the controversy made frequent reference to similar themes: the innocence of children and the obvious appeal of their cooperative statement in favor of peace. Children, then, through their associations with innocence as well as through the years of organizing, fundraising, and publicity that predated Los Alamos's rejection, *were* capable of influencing public perceptions, and in this way residents lost some symbolic control over what their town signified. In

16. Library Board, letter to LACC, November 21, 1994.

17. LACC 1994, 11–12.

18. "Eruption in Los Alamos," *Boston Globe,* November 30, 1994.

other words, refusing to allow the statue to be located in Los Alamos county did not fully prevent young activists from intervening in public meanings and associations.

But in their grappling with youth over the placement of the statue, adults held all actual power. As sociologist Jessica Taft has argued, differences in age are "also differences of access to power and resources," although "this inequality is often invisible and normalized; it is taken for granted in most inter-generational contexts that adults should be the ones who are 'in charge.'"[19] The children and teens who spoke at meetings were not voters, even those who were residents of Los Alamos, and thus they approached the council not as constituents but as petitioners, as I discuss more fully below. Some youth reflected afterwards that they had not been able to mobilize their supporters to show up in sufficient numbers at these contentious meetings, allowing the vehemence of their opposition to have an outsized impact on the council's decision-making.[20] For instance, supporters within Los Alamos who weren't able to be present at the meetings asked others to speak on their behalf, to offer reassurance that "there are many here in Los Alamos who want the statue here"—but without a visible (and vociferous) presence at the County Council meetings, that support appeared much weaker than the opposition.[21] The age of many of the statue's proponents mitigated against them appearing in full numbers at the meetings that determined the statue's fate; children and teens who lived in northern New Mexico needed adults to drive them to the meetings, and not many could participate in public meetings that ran from roughly 6:00 p.m. to 9:00 p.m. on Monday nights in a town a hundred miles north of Albuquerque. In light of these imbalances, it may not be surprising that these young activists failed to accomplish a significant dimension of their project: namely, placing the statue in Los Alamos.

Yet this chapter ultimately reconsiders questions of success and failure in relation to this case. That reconsideration is enabled in part by attending to the materiality and durability of the statue as an object—nine feet tall, cast in bronze—that, in Richard Marback's words, "could not [be made] other than" it is.[22] That is, while petitions may be filed away and disregarded, a large bronze statue unavoidably takes up space. This particular statue has moved nomadically between Albuquerque and Santa Fe, continuing to generate meanings in relation to Los Alamos long past its dedication in 1995. That same durability also shifts the time frame for the participants I spoke with later about their

---

19. Taft, *Kids Are In Charge*, 7.
20. Dingmann, "Peace and Perseverance."
21. LACC 1995.
22. Marback, "Unclenching the Fist," 48.

own sense of the project's success and failure. Although media coverage at the time tended to treat the statue's rejection from Los Alamos as a significant failure—echoes of which can be seen in similar media coverage of im/migration activism and March For Our Lives activism in chapters 2 and 3—I reconsider those assessments in conversation with the several activists I interviewed about their involvement when they were children. Consequently, in this chapter I assess the rhetorical strategies that children and teens employed in their efforts to generate support for, fund, design, build, and dedicate the Children's Peace Statue. I then demonstrate how childhood constrains rhetorical possibility, arguing that adult opponents of the statue were able to draw upon those constraints as they rearticulated children's strategies in ways that undermined the project's ability to gain ground in Los Alamos. Through retrospective reflections, however, participants who were involved in the project as children consider how their embodied practices extend the significance of their activism across time and how their prior perspectives related to the statue's rejection have subsequently shifted. Reflexive agency—a mode of agency formed through relations among prior, present, and future selves, rooted in embodied experienced and inflected by temporal change—offers these participants an open-ended perspective for reconsidering their activism and its outcomes. In reflection, these activists affirm the present value of their prior experience and revisit their felt sensations of failure and disappointment to generate a reconfigured understanding of the agency children can exercise in relation to complex public issues.

ORGANIZING FOR PEACE AT THE END OF THE COLD WAR

The children who initiated the Children's Peace Statue were adults when I spoke to them in retrospective interviews in 2017 and 2021, recalling events that had taken place more than twenty years previously.[23] As one of my interview participants explained, she remembers the project's beginnings in outline but not "the specifics of it, because it's a story that's been retold so many times." Indeed, the children who advocated on behalf of the peace statue had recounted their project's origins repeatedly: in issues of their newsletter, *The Crane*; in interviews with local and national journalists; and repeatedly during their efforts to persuade the Los Alamos County Council to provide land for

---

23. Directly contacting individuals who were named in the news coverage, I sent interview requests and IRB-approved interview questions to approximately ten individuals. I ultimately conducted interviews with four of the former organizers of the project, which I recorded and transcribed. See appendix 1 for the full interview questionnaire.

the statue. Their version of the statue's origins became contested, however, as adult opposition to the statue heightened within Los Alamos and opponents charged that the statue was, in the words of the councilor most opposed to the project, "all part of an adult put-up plan."[24]

The project began in late 1989 in an elementary school classroom in Albuquerque, where teachers Christine Luke and Caroline Gassner involved their third and fourth graders in a Future Problem Solvers brainstorming session aimed at addressing the problem of nuclear proliferation and the threat of nuclear war. Though it began at school, the project moved quickly beyond the classroom—to the cafeteria, where students held a popcorn sale to raise money; to a local bank, where students marched to deposit the first $12 raised toward their project; and outward to an expanding range of sites, including local libraries, bookstores, and churches, a pizza place where monthly planning meetings were held, County Council meetings in Los Alamos, local press conferences, TV and radio interviews, classrooms around the country where children created designs for the proposed statue, and peace conferences in Salt Lake City, Seattle, and Hiroshima.

Though their message in support of peace struck many media commentators as innocuous, even inarguable, that message in fact emerged from and spoke back to a specific political context. One participant, who described himself as a kid who had always been "drawn to pacificist ideas," recalled learning about the project late in 1990, when "the run-up to the Gulf War" was taking place, something he found "very upsetting to me as a ten-year-old kid." He felt that "getting involved in this group of other kids who wanted to work for peace in some way—in the ways that are available to children—really appealed to me." Another participant recalled this period as one in which young people felt deeply vulnerable to the decisions of adults. Although the Berlin Wall fell in late 1989, around the time of the pivotal classroom discussion, many elementary students had performed "duck-and-cover" drills throughout the 1980s, lining up in hallways and covering their necks with their hands or ducking underneath classroom desks. As this participant explained, the 1980s "felt . . . apocalyptic in a lot of ways, for kids." He elaborated that "when we came up with this idea, there was still a nuclear arms race with the USSR and it just felt like adults were totally out of control. The world seemed insane in a lot of ways, that people were just building bigger and bigger missiles. Probably as an adult you're looking at it and there had been some arms treaties and things like that, but as a kid it just felt like what we were learning about the

---

24. Kathleene Parker, "Councilor: Peace Park Adults' Idea," *Santa Fe New Mexican*, February 13, 1995, B1.

world was that it could be gone at any moment." The prompt for the classroom brainstorming session emerged from this context, with students agreeing that a statue created by children from around the world could carry a message that would intervene in a global political context that felt "out of control."

Over the next five years, the students who organized in support of the Children's Peace Statue wrote in an incredible variety of forms and genres. They wrote personal letters to solicit donations and thank supporters in Russia, Japan, and other international communities of peace activists; drafted flyers and donation forms that they sent to schools, churches, and community groups throughout the US and beyond; composed and sent press releases to newspapers and magazines; prepared formal presentations that they delivered at local government meetings; devised T-shirt designs, competition guidelines, and informational brochures about the project; composed, designed, printed, and distributed thousands of copies of their official newsletter, *The Crane*, which featured letters, narratives, fundraising and peace-building ideas, poetry, and artwork by children; and created an early computer database to record all donors who contributed to the project—a database of names, entered by hand, that numbered fifty thousand by the time of the statue's dedication.

The organizing, fundraising, and persuasive work required to move the project from idea to materiality was distributed during these five years among a shifting and largely unstructured collective. Although several older students came to perform key leadership roles—such as editing *The Crane* and developing a database of supporters' names—the Kids' Committee itself included children of wide-ranging ages who moved into and out of positions of leadership over time. Beginning in 1990, the Kids' Committee held monthly meetings at a pizza restaurant in Albuquerque; these meetings were advertised in the *Albuquerque Journal* and open to interested students from any school. It was at the first such meeting, in February 1990, that the Kids' Committee formed and identified themselves, and those in attendance signed their names to a public letter that ultimately circulated quite broadly as a collective statement of the group's purpose. Some of the original thirty-six members who attended that initial meeting moved away or lost interest, while others who were not part of the original committee became deeply involved in subsequent years. One of the original students in Gassner and Luke's classroom explained to me in our retrospective interview how important it was that "older kids [came] to help," providing expertise and leadership that was crucial to the elementary-aged kids who were involved. For instance, "one [high school student] had some computer skills and started building a database so that we could collect the names" of supporters. Another interview participant suggested that age itself provided a kind of leadership structure, noting that kids' participation varied according to age, as younger students graduated from "setting goals, selling t-shirts, maybe talking to reporters" to "when you're older . . . getting events going, teaching kids to fold cranes." One participant recalled seeing some other children lose interest in the project as they got older, which prompted him to keep working on it, because "it didn't seem fair to just let it go" after so many supporters globally had contributed to it. Adult advisors, including Luke and Gassner and an Albuquerque-based international educator, Camy Condon, provided a degree of stability; nevertheless, the distributed structure of the committee, as well as their ambitious conception of the public that the statue would speak for, required the young people involved in this project to confront one of the major challenges of grassroots organizing: persuading a shifting collective to invest time and energy toward ends that might not be realized for some time.

The way this collective operated underscores the complexity of what Jessica Taft would call "horizontal intergenerational" activism, as well as the difficulty many audiences have believing that adults and children can share agency in this way.[25] One participant recalled "being aware of the suspicions of other adults, that we were sort of unwitting pawns of these old hippies, that we were getting inculcated somehow or indoctrinated with these filthy Communist ideas." He found it dismaying that "so many people . . . seemed to reach that conclusion on their own, that there was really no way that all these children can feel so powerfully about this and be participating of our own free will." In his recollection, the relationship between adult guidance and child agency was complex and mutual; as he recalls, the group *did* rely on the adults who were supporting the project, explaining, "I do think a roomful of twelve-year-olds cannot keep organized without some guidance," just like "a roomful of twenty-year-olds cannot keep organized without some guidance." But such guidance does not turn young people into the puppets of older activists "just using us for their nefarious ends," as opponents charged.

Instead, interview participants recalled forcefully their unusual experience of being treated as partners—or leaders—with adults following supportively rather than directing. As one participant shared with me later, "I never doubted that they wanted us to decide. They wanted us to be the ones who were making the decisions about what should happen with the project. That really stuck with me." It was a fourteen-year-old committee member who proposed at the first press conference in 1990 to locate the statue in Los Alamos, and children who decided what to say during unscripted public events at bookstores,

25. Taft, *Kids Are In Charge*, 8.

churches, convention centers, and in radio and television interviews. Another participant characterized this dynamic as one in which kids generated ideas but needed help to "put them into action" or to figure out precisely "what a project was, what [it] even meant to be taking this more seriously as an idea." He recounted that "a lot of the big decisions really were set by the kids, but then the adults and older kids [would] help channel some of those ideas and try to make them actual feasible things to do." For instance, this participant recalled the group holding a press conference attended by local news stations and recollected being "wired up with a microphone" and "being on camera while they asked questions," even though the kids had not been "prepped for any of that. It was just kind of like, these are the kids that are active in the project, and then there's an adult asking you a question on camera." Countering opponents' later allegations that the children were being manipulated by adults to voice opinions they didn't understand, this participant reflects, "I don't even remember what I would have said or what was asked of me, but it was probably . . . whatever pops into my head about the importance of peace in the world, because that's mostly what we were interested in telling adults." Sharing power between children leaders and adult supporters shifted expected relationships in ways that the project's opponents found difficult to countenance. Another participant recalled that being youth-led was the most important dimension of the project for her; she explained that the "adult leaders were really good about making sure that children's voices were heard at every stage," and noted that although she "didn't have any associations with the term 'activist' at the time," she "felt like [she] was being an activist" by "being a spokesperson" for the project and contributing to its success in every way she could.

The belief that young people had ideas that were worth listening to was an overriding characteristic of this project. One participant that I interviewed emphasized that what mattered most at the time was "for kids to have a voice and speak up, and say, We don't agree with [nuclear proliferation], we want a future. That seemed . . . important." As he explained, "the physical statue itself [was not] the first idea," but instead, that became the means the group chose to "tell the world somehow how we feel about this situation." Nearly twenty years later, the experience of "saying something important enough that adults were going to listen" remained noteworthy for the people I spoke with, suggesting, in part, that the experience of being listened to was memorably out of the ordinary. Another participant felt that her involvement in the project "taught [her] to speak to [her] ideals" with conviction that her voice mattered even if, as a child, she wasn't "the expert" or the most authoritative person in the room. In the words of another participant, the adults explicitly avowed an approach he characterized as "Let kids speak their mind, maybe you'll learn something from them." Though he granted that kids' leadership probably meant they "made lots of mistakes and didn't realize the connotations of our arguments or [of] the things that we were saying in public," nevertheless, he felt the adults embraced the question "What happens if kids are in charge of doing something like this?"

Perhaps in retrospect it seems inevitable, given the youth-led nature of the project, that their attempt to dedicate a peace statue in Los Alamos on the fiftieth anniversary of the bombing of Hiroshima would fail. One of my goals in approaching these materials, however, has been *not* to assume that failure was inevitable. As I show below, one tactic of opponents was to characterize the children as out of their depth, unaware of effective avenues for activism and uninformed about the broader context that made their arguments threatening to residents of Los Alamos. Approaching these children as rhetorical agents means holding open the prospect of their success, rather than recapitulating to the assertions of opponents, who drew substantial rhetorical power from characterizing the children who addressed them as naïvely unaware of the complexities of adult conflicts. Consequently, I show how these children acted strategically through their efforts to create a material object meant to concretize children *as* a collectivity capable of engaging in public acts of meaning-making. Turning later to adult responses, I show how the association of children with innocence provided adult opponents with argumentative resources for subverting these activists' attempts to act as meaning-making agents in public life. Drawing upon a range of materials, including minutes from Los Alamos County Council meetings, news coverage of these meetings, and archival materials retained by participants in the project, I highlight the strategies children adopted, then trace the tactics by which adult opponents subverted these speakers' agency.

AMPLIFICATION AND THE RHETORICAL POWER OF COLLECTIVITY

From the project's beginnings in 1990 through the dedication of the statue in 1995, children organizers worked persistently to intervene in public life. This section analyzes the rhetorical strategies employed in the diverse activities they pursued—speaking at public events, composing and distributing a newsletter, coordinating their petition to the Los Alamos County Council, and so on—in their efforts to constitute an international constituency, capable of speaking persuasively to powerful publics. Through rhetorical tactics of amplification and through strategic spatial and temporal linkages that asserted their existence as a powerful speaking body, supporters of the Children's Peace Statue asserted their agency and the legitimacy of their political collective. These tactics were subverted by adult dissent, which not only reasserted dominant understandings of the atomic bomb as necessary and peace-initiating but also resisted recognizing the agency of children speakers. In the analysis that follows, I read promotional material and correspondence alongside news coverage and meeting minutes to locate evidence of the rhetorical strategies children employed. These materials suggest that children speaking in support of the statue employed three major rhetorical tactics: *amplification, spatial linkages,* and *temporal identifications.*

Amplification

Children used amplification as a rhetorical strategy to increase the force of their voices by positioning themselves as speaking for thousands of other children.[26] At the 1992 meeting when the group first petitioned the council for land, numerous students asserted that they were speaking for others; one student spoke on behalf of a group of youth at Los Alamos High School, for instance, while others spoke for those who had sent their signatures, letters,

---

26. I use the term *amplification* to describe several tactics used by the Kids' Committee, because these tactics seem to me to attempt to augment the small-scale agency of individual young people through accumulation. Jeanne Fahnestock defines amplification as "endowing an element with conceptual importance by making it salient in a text and prominent in perception," a prominence often achieved "through tactics of *copia,* which involve expanding the amount of text devoted to an item in order to preoccupy the audience's attention." See Fahnestock, *Rhetorical Style,* 16. Referencing Chaim Perelman and Lucie Olbrechts-Tyteca, Fahnestock elaborates further: "Emphasis and presence are twentieth-century terms for classical rhetoric's insistence on amplification" (203), and emphasis and presence are clearly pursued through the tactics of amplification used by Peace Statue activists. Relevant to my use of amplification is Temptaous McKoy's theorization of what she calls amplification rhetorics (AR) as "discursive and communicative practices, both written/textual and embodied/performative, typically performed/used by Black/African-Americans that center the lived experiences and epistemologies of Black/African-American people and other historically marginalized groups. AR are characterized by three tenets: (1) the reclamation of agency (ownership of embodied rhetorical practices), (2) the accentuation and acknowledgment of narratives (validated lived experiences), and (3) the inclusion of marginalized epistemologies (that add to new ways of learning)." See McKoy, "Y'All Call It Technical," 28. Although the young white and Latinx leaders of the Peace Statue Project are positioned differently than the Black performers, writers, and institutions that McKoy focuses on, her theorization of amplification as a tactic for reclaiming agency and foregrounding marginalized epistemologies suggests potential overlap between her study and the practices employed by the transnational network of young people included here.

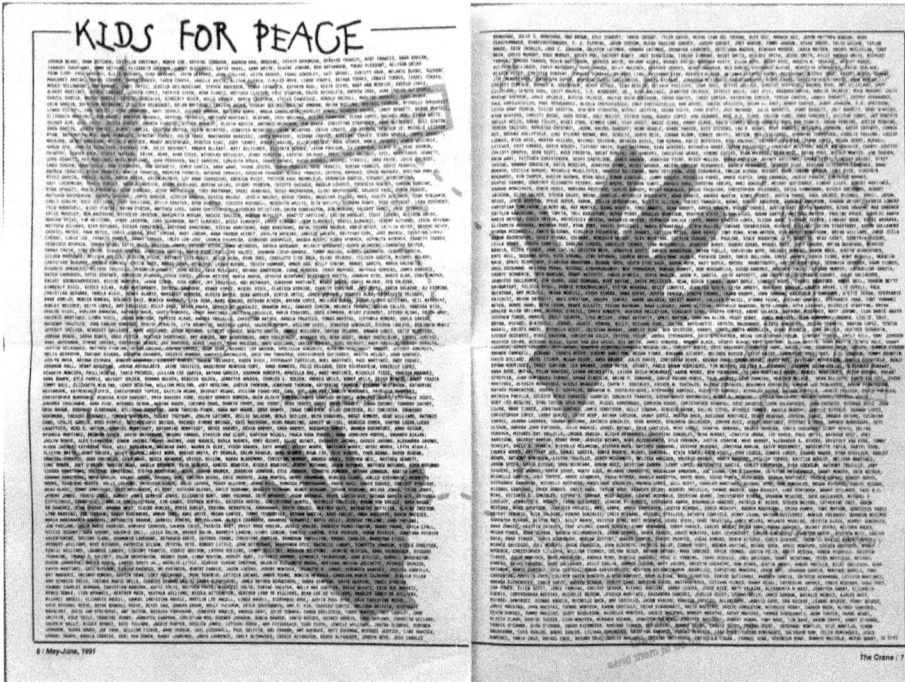

FIGURE 4. "Kids for Peace." Names of supporters, printed in *The Crane* 1.1 (1991).

and dollars in support. One said: "I got several letters from kids in Silver City and I am sending these to you but I decided that I'd read one. . . . 'Dear City Council People, My name is Crystal Ness. Please give the land for the Peace Statue because I would like to see a statue for peace.'"[27] Many of the promotional materials circulated by the Kids' Committee recount the support the project had received from others—both adult and child, individual and collective—in ways that frame the statue as a project pursued by a broad national and international collective. For instance, the first issue of *The Crane*, the kid-produced newsletter mailed to supporters of the project, features a large two-page spread containing all the names of supporters collected through May 1991 (see figures 4 and 5). The numerous names in extremely small print that cover these pages have an augmentative effect, becoming not merely a list but accumulating into a visual representation of mass support. Blue text behind the printed names invites readers to join this collective by suggesting "Fun Ideas for Building Peace," such as "Take photos of peace events and send them to us" or "Have an art show or auction." Blue handprints stand out against the

---

27. *On Wings of Peace*, 6–7.

IACSHANE, NINO ANGELINO, ASHLEY WEITZEL, REBECCA COHEN, SHAYNA LAZAR,LUCAS
/IN HARVEY, KARA HARVEY, MARGARET HARVEY, AMANDA KUEHNTOPZ, ANNA KUISUR,
KARISSA MCCALL, PAULA ROSA PODEHL, ANNA JENNIFER PODEHL, SHOHREH BIAJAR,
, CORY GUINEE, ELISE GUINEE, ZACHARIE JACOBS, CASSIE JACOBS, ALEXANDRA JACOB
ISEN, KATY MOSES, JEFFRY MOSES, GRETCHEN MOSES, HEIDI MOSES, LETTA NIGGLI,
AN DEWALD, SARA SCHMOE, MIWA ITO, CHIE HIROSE, YOKO AKANA, SASHA SCHENK,
KEMORE, CHRISTINE MURRAY, ANDREA GOULD, STEPHEN WEIL, MATTHEW GENNETT,
, NICOLE BOWDICH, JEREMY ROTUNNO, JASON ROTUNNO, MATTHEW ROTUNNO, KIAH ROTUN
AH JOHNSON, KYLE JOHNSON, KENNETH JOHNSON, NATHAN JOHNSON, MARTIN LOPEZ,
TE, JUAN MONTES, GRANT DRUMMOND, REBECCA CLARK, JOELLE STEINBECK, HERMETTA
JENNY RILL, REBECCA SYNDERGUARD, ANGIE RUIZ, CHRIS CHAVEZ, CHRISTY STRAIGHT
I, BRADLEY SCHRAMM, MINDY SCHRAMM, TREVOR SCHRAMM, MELISA JONES, TYLER JONES,
IN, ERIK BROADUS, JASON BROADUS, SKHYE GARCIA-WIX, BRIANA GARCIA-WIX, ERTUGRUI
IERTEL, CHRISTIANNE HERTEL, MICHELLE TRUJILLO, SHAWN VON DREELE, ROSA HAGAR,
IN, SHOSHANNA, DAVID CHAVEZ, HEATHER GATT, NATHANIEL GOTTLIEB, BLAISE TREESON,
TOMMY TECHENTIEN, NATHAN GARCIA, SARA TWEIST, ABRA ANCLIFFE, DAVID MAESTES,
ARRASCO, ANNAROSE SCHWARTZ, KATIE KELLY, JESSICA FRELUND, JUDD FRELUND,
LY ROSE VOGLER, JESSIE VOGLER, PHOENIX YOUNG-TANTUM, SARAH YOUNG, KAYLA LYALL,
ON, LINDI LANCON, CAMILLE LANCON, KYLE POIRIER, SHAWN POIRIER, JONATHAN POIRIE
STINE PAPPIAN, BRANDDON PAPILLION, RAQUEL CHARLES, MARKEYNA DICKS,
WITHERWAX, SHARHONDA OTIS, RACHELLE LANDRY, VINDETTA JOHNSON, NICOLE CHRETIEN
JIMMY GUILLORY, BRANDON RELEFORD, JASMINE OLIVIER, ADAM THIBODEAUX, RICHARD
UNT, TIFFANIE HARMON, KIMBERLY THIBODEAUX, JOHN BILLIOT, DURRELL WASHINGTON,
THON, MAJORIE ELIZABETH BREDA, ADRIENNE BELLOW JOLIVETTE, MICHAEL GAVAZZA,
CERO, JEREMY MONTOYA, JEANETTE R. LONGO, VERONICA SANCHEZ, JESSICA CARRILLO,
ALBAS, AMBER YOUNG, MONICA MENDOZA, CAROLINA MARIE CALDERON, JESSICA ELLEN
MES MATHEW SCHWECHERL, SARAH SIMPSON, KATIE GUIFFRE, TRACY O'BRIEN,
ILTS, CORINE CHESTER, MOLLY MAE CHESTER, ERIKA GUISTI, ERIN SUE MOCHRIE,
THER LYNN DE VILLIERS, RYAN LEE DE VILLIERS, BRADLEY JAMES DE VILLIERS,
IDA ANGELL, STEPHANIE HYDE, JUSTIN PAUL HYDE, ERIN CHRISTINE REEVE,
RICA SOUTHWORTH, AMY C. PIA, CHARLES CORTEZ, MELISSA GRIFFIN, STEPHANIE
IREW GRAY, JULIE CONNER, CHAVA EDELSTEIN, TORRE HUNTER, TREY LANGLEY, ANNE
ION, ROBIN BANKER, CHRIS REEVES, QUINCY HARRIS, TODD GAYLORD, CHAQUITA WILLARD,
HODGE, AMY FITZGERALD, CHAD FLOYD, JENELLE WILLIAMS, JANIKA FLOWERS, DURENDA
GRIFFIN, AMY PARHAM, AMY ROEBUCK, MATT SHERMAN, MICHAEL JUSTICE, LINC HANCOCK,
LY ALTHAUSER, CASSIE ALTHAUSER, DEREK ALTHAUSER, JOSEPH BECK, JESS CHARLES

FIGURE 5. Detail from "Kids for Peace."

names, signaling the members of this collective as children, even as the names
themselves evoke the (typically adult) political project of petitioning—a time-
honored amplification strategy employed by the disenfranchised, which I discuss more fully below.

Children's amplification strategies took embodied and material forms
as well. Although approximately twenty children spoke at the 1992 County
Council meeting, their presence was augmented by a large, visible group of
supporters in the audience—roughly one hundred children and two dozen
parents and teachers who attended to show their support. In addition, one
speaker presented the council with a list of names of more than ten thousand
other children who had contributed money in support of the project. A document of this size is obviously not meant to be read; its purpose is to amplify

the force of the children's petition by portraying—and helping the council to visualize—thousands of absent others who likewise support the project. As she presented this list to the council, Bonnie Malcolm said, "in these names, of 10,000 children, we ask for land."[28]

Presenting the list of names to the council as a request on behalf of ten thousand individuals connects this amplification strategy to the long-standing practice of public petition. Petitioning was a rhetorical and political tactic employed by white women and African Americans in the nineteenth century—disenfranchised groups for whom the act of petitioning signaled not only specific political desires but also their right to speak to a governing body that granted them no voting rights. Through antiremoval campaigns, for instance, women "intruded into an exclusive discourse community" and laid claim to national, political space.[29] Likewise, women who participated in abolitionist petition campaigns "bypassed the requirement of suffrage to participate publicly in the political debate over the heated national issue of slavery."[30] The strategy of amplification employed by children supporters of the Peace Statue functioned similarly by simultaneously strengthening the speakers' request and constituting the speakers themselves within a civic space that grants children no legal right of address. As Susan Zaeske argues, understanding public petitions in this way focuses our attention on petitioning as a political act that "reformulate[s] . . . the political subjectivity of the rhetors themselves."[31] In the antebellum United States, exclusions from voting were based on an ideal political subject "who was to be a rational actor capable of independent thought and action."[32] Many disenfranchised residents "fell outside" categorization as political subjects because of "their status as dependents . . . believed to lack capacity for rational thought."[33] The amplification tactics of peace statue supporters likewise drew attention to political exclusion; supporters amplified their claims and asserted political subjectivity not only at council meetings but also—perhaps most insistently—at the dedication itself, when the names of all fifty thousand supporters were read aloud during a month of events held throughout August 1995. Reading supporters' names aloud extends the act of petition into public space, claiming their status as members of a collective who speak their desires through the statue.

---

28. *On Wings of Peace*, 2.
29. Portnoy, "Right to Speak," 603.
30. Zaeske, "Signatures of Citizenship," 148.
31. Zaeske, 148.
32. Zaeske, 149.
33. Zaeske, 149.

The strands of folded paper cranes that frequently figured in the public discourse of children supporters constituted a further form of material amplification. The children often linked their project to the narrative of Sadako Sasaki, a Japanese girl who died of leukemia at age twelve in 1955; Sasaki, following a Japanese folk belief, hoped to be granted her wish for health if she folded one thousand paper cranes. After Sasaki's death, her classmates organized a youth movement to dedicate a peace memorial in her honor; strands of one thousand paper cranes are still left at this statue in Hiroshima. While single origami cranes symbolize peace, the chains of one thousand cranes folded by student supporters of the statue make visible and material both the care of individual children and the collective power of their work together. Though each crane is folded by a particular individual, an act that takes only a slight amount of skill, time, and resources, these individual contributions become substantial when linked into chains of one thousand. Strands of folded cranes consequently emblematize the pooling of energies toward a project that would be, similarly, the linked, larger result of small individual efforts joined together.

In 1992, in addition to a massive list of names, the children employed the visible, material abundance of nine thousand folded paper cranes to augment the presence of speakers in the room by recalling the presence of thousands of other supporters elsewhere. This connection was reinforced by the student who presented the cranes, saying, "In addition to the 10,000 children [who contributed their money and names], we represent many other thousands of children who have sent their support in the form of paper cranes. . . . I guess what this means to you is that those of us here tonight represent the 10,000 people and others who have helped us make all these cranes. We all ask for your support."[34] Students' amplification strategies attempted to make manifest to the council the size of their collective, and they suggest that the children anticipated the difficulty they faced in addressing an elected body where their collective had no formal standing.

Spatial Linkages

Forming spatial linkages with children around the world offered supporters a further avenue for amplification, by constituting their discourse as originating from a national and international rather than merely local community. Presenting their original petition to the council, children highlighted

---

34. *On Wings of Peace*, 4–5.

the geographic scope of the letters and donations they had received. One speaker emphasized that the children in the room "have come from all over New Mexico tonight; from Albuquerque, from Los Alamos, from Espanola."[35] Another explained that the ten thousand names presented to the council come from "49 states in the US" as well as kids in "53 countries who support our dream."[36] A flyer created by the Kids' Committee in 1994 likewise emphasized that the project had "received support from all over the world with names of over 41,000 children from all 50 states and 63 different countries." Highlighting origins of donations helped the Albuquerque-based group invoke a global collective of children supporting the statue's message of peace.

In addition, the Kids' Committee created more specific spatial linkages with Japan. They identified their proposed statue as a "sister statue" to Japan's Children's Peace Monument, Genbaku no Ko no Zō, dedicated in 1958 in Hiroshima Peace Memorial Park, which occupies central Hiroshima. Through the "sister statue" designation, the Kids' Committee highlighted the precedent-setting nature of that earlier statue as one proposed and funded by children. For instance, a photograph and drawing of the Japanese statue were featured in the initial issue of *The Crane,* with a narrative explaining that the current project

> was inspired by the Japanese statue called "Genbaku No Ko No Zo" (Atomic Bombed Children), constructed in the Hiroshima Peace Park after the Second World War. Following the war, Japanese children raised funds and urged the building of a peace statue. They were led by the classmates of Sadako Sasaki, a young girl who was a victim of radiation sickness and who died ten years after the war. The dream of U.S. children today is to design and build a "sister" statue, to be created by student design and student raised funds, in New Mexico, the state in which the first nuclear bombs were built and where the first nuclear test bomb was dropped on July 16, 1945.[37]

The Japanese statue is likewise depicted on a 1990 flyer that was reprinted in numerous periodicals, and a prayer attributed to Sasaki, "I will write peace on your wings and you will fly all over the world," was printed on promotional materials and donation forms. During the initial presentation to the council in 1992, one student supporter recounted Sasaki's story in detail, beginning with the bombing of Hiroshima during her childhood and concluding with the unveiling of the Japanese statue in 1958, arguing that this story "shows even

---

35. *On Wings of Peace,* 2.
36. *On Wings of Peace,* 2.
37. Condon, "Kids Invited," 1.

little children have big dreams and I think this story inspires young minds."[38] Kids' promotional materials and public presentation together articulate this linkage to Japan as centered on children's agency—on Japanese youth offering a positive model of what young people can accomplish through collective action. Even as the Kids' Committee recirculated Sasaki's story, they emphasized the uptakes generated through the collective labors of Sasaki's classmates and the movement for peace her classmates helped to promote. This framing differs markedly from the xenophobic associations with Japan that adult opponents repeatedly reinforced, insisting upon articulating Japan as a racialized enemy, as I show below.

In addition to portraying the Japanese statue as offering a precedent for the children's public action, the Kids' Committee cultivated other links between Los Alamos and Hiroshima as well. Most significantly, they argued that placing a statue in Los Alamos parallel to the Children's Peace Statue in Hiroshima would revise the line of violence that ran between the two locations through the trajectory of nuclear destruction. In a 1990 flyer distributed to periodicals across the country, members of the Kids' Committee explained:

> Maybe you don't know it, but Los Alamos, New Mexico was the place where the first nuclear bombs were made during World War II. From Los Alamos, two atomic bombs named "Little Boy" and "Fat Man" were carried by plane to Japan and dropped on the cities of Hiroshima and Nagasaki at the end of the war in 1945. . . . Now we want to create a Children's Peace Statue in the United States in the city of Los Alamos. By this action we are saying NO to war.

The image developed here, which traces the line of flight from Los Alamos to Hiroshima, inverts that trajectory by seeking to bring *back* from Hiroshima the idea of a statue that materializes and communicates kids' collective desire for peace. When addressing the Los Alamos County council, supporters did not invoke the trajectory of the bombs so directly but instead emphasized the message of peace the statue in Hiroshima bears. The children deployed the project's links to Japan in a polysemic fashion, finding this spatial connection useful for different arguments and audiences. In contrast, their adult opponents resisted these spatial connections, as I show below, by repeatedly reiterating racialized characterizations of Japanese as enemies and "outsiders" and by refusing to countenance the articulations offered by the Kids' Committee, who located in Hiroshima valuable models of collective youth organizing.

---

38. *On Wings of Peace,* 3–4.

The Kids' Committee forged these spatial connections in myriad material ways: through exchanges of letters and donations with supporters around the globe, of course, but perhaps most significantly through the practice of the groups of supporters who assembled and mailed chains of one thousand folded paper cranes, which figured prominently in public events the Kids' Committee held to promote the project. The weight and size of such strands of cranes should not be discounted: each strand required a roughly 3′ × 3′ box to ship to Albuquerque. At the time of the dedication in 1995, although the Kids' Committee had not received the million names they originally sought to collect, they *had* received more than a million folded paper cranes from supporters worldwide.[39] Such links formed material as well as symbolic connections between project leaders in Albuquerque and Los Alamos and the supporters they sought to engage with worldwide.

Temporal Identifications

In addition to creating international linkages, children used temporal tactics to constitute their collective. Supporters emphasized age, rather than language or nationality, as the primary identification organizing the dispersed global community they sought to construct. For instance, they reprinted in *The Crane*, in their original languages, letters from Russian and Japanese supporters; poetry, drawings, and photographs printed in the newsletter usually included the age of the children who submitted them. Promotional press releases that the group wrote and circulated to other periodicals asked, "Can children have a significant impact on the world?"[40] The title of their governing organization, the Kids' Committee for Peace, itself reinforces this age-based identification, attaching "kid" as a possessive modifier to the bureaucratic, adult structure of a "committee." In their ambition to "reach one million kids who want peace," the Kids' Committee reinforced their agency by reminding readers that kids were in charge of the project, generating its energy and scope.[41] Their "one dollar, one name" fundraising strategy similarly emphasized the possibility of even young children making direct contributions to show their support, and a newsletter circulated in late 1992 emphasized that "*only money from children will be used to build the peace statue*," though adult supporters could provide

---

39. They had received 1,015,000 cranes by August 1995, in strands of one thousand, many of which festooned the statue during the month-long dedication.

40. "Tomorrow's Child," flyer, 1992.

41. "Dear Friends," flyer, 1990.

financial support by sending postage stamps for the kids to use in responding to the many letters they received.

They also oriented their project toward the future rather than the past. In public statements and printed documents, supporters reiterated the statue's message: that kids want peace for the future. In their widely reprinted 1990 flyer, members of the Kids' Committee introduce themselves as "36 kids in New Mexico who have a dream of making a peaceful future for our world" and ask for support because "the future of the earth needs us to be united." A flyer from 1994 places this message in bold and all caps: "The Albuquerque children decided that their statue would represent their **HOPE FOR A PEACEFUL FUTURE.**" Students worked to create a collective that could overcome geographical, national, and linguistic differences, unified around its members' identities as children who shared this desire for the future.

By emphasizing the statue's orientation to the future, supporters sought to eschew the perception that the statue would memorialize past events. For instance, responding to residents' concerns over "rewriting history," one member of the Kids' Committee, Jack Thornton, tried to redirect discussion toward the statue's orientation to the future, explaining:

> If we didn't make it sufficiently clear earlier, this monument is not intended as a reminder that Hiroshima happened. Rather, this monument is intended as a sister statue to one that happens to be in Hiroshima, for peace. Our purpose here is not to remember wars that have happened, not to forget them or the people who died serving our country, or other countries. Rather, our purpose here is to look forward into time and do at least, in our way, some small project or something that will hopefully lead to a peaceful future where we won't have to be remembering wars and people who have died protecting others.[42]

Here Thornton emphasizes that exercising agency—in trying to "do at least, in our way, . . . something" that could lead toward the future they desire—is key to their efforts. Another student invited the audience to "all look forward towards peace and not back on pain and suffering."[43] At the 1994 meeting, asked to comment on why Los Alamos was chosen, Bonnie Malcolm explained that the members of the Kids' Committee "want a peaceful future, nothing more, nothing less . . . [and] to work together to get over the past."[44] Similarly, David Rosoff reiterated that "the statue's message would be that adults of today

42. *On Wings of Peace*, 3, 7.
43. *On Wings of Peace*, 5.
44. LACC 1994, 10.

would use their power to create a peaceful future for those of tomorrow."[45] At the final meeting in 1995, Dana Kaplan insisted "that the project evolved beyond World War II. It is a hope for a peaceful future, and has nothing to do with Hiroshima or the atomic bomb."[46] Adult supporters likewise reinforced this future orientation; Councilor Ginger Welch, the member of the council who most strongly supported the statue, said at the final meeting, "the children . . . want peace for the future of the world and . . . that is what [the statue] stands for."[47] A nun representing the Sisters of Loretto argued that the statue was "not a statement about the past, it is not about whether or not to have a defense program, Los Alamos bashing, or about making anyone feel guilty . . . it is a children's prayer that the future of the world be without war."[48] Such repeated assertions highlight the importance supporters accorded to the statue's orientation to the future, yet the necessity of insisting upon that orientation reflects the extent to which future meanings, present desires, and past narratives remain deeply, irresistibly enmeshed.

DUPES, PUPPETS, AND PEOPLE
"GENERATIONS AWAY FROM THE TIMES"

Circulating discourses that figure children as naïve, uniformed, and apolitical form a powerful constraint that young activists must work to mitigate, leaving them susceptible to opponents' rearticulations. Despite efforts of children rhetors to garner support for the future-oriented meanings they hoped the statue would generate, opponents of the statue disputed these meanings, countering the kids' rhetorical strategies in multiple ways. Adult opponents reasserted dominant narratives of the bombings of Hiroshima and Nagasaki as peace-initiating, and they resisted engaging with children as speaking agents, figuring the children instead as (at best) innocent idealists and (at worst) puppets being maneuvered by adults into arguments and agendas they were incapable of understanding. Recognizing agency as something children exercise in complex ways requires that we register the diverse effects of their public activism, even when their efforts appear to fail. Although opponents prevailed in preventing the statue from being located in Los Alamos, the intensity and variety of opponents' responses provide evidence of children's

---

45. LACC 1994, 10.
46. LACC 1995, 11.
47. LACC 1995, 9.
48. LACC 1995, 11.

rhetorical agency. If children were incapable of public action, rejecting their project would not have demanded so much urgent rhetorical effort.

The nature of the children's project—its opposition to Cold War–era political formations, its posing of alternative forms of collectivities, and its supporters' status as unauthorized speakers—prompted the range and vigor of the oppositional tactics I chart below. This analysis invites rhetorical scholars to attend to how ideological opposition can be masked by strategies of rearticulation that draw upon pervasive figurations of children as innocent, naïve, and lacking in agency. Opponents in Los Alamos masked not only their ideological opposition but more fundamentally the racialized and xenophobic nature of that opposition, reasserting dominant narratives of white innocence that were threatened by the revised linkages the project attempted to generate. In this way, age operated as a liability for these young rhetors despite their efforts to manage and mitigate its constraints. Widespread representations of children as politically ineffectual served as an argumentative resource for opponents who employed such representations to resist the public action these children pursued and thus to reinforce the impossibility of children acting publicly.

Adults who opposed the statue resisted children's agency in myriad ways. For instance, some adults' tactics of heckling and shouting to prevent teenagers from speaking during council meetings served as an effective, if uncivil, way to foreclose the possibility of rhetorical exchange. Such behavior bespeaks not only the intensity of local investment in dominant understandings of Los Alamos's wartime role but also a deep reluctance to address and be addressed by children. Other tactics of resistance operate more subtly—and more civilly—than simply shouting to prevent a child from speaking. These tactics enable adult opponents to refuse not only the children's petition but more fundamentally the claim to agency and political subjectivity they staged through the project.

Adult opponents subjected the students who addressed the Los Alamos County Council to a range of kinds of dismissal. Some raised concerns about the "process" the students had adopted in petitioning the council for land. Councilor Morris Pongratz, for instance, who was fiercely opposed to the statue, argued that "the United States has a ratified way for addressing ways to change government policies and he is concerned that the process that is being advocated is not one of electing people and changing something if you don't like it."[49] Pongratz had spoken at length against the statue as a member of the public during the initial discussion of the project in 1992, when he was a councilor-elect but not yet a voting member; despite his objections, which

---

49. LACC 1995, 7–8.

ranged from opposition to "outsiders" to uncertainty about "wording" on the statue to general disapproval of "monuments" as ineffectual, the motion to find county land for the statue passed 5–0 at this earlier meeting.[50] Concerns with the "process" by which the statue was being considered were raised by other Los Alamos residents, who proposed that the issue "should be referred to the voters."[51] Yet children do not have access to the electoral citizenship Pongratz privileges, and resistance to the *form* of children's advocacy ignores the extent to which these petitioners are excluded from electoral channels, while also masking the nature of their opposition in neutral language of "process" that shields their politics from scrutiny.

Frequently children were subjected to lessons about the futility of their project. Pongratz, for instance, argued that "the real place where we need peace is within our hearts and he is not sure how much a monument does for that."[52] Praising "actions" over "monuments," Pongratz "would rather see $1 million spent trying to feed the hungry people in Somalia rather than spend $1 million on a statue."[53] Many others repeated the idea that more good could be accomplished in some other way—by providing food or housing for the poor, assistance for children whose parents are unemployed, medications for children in Russia, and so on. This list of ostensibly effective alternatives taps into circulating images—in particular media coverage in 1992 of the famine in Somalia—and reasserts comforting tropes of the US as force of benevolence, using the familiar figure of the child-in-peril that Wendy Hesford has shown shores up violent US exceptionalism.[54] Opponents characterized the project as "dewy-eyed sentiment" or "wishful thinking" that could never accomplish the children's ambitious goals.[55] These dismissive characterizations denied children's agency by denying that the project could have the effects children claimed for it.

Adult opponents (as well as many supporters) repeatedly asserted the children's innocence. Many who voiced concern about the potential message of the statue tempered their critiques by affirming that they trusted the children's "pure" motives. One critical resident, for instance, granted that "the project has been promulgated with excellent intentions, but is misdirected," and Councilor Bob Fisher noted that, although he opposed the statue, "no one in

---

50. LACC 1992, 5–6.
51. LACC 1995, 9.
52. LACC 1992, 5.
53. LACC 1992, 6.
54. Hesford, *Violent Exceptions*.
55. Charmian Schaller, "What Was Said about the Statue," *Los Alamos Monitor*, February 15, 1995, A3; and LACC 1995, 9.

the room doubts the intentions of the children here tonight."[56] Adult supporters of the project voiced similar affirmations; JoAnn Dowler, a Los Alamos teacher, introduced the children by stating that their "motives are pure and uncomplicated," and Councilor Welch affirmed numerous times that "the children have a sincere and honest motive."[57] The availability of such assertions of innocence registers the fact that the children who organized through the Kids' Committee were predominantly, though not exclusively, white, as both childhood and the innocence it requires "has never been available to all."[58] Such assertions of innocence, even when intended as support, represented the children as incapable of voicing any serious challenge to dominant political formations, effectively blunting and subverting the power they claimed—both in the act of petitioning the council and in the possibilities they ascribed to the statue in their own letters and promotional flyers.

The insistence upon viewing children as innocent also reveals the contingent nature of adult protection, which children can expect only so long as they refrain from challenging adult power. Many opponents' civility diminished as their certainty of the children's innocence weakened. One city official wrote to the council that she was "forced to question the motives of the Kids Committee and their adult advisors," because the children's stubborn resolve to hold an August dedication caused her to suspect that they were planning disruptive anti-war demonstrations.[59] Pongratz likewise expressed skepticism regarding the children's innocence, complaining that the council was "told that they are innocent children, pure of heart and untainted by the adult world and that the Council should not question that."[60] Pongratz was particularly willing to engage with children confrontationally. In the 1994 meeting, after teenager Bonnie Malcolm reiterated that "the point is that [Sasaki's] statue was built and funded by children," Pongratz responded that he "did not 'buy' her comments. If it is to be a sister image to the one in Hiroshima, Japan, one might think that it would be dedicated in the month in which [Sasaki] died."[61] Through strong associations between innocence and incapacity, the tolerant attitude adopted by some opponents eroded as the children's requests threatened to become reality.

One consequence of opponents' resistance to children's agency is that statements about the children as *innocent* could be converted into assertions

---

56. LACC 1992, 4; LACC 1992, 6.
57. LACC 1992, 3; LACC 1995, 9.
58. Meiners, *For the Children?*, 32.
59. LACC 1994, 11.
60. LACC 1995, 8.
61. LACC 1994, 10; LACC 1994, 10.

about the children as *dupes*. As Kathleene Parker, writer for the *Santa Fe New Mexican,* reported in 1995, "opponents have claimed the idea in fact originated with adult peace activists who are exploiting children as a way to get the statue built in Los Alamos."[62] Councilor Pongratz circulated an agenda packet before the 1995 meeting that asserted that the entire project, in Pongratz's words, was "all part of an adult put-up plan," specifically by Camy Condon, the adult advisor who Pongratz said "went shopping for kids gullible enough to think [the idea] was their own."[63] Pongratz asserted that a letter Condon mailed to a friend in Los Alamos in February 1990 constituted "physical evidence that the concept [of a peace statue] was 'sold' to young children via unbalanced presentation" and "clearly proves that this concept did not arise from a class of students . . . as the press release claims."[64] Letters to the *Los Alamos Monitor* likewise asserted that adult activists were exploiting the children "to further their questionable cause."[65] Under the guise of concern over "exploitation," these portrayals reveal a reluctance to engage with children as speaking agents. If children are innocent, they are not agents but puppets, which allows opponents to argue more comfortably against the adult activists who are seen as ultimately generating their discourse. This tactic suggests analytically what childhood studies scholars have argued more theoretically: that our ideas and language characterizing children as powerless help to constitute that powerlessness.

Opponents also adopted tactics of rearticulation by which they revised the children's lines of argument. Specifically, adult opponents reframed the project's spatial and temporal linkages through xenophobic constructions that recast supporters as outsiders, irrelevantly distant from the meaningful community of Los Alamos residents, and that generated anxiety about future uses of the statue—especially future demonstrations by antinuclear activists.

Children's efforts to forge spatial links with Japan in particular and with an international community of children more generally were rearticulated by adult opponents in ways that turned supporters of the statue into community outsiders. Despite the presence of many Los Alamos students and teachers among supporters, councilors and members of the public who spoke against the statue effectively reframed the project as one originating outside Los Alamos and consequently without jurisdiction. For instance, in the final meeting in 1995, when Councilor Greenwood "stated that he was elected to

---

62. Parker, "Councilor," B1.
63. Parker, B1.
64. LACC 1995, agenda documentation.
65. Letter to *Los Alamos Monitor,* December 7, 1994, 4.

represent Los Alamos, not Northern New Mexico, Albuquerque, etc.,"[66] this statement was greeted with applause.[67] Even though two hundred Los Alamos residents submitted their signatures in support of the statue, opponents who attended the meeting referred to the statue's supporters as "external people" and asserted that Los Alamos "should not accept anything from outside the community."[68] After voting again to reject the statue, Councilor Greenwood closed discussion of the matter by reminding the audience that the council would not "prohibit doing something like this if there is an interest within the community. His opposition is primarily the external nature of it."[69] Both "external people" and "external nature" function here to maintain white innocence in relation to a perceived challenge to the centrality of Los Alamos residents' construal of global politics and history. Framing the children as outsiders permits opponents to reject the statue while insisting that their community supports both children and peace, casting their opposition as a problem of jurisdiction rather than of message. The language of "outsiders" used by opponents operates flexibly, drawing sharp but unstated lines around who can and cannot speak about Los Alamos or about nuclear warfare and who can and cannot legibly articulate what they hope for the future. Using "outsiders" in this euphemistic way allows opponents to reject the prefigurative politics articulated by the Kids' Committee and to recenter dominant white memories and meanings (while obscuring that very recentering). The project's links to Japan—which Malcolm and other youth repeatedly articulated as an assertion of children's political agency and capacity for collective organizing—both racialized and politicized the meaning of *future peace* in ways that opponents refused to accept.

The project's specific spatial linkages with Japan provided opponents with further resources for positioning it as inappropriate for Los Alamos. These included racist and xenophobic responses from opponents who figured Japan as an ever-threatening enemy. One woman asserted that if not for the atomic bomb, "everyone in the room" would be "speaking Japanese and bowing to the Japanese" if not "being kicked by them."[70] Another opponent, Al Charmatz, proposed a design for the statue that would feature "a panel showing Battleship Row at Pearl Harbor listing the names of the thousands of seamen who are still inside the Arizona . . . another panel showing the New Mexico National

66. LACC 1995, 8.

67. Schaller, "What Was Said About the Statue," A3.

68. Kathleene Parker, "Los Alamos Gives Kids' Peace Park Another Chance," *Santa Fe New Mexican,* February 2, 1995, A1; LACC 1995, 10; and LACC 1995, 10.

69. LACC 1995, 13.

70. Schaller, "What Was Said."

Guard and the Bataan Death March with soldiers being decapitated and shot
. . . right across the top should be the immortal words of Harold Agnew,
former Director [of Los Alamos National Labs], 'They bloody well deserved
it.'"[71] The availability of racialized anti-Japanese antagonism is evident in these
statements, and the hostility of these responses underscores how deeply the
project threatened dominant exceptionalist narratives within Los Alamos
(and the US more broadly), which insist upon the US as a peace-maintaining
global savior, even in the act of detonating nuclear weapons on civilian cities.
The designation of the project as a "sister statue" to the peace statue in Hiroshima prompted many opponents to propose alternate locations, especially
Pearl Harbor and Washington, DC, as more "parallel" to Hiroshima. Councilor Denise Smith, for instance, suggested Washington, DC, as "a place where
decisions are really made as to whether we enter into conflicts," and Councilor
Pongratz argued that "symmetry" with the peace statue in Hiroshima "would
suggest a Pearl Harbor memorial—perhaps in Japan."[72] Although the children
repeatedly asserted that their project found in Hiroshima a vital origin for a
youth-initiated peace movement, opponents refused to consider the specific
associations with Hiroshima that the children avowed. Instead, using a racialized tactic for maintaining white supremacy and white innocence, opponents
fixed the meaning of Hiroshima, insisting on World War II as its meaning, in
order to erase the possibility that Hiroshima could signify the global prefigurative politics young people claimed.

Likewise, although the children used age to constitute an international
community of supporters, opponents used this to position them as outsiders
in a temporal sense, arguing that children could not legitimately contribute
to public discussion about events they had not witnessed. This is evident in
opponents' characterization of children as "people generations away from the
times, people who seem never to have heard of Pearl Harbor."[73] Not only the
specific children who represented the statue at meetings, but children and
teenagers in general were depicted as disqualified from participating in public memories and political meanings broadly. For instance, a long editorial
by Evelyn Vigil, publisher of the *Los Alamos Monitor,* recounted a visit to the
USS *Arizona* Memorial during which "a couple of teen-agers in front of me
. . . giggled and pointed and acted up enough to draw a sharp retort from the
tour guide" and, eventually, to be prevented from entering the memorial.[74]

---

71. LACC 1992, 5.

72. LACC 1994, 10; and Morris B. Pongratz, "This and That," *Los Alamos Monitor,* December 6, 1994, 4.

73. LACC 1995, 10.

74. Evelyn Vigil, "Remembering Pearl Harbor," *Los Alamos Monitor,* December 7, 1994, 4.

Vigil's diagnosis was that "these kids didn't know history. They had no sense of what had happened at this site, no sense of what it means to go to war, and so they had no sense of what is proper respect at a place like this."[75] These unruly teenagers were excluded, Vigil suggested, not only because they misbehaved, but more fundamentally because of their inability to access the wartime experience of earlier generations. Vigil linked the teenagers in this anecdote with those supporting the peace statue, writing that "while it's right to seek peace at every opportunity . . . the teen-agers who acted up . . . probably never knew anyone who went to war. They probably never really thought about the sacrifice a war demands. And, I wonder, would they be tough enough to answer the call, if they were needed?"[76] This perennial complaint about disrespectful teenagers serves, in the context of the peace statue controversy, to substitute disruptive teenagers, ignorant of history, for the collective of thousands of children working together to create a monument to peace. In place of the specific children who had attended County Council meetings and endeavored to speak while opponents shouted them down, Vigil substitutes generic teenagers at a memorial site where the only way to behave respectfully is to be silent. Furthermore, she shows these teenagers receiving a lesson in which their unruly behavior secures their exclusion. The anecdote depicts children simultaneously as disruptive—for failing to sustain imperiled public memories—and incapable of action, as figures who cannot be trusted with the future, because they will fail to act.

Finally, opponents shifted the temporal orientation of the statue into a source of fear about its durability—its capacity to enable unsanctioned uses in the future. Councilor Greenwood, for instance, called the statue a "soap box for people to come to Los Alamos to speak general opposition to what the community has believed over the years."[77] Others asked for reassurance that, as a "donation to the County of Los Alamos," the statue "could be removed" in the future if the council so desired.[78] Councilors were "worried that peace activists would employ the park for rallies,"[79] and Councilor Greenwood asked "peace activists" who were in attendance at the 1994 meeting to promise they would not use the statue for antinuclear demonstrations in the future. Though the supporters who were present were willing to offer such a "promise," another Los Alamos resident spoke up to remind the audience that "there are no guarantees that people are going to use the site" in the peaceful

75. Vigil, 4.
76. Vigil, 4.
77. LACC 1995, 12.
78. LACC 1994, 9.
79. "Editorial," *Los Alamos Monitor,* November 27, 1994, A4.

ways the Kids' Committee recommends.[80] Even in an editorial supporting the statue, the *Los Alamos Monitor* conceded residents' "genuine concern about just what will happen in Los Alamos . . . on the 50th anniversary of Hiroshima Day, when demonstrators who feel the bombing was wrong might interact with veterans . . . and the presence of hundreds of children wouldn't help."[81] The statue's design, open-ended and implicit as it was, could not sufficiently stabilize its potential meanings; Councilor Pongratz "expressed concern about the [statue's] symbolism, especially . . . [its] dual meaning," which I take to mean its implicit or assumed message of blame.[82] Although he "does not challenge the interpretation of the children," he asserted that "to many people in Los Alamos this action is casting a stone."[83] Pongratz's anxiety announces the necessity of maintaining white innocence and US exceptionalism. As one of my participants reflected in his retrospective interview, recalling Pongratz's virulent antagonism to the project, "I don't think you would be this mad at us if you didn't feel bad about this. Why are you so defensive if everything is as justified as you say?" But the fear that opponents voiced of unstable interpretations of the statue, their anxiety over who might control the statue's future meanings, underscores the vulnerability of young activists' arguments to adult rearticulations that undermine their rhetorical agency.

LOCATING AGENCY THROUGH DURABLE OBJECTS AND ENDURING EXPERIENCES

For the County Council to vote, twice, *not* to provide a site for the statue felt like a stinging rejection to the young people who had labored for years toward the goal of dedicating the statue in Los Alamos. As one of my participants explained, "the feeling that Los Alamos didn't want it felt like they rejected our message, . . . our message of peace across continents." As this participant reflected, it was easy for the council to dismiss their project, to say in essence, "whatever, it's a statue, we don't have twenty square feet of land that we can give to you," while that decision had "a lot of weight for the rest of us" who had worked for years to materialize this object. As a consequence, even the Kids' Committee's notable successes—raising nearly $50,000, incorporating young people expansively in the statue's design, successfully having the statue

---

80. LACC 1994, 11.
81. Charmian Schaller, "Peace Statue Should Live in LA," *Los Alamos Monitor*, December 6, 1994, 4.
82. LACC 1994, 14.
83. LACC 1994, 14.

fabricated, staging a full month of dedication ceremonies in August 1995—
remained, as this participant recalled, "bittersweet," tinged by the sense that
its location in Albuquerque was "temporary," and bolstered by the hope that
"someday we'll get it to Los Alamos."

These mixed experiences of success and failure prompt the analysis of this
final section, where I shift from the immediate context of young people's strategies to a wider consideration of how these activist experiences intersected
with children's agency—a long-term perspective enabled by the Children's
Peace Statue project's long duration, having begun now more than thirty years
ago. I follow Taft's caution that "social movements should not be judged by
their ability to fulfill their most lofty goals: ending poverty, creating sustainable communities, and dismantling global inequality are not straightforward
tasks that can be checked off an organization's to-do list. Social movement
'success' is not an either/or question."[84] Instead, Taft's ethnographic work with
the movement of working children in Peru reveals numerous "modest successes," such as "challenging children's exclusion and increasing their social
and political power in everyday life," which demonstrate that "children themselves can actively participate in [and] collectively contribut[e] to remaking
the world around them."[85] As she argues, children's embodied experiences of
political organizing and collective, nonhierarchical decision-making generate significant—even transformative—forms of power that scholars should be
careful not to disregard.

Reflexive agency animates the reconsideration these participants undertook as they revisited experiences that felt like failure and returned to the
lessons they carried forward about politics, activism, organizing, and social
change. Inviting participants to reconsider their experiences and eliciting
their own assessments of the significance of their activism over time, these
interviews articulate agency as rooted in embodied experiences that endure,
making those experiences available through reflection to create new conceptions of their significance. Likewise the durability of the statue this collective
materialized allows it to function as an ongoing discursive opening—one that
generates new meanings in relation to its material context in New Mexico and
in relation to the ever-changing perspectives of these participants, who forge
new links between their past and present selves and remake their rhetorical
agency in the process.

---

84. Taft, *Kids Are In Charge*, 214.
85. Taft, 214–15.

Durable Objects

The durability of the statue itself helps to extend the children's agency over time, though not in the precise way opponents in Los Alamos feared—it did not become the dreaded "soap box" capable of gathering those who wish to oppose all that Los Alamos has "believed over the years." Yet making a statue offered a highly durable way for this collective of children to concretize their "message of peace across continents" and to communicate that message to future communities. As new materialist philosophers such as Bruno Latour have argued, material objects crystallize, extend, and solidify the power of social forces that are otherwise ephemeral, generating what Latour describes as the "steely" quality of particular relations and associations.[86] Objects, institutions, architecture—these can all be seen as ways of materially "loading" social interactions with a greater force, beyond the weight of our more momentary persuasive capacity.

This perspective illustrates how building a statue offers marginalized speakers a way of communicating their argument—that children around the world desire a peaceful future—with greater material force, allying their collective agency with that of a durable material object. And as Richard Marback has argued, objects themselves have an agency that exists apart from our intentions toward and interpretations of them; objects "have an effect on us, they do things for and to us," and they "demand from us responses we might not otherwise have were it not for our encounters with them."[87] Marshaling their resources of time, money, energy, and the amplification of their network of supporters in order to design and fund a large bronze statue—an object that takes up space, generating "extensive and intensive embodied" encounters—extends the Kids' Committee's (amorphous, distributed) agency across time, through alliance with a durable material object.[88]

The statue's design, in fact, materializes the rhetorical tactics the collective pursued discursively. Amplification through collectivity—the strategy they employed when delivering ten thousand supporters' names to the County Council—reappears in the statue through continents that are composed of individual kids' small sculptural contributions. Another key discursive tactic was forming a network that spanned *space* but was linked by *age*, and sculptor Tim Joseph's fabrication process replicated this, by inviting children to mold wax figures of plants and animals and mail these to his foundry. These practices define age as the primary unifying characteristic of the collective they

---

86. Latour, "Technology Is Society Made Durable," 70.
87. Marback, "Unclenching the Fist," 56–57.
88. Marback, 56.

form, cutting across differences of nationality, race, language, and geography, and eschewing in particular the capitalist/communist dichotomy that had so powerfully structured Cold War–era political formations. Although the participatory dimension that Noe Martinez envisioned in his design—in which visitors to the statue would plant seeds to contribute to an ever-changing garden—was determined to be unsustainable in the desert environment around Los Alamos, Joseph's adaptation retained this participatory dimension.[89] In short, the statue reenacts the tactics of the collective that preceded it, with individual statements subsumed in the statue into a single, nonverbal assertion of collective desire for peace.[90]

The durability of the bronze statue not only extends and materializes the agency of the collective that produced it, but also generates ongoing associations with Los Alamos across changing historical contexts. The statue was dedicated at the Albuquerque Museum through thirty-one days of events throughout the month of August 1995, including a brief relocation to Santa Fe for a weeklong peace conference at which *hibakusha* (or bomb-affected people) spoke about their experiences surviving the atomic blasts in Hiroshima and Nagasaki. Throughout that period, news coverage reiterated the project's origin story and recounted the thwarted efforts of the children to locate the statue in Los Alamos, describing the statue repeatedly as "originally intended for Los Alamos" and "rejected" by that city.[91] For instance, an Associated Press story reported that "a statue created by schoolchildren as a peace symbol and rejected by the birthplace of the atomic bomb became the focus of a month-long dedication . . . after a four-year search for a home."[92] One of the adult advisors shared with the press that "the statue will be offered to Los Alamos each year,"[93] and indeed, public records of the Los Alamos County Council show ongoing (but unsuccessful) subsequent efforts to get the statue back on the council's agenda.

The statue generates ever-changing linkages through its materiality. Periodically over the past two decades, the statue has been moved from one location to another, and these occasions have prompted further news coverage linking the statue with Los Alamos. For instance, after residing for three years at the Albuquerque Museum, the statue was rededicated in August 1998 at the Plaza Resolana, a conference center in Santa Fe, occasioning news coverage that reiterated that although the statue was "originally intended . . . to

---

89. Dingmann, "Statue Unites World's Kids."
90. See Blair and Michel, "Reproducing."
91. Emiliana Sandoval, "Monument to Peace," *Santa Fe New Mexican,* August 10, 1995, B1.
92. "Children Dedicate Statue for Peace," Associated Press, August 2, 1995.
93. Sandoval, "Monument to Peace."

be dedicated in Los Alamos," "the Los Alamos County Council refused to provide a site for the statue" out of "fear the statue would become a rallying point for anti-war activists."[94] This coverage repeated the idea that the statue might be accepted in Los Alamos eventually, explaining that "the Albuquerque children's group still hopes eventually to dedicate the New Mexico statue—a globe-shaped bronze artwork—in Los Alamos."[95] Later coverage continued to characterize the statue in this way, explaining it was "originally made as a gift to the city of Los Alamos. It was refused."[96] The statue's existence can be seen as eliciting this association with Los Alamos, reaching into interaction with that location despite its exclusion from the town's boundaries.

Through its materiality, the statue is enlisted into other forms of community formation as well. In particular, its materiality has enabled it not only to form repeated links to Los Alamos through that city's rejection but also to serve as a site for peace-building efforts, echoing Marback's insight that we interact with objects in an "ongoing series of actions in the perpetual present."[97] For instance, from 1998 to 2013 the Children's Peace Statue was the site of Peace Day events celebrated each year on August 6 in Santa Fe, and beginning in 1999, a program called Cranes for Peace used the practice of folding paper cranes to teach "about the realities of nuclear weapons and nuclear war" and to "inspire a culture of peace" in elementary, middle, and high schools throughout northern New Mexico; students involved in that project "fold[ed] cranes every year to put on the Children's Peace Statue" in advance of Santa Fe's Peace Day celebrations. Strands of one thousand paper cranes have long been sent to the statue from around the world, and the statue had been regularly adorned with strands—from twenty thousand up to one hundred thousand—during Peace Day celebrations.[98] Significantly, the statue's materiality—its location, visibility, and availability for adornment—organized this dispersed activity, which spanned numerous schools and involved hundreds of young people in embodied actions—folding cranes, discussing global connections, and articulating future desires—that echo those recounted during my interviews with participants.

The statue's materiality makes it available for reconsideration through acts of reflection as well. All my participants mentioned their experiences of reencountering the statue at later points—while on field trips in high school or

---

94. Monica Soto, "Children's Peace Statue Finds a Home in Santa Fe," *Santa Fe New Mexican*, August 12, 1998, B1.

95. Soto.

96. "Peace Cranes Draw Schools into Projects," *Santa Fe New Mexican*, May 6, 2007, E4.

97. Marback, "Unclenching the Fist," 54.

98. Erika Davila, "Cranes for Peace," *Santa Fe New Mexican*, August 7, 2001, B1.

when returning to Albuquerque much later. Several noted a complex range of responses when returning to the statue with their own children or forging new relationships with it from their adult perspectives, suggesting again the way the statue's materiality enables reformulation and supports the reflexive agency of these activists. One participant articulated this openness to new articulations especially memorably: she recalled the deep feeling of disillusionment and defeat she and others had experienced when the statue was rejected by the Los Alamos County Council for the final time, explaining, "I remember there being a really strong attachment to Los Alamos, as the place that the statue belonged, and when the Albuquerque Museum decided that they wanted it, it was positive that we got a home for it, [but] I also remember it always being accepted as temporary, [that] someday we'll get it to Los Alamos." But reflecting on that disappointment twenty years later, she continues, "I just think, now—I don't know that the location matters as much—that [what matters] is more the spirit of it, and that New Mexico carries with it a whole history of military testing outside of just Los Alamos, and so I think that it resonates probably around the state in a different way." The contrast she draws—between participants' felt sense of frustration and defeat in 1995 and her more recent understanding of the capacity of the Children's Peace Statue to make new meanings as it "resonates . . . around the state" in relation to a wider, regional history of nuclear testing—suggests one way in which the materiality of the statue undergirds participants' reflexive agency, keeping activist experiences available for reconsideration through shifting perspectives. This response locates agency in the act of reconsideration, identifying new significance for her earlier work by revisiting it from her current perspective.

Enduring Experiences

As one might expect, certain dimensions of the activism that these individuals undertook when they were ten or twelve or fifteen years old have faded with time. My interview questions invited participants to reflect on what they recalled of their experiences, what they felt had been most significant about their involvement in the project, and what connections they could see between their Peace Statue advocacy and their later interests, experiences, and pursuits.[99] In contrast to my interviews with undocumented activists and March For Our Lives activists, these participants ran up against the uncertainty many

---

99. See appendix 1 for the full interview questionnaire.

feel when asked to recall events more than two decades past. For instance, participants were not always certain what writing or speaking they had undertaken; some recalled collaborative discussions when the group planned what they would say at public events, but expressed hesitation about recalling specific writing or speaking they had contributed, saying, for instance, "I don't remember if I wrote for [*The Crane*], I might have," or "There's a good chance I have some writing in *The Crane* . . . but I don't have memories of composing an essay for *The Crane,* although maybe there is something in there I don't remember." These hesitations suggest that some capacities this project cultivated have faded. Nevertheless, the new linkages and explanations participants articulated during our interviews reconstitute their rhetorical agency, forging links between their past and present selves.

Participants were able to identify certain throughlines between their experiences working toward the Peace Statue and their later academic or activist pursuits. One participant, for instance, tied this experience to an enduring interest in Japan, leading to Japanese language study and an East Asian studies concentration in college and graduate school. Another identified not activism per se but advocacy as a durable orientation born out of her work for the Peace Statue. She continued to pursue international experiences through a junior Peace Corps–style program as a teenager and then pursued social justice advocacy through her professional work as a lawyer and courtroom advocate for children. Another participant connected her early activism with an ongoing commitment to speak to and act according to her beliefs, which connected her academic work in community development with her personal commitments. She felt the project "taught me to speak to my ideals" even in the face of opposition, and she elaborated later in our interview that the experience cultivated her determination to be "principled" and to "act on those principles."

Many embodied experiences connected to activism remained significant for these participants and available for reflection. First of these was the experience of folding cranes and teaching others to fold cranes. Many of the public events staged by the Kids' Committee included teaching others how to fold paper cranes, and consequently this perpetual activity resonated strongly across their recollections. Three of the respondents mentioned, unprompted, that they still teach others to fold cranes and find this activity provides ongoing occasions for talking to others about their earlier involvement with the Children's Peace Statue. As one explained, "I also remember folding paper cranes, like, all the time. I kind of feel like actually everything . . . I have this memory of everything that happens, happens in conjunction with folding paper cranes. There was never a time you weren't folding paper cranes."

Another recounted how this embodied practice, which had been so central to her engagement with the project, had persisted: "we have a little boy down the block who's really into origami and I was like, *Oh, let me show you what I can do.* I made him some cranes and my son was like 'Why do you know how to do that?' and so it went into a whole discussion of this thing I had done in elementary school, how I wasn't much older than him and we had this idea." As these recollections emphasize, the repeated, embodied activity of folding cranes, which formed a node of activity and exchange across the duration of the project, persisted into the present, providing ongoing occasions for connecting to others around peace and activism.

Second, one of the primary things that participants found valuable about their involvement in the Peace Statue Project was their embodied experiences of speaking in public, which remained significant to them. For instance, one participant I spoke with had traveled to a peace conference in Seattle on behalf of the Kids' Committee when she was fourteen, with an adult advisor and several other Kids' Committee members, and three of my interview participants had traveled together to Hiroshima on behalf of the project to speak to enormous audiences at a peace conference on the fiftieth anniversary of the bombing. These individuals recalled at length the embodied experience of speaking before such enormous crowds. One who had been informally chosen as "the spokesperson for the group" did "a lot of our speaking on that trip," including speaking "on stage" to tens of thousands of attendees at the conference, addressing through translators a "*stadium* full of people." Another participant recalled participating in highly formal meetings with the mayor of Hiroshima and with international peace activists in attendance; he recalled the striking experience of being in "a country that had a real peace movement in it, where it didn't just seem like this one little idea that these kids had, but it had been something that adults," including "teachers . . . were very active" in. In his words, the experience of "being accepted and taken seriously . . . [even] while it feels like we're representing the people who did this act of dropping the bomb, that experience of realizing . . . that people could listen to kids was very powerful." As another participant explained, through his experience addressing various audiences over the course of the project, "I learned that I had a way of speaking and a voice inside me that I could command, and that with the right preparation I could get people to listen to."

Such an experience—being listened to and treated as though their ideas were meaningful—resonated powerfully in participants' reflections. Participants recalled that a team of journalists from NHK, Japan's public broadcasting network, made repeated visits to New Mexico to report on the Children's Peace Statue project for Japanese audiences, as did US-based news teams from

Nickelodeon and many local and regional news crews. One participant, who characterized himself as "probably shyer than a lot of other kids on the project," explained that overcoming his discomfort to speak about the project was valuable, because it "did feel like we were saying something important enough that adults were going to listen, so that being on camera and speaking up for the project was . . . important even if that wasn't a natural thing for me to do." As I heard in interviews with other young organizers, pursuing a public project can prompt this kind of development, spurring capacities that lay outside participants' prior skills and self-understanding.

Intense, embodied experiences structured participants' new articulations of agency through reflection. For instance, one reflected that her efforts to speak at raucous County Council meetings represented her "first time speaking in any sort of political context, and it was an intense one. It wasn't some cutesy kid project. They were pissed." Another explained, "I don't really remember if I spoke at the Los Alamos County Council, but I remember that experience of being there, waiting forever and having one minute to talk to the council . . . [and] the disappointment in not getting [the statue accepted] there at that time." Emotions such as anger, frustration, disappointment, and confusion infused these recollections. One explained, "I wouldn't say that all the feelings [associated with the meetings] were negative, but I certainly learned that adults didn't have to be honest, that they could conceal their motives, and that people's motives in politics were often completely at odds with what they purported to believe and say." This participant found it "ridiculous . . . that there could be no middle ground . . . between the total and abject worship of Los Alamos as the savior of the West and the winner of the war, and . . . what they perceived as an outright attack on the facility and everything it had ever done or stood for. There was just no room for anything in between."

Participants also encountered opposing perspectives in quieter spaces outside of the council meetings; one participant recalled a more civil meeting the Kids' Committee held with a veterans group, in which "they voiced some of those [same] concerns" but in a less intense, more "arms-length" manner, while the Kids' Committee "present[ed] our case and tr[ied] to connect with them." This participant charted his own gradually emerging realization "that [our project] could be provocative to people . . . even though I didn't really understand exactly why." As he put it, "We just want adults not to blow up the whole world, so it seems like everybody should agree about that." But the intensity of some adult responses led to expanded awareness that agreement couldn't be taken for granted. For another participant, the experience of engaging with such strong opposition helped her "to not feel like you have to be the expert in the room to talk about" something, and "also probably taught me that if you are told no by one authority, you just ask another author-ity, and eventually somebody will tell you yes." One participant found sig-nificance in what his earlier experiences underscored about the contradictory nature of adult adulation for young people as symbols rather than political agents, explaining, "this is a society where children generally are not listened to despite what everyone pretends to believe. . . . You can't really be a child or a young person in our society without realizing this, that the society is full of adults who are happy to pretend to believe that they want to hear what you have to say and that what you have to say matters at all. But this doesn't play out, I don't think, in the experiences of young people." This participant pointed to Greta Thunberg as an example of this tension, evincing "the rush to canonize her and put her on a pedestal so that she can be more quickly and thoroughly ignored." Suggesting some of the ways that political subjectivities can be connected to earlier activism, he explains, "for me, I am going to try to live differently," noting, for instance, "when the time comes to work for causes like lowering the voting age to 16 or 14, I will be on board."

CONCLUSION: EMBODIED AGENCY IN RETROSPECT

Ultimately, these interviews suggest that their involvement in the Children's Peace Statue project provided these young people with the unusual experience of having their voice and ideas valued by adults around them—an embodied experience with implications for their rhetorical agency. One reflected that she learned from her involvement in the project that she "ha[d] something to say about nuclear war," even though she "was just a kid." She remembered "feeling like my opinion was really valued in those meetings," where "people would ask" for her thoughts and ideas in relation to a large-scale and collec-tive undertaking; this experience, she felt, "was a formative thing." Because this participant was younger than some of the other leaders—only ten around the time the statue was fabricated—she felt in retrospect that she wasn't sure how much she had contributed; nevertheless, she recalled feeling "pride" and "ownership" in relation to the project. Because "the adult leaders were really good about making sure that children's voices were heard at every stage," she still found herself "being a spokesperson . . . and an active participant." Another participant responded to my query about what was most significant to him about the project with a statement tinged with incredulity: "Kids can do stuff in the world. They have a voice. We had adults who believed that."

As a child-led, large-scale collective endeavor, the Children's Peace Statue project challenged what Taft calls "the exclusion assumption, or the assumption that children should be prevented from participation in both work and politics."[100] In retrospective interviews, my participants identified these experiences as enduring; consequently, I understand their reflections as suggesting critical insights regarding rhetorical agency. That is, their words provide a way to view their experiences—such as being treated by adults as though their words and ideas could make an impact in the world—as reflecting what Taft calls "prefigurative politics," or practices that attempt to "prefigure" the "social relations" a movement is seeking to see enacted "in the wider society."[101] In contrast, treating children as "tokens of futurity" discounts the efficacy of their words and actions while also enabling rhetorical practices that weaken children's political possibilities in the present.[102] The vehemence of efforts on the part of adult opponents to refuse the children's project ultimately underscores the viability of their strategies, the fact of their rhetorical power, even in the face of arguments asserting their project's futility. Children's complex rhetorical agency can be seen in the constellated effects their project generated, which included creating a transnational network of supporters, provoking opposition, materializing a statue, sustaining participation, generating encounters between many thousands of individuals and the statue itself, and cultivating embodied experiences with enduring significance for those who participated. Through embodied practices and material objects that endure, activism resonates across the life span of these individuals, structuring their opportunities for reflection and generating new formulations of significance for their activist work.

---

100. Taft, *Kids Are In Charge*, 4.
101. Taft, 8.
102. Edelman, *No Future*.

CHAPTER 2

Agency as Perspectival

Vulnerable Undocumented Activism

At the start of a new year, on January 1, 2010, four young undocumented activists set out on a four-month walk they called the "Trail of Dreams." Walking 1,500 miles from Miami, Florida, to Washington, DC, on a trek inspired by "migrant farmworkers who walked the length of California in the 1970s," the four students—Gaby Pacheco, Felipe Matos (later Sousa-Lazaballet), Carlos Roa, and Juan Rodriguez—performed this walk as a tactic for catalyzing public discourse and intervening in immigration policy.[1] They hoped in particular that the extreme distance and duration of their effort would generate sustained news coverage and consequently put pressure on Congress to bring the DREAM Act to a vote. This legislation, first introduced in 2001, offered conditional protections and a path to legal citizenship for some undocumented children who had first migrated to the US at age sixteen or younger, and in 2010—with a Democratic president and looming midterm elections—many young undocumented people voiced their impatience with continuing to wait for more comprehensive immigration reforms that seemed unlikely to materialize. As Felipe explained to me when I interviewed him in 2021, the decision to perform this walk from Miami to DC "started with . . . impatience

---

1. Laura Wides-Muñoz, "Youths Trek from Miami to D.C. for Immigrant Rights," Associated Press, January 1, 2010.

and feeling like not enough was [being] done."[2] By walking to DC, these four activists aimed to leverage their identities—as young, undocumented, and, for two participants, queer immigrants—to direct media attention and create greater urgency for this legislation.

To harness this impatience to pressure legislators toward action, the four activists adopted a rhetorical strategy in which they embraced the vulnerability created by their undocumented status. In Felipe's terms, they "needed to do something really extraordinary that could put us in jeopardy," because they felt that the immigration reform movement needed "a real sacrifice . . . to be made." The activists characterized their trek as an embodied demonstration of the urgency of the need for legislative action and their willingness to risk exposure in pursuit of change. Speaking with me a decade later, Felipe emphasized how precarious it felt at the time to walk through "the Deep South" while "being an immigrant, being undocumented, and being queer" and the risk they took on by their determination "to unapologetically talk about who we were completely." One of the legal counselors who advised the Trail of Dreams organizers explained that the activists were "willing to put their lives on the line, but they are going to be walking through some very unfriendly places for immigrants."[3] Walking through unfamiliar and unfriendly communities while publicizing their stigmatized status exposed their vulnerability; it also transformed that vulnerability into a tactic for marshaling rhetorical agency. That is, their strategy aimed to transform an ostensibly private experience—one marked by the risks and vulnerabilities borne by undocumented people in a nation deeply committed to policing and criminalizing border crossings—into a public matter. As the four activists explained in an interview on CBS news, "We felt talking to legislatures and leaders was not changing anything. Doing demonstrations was not doing anything. We had to prove and show with our bodies how much we decided to be in this country, how much we love this country." As a strategic event staged by undocumented young people, the Trail of Dreams highlights how childhood functions to both facilitate and constrain rhetorical possibility. The young activists whose labor is analyzed in this chapter negotiated their symbolic power, leveraging their youth to generate wide-

---

2. Interview participants chose the names by which I refer to them in this chapter. Directly contacting individuals who were named in news coverage of im/migration activism, and sharing information about my research with adults in my social networks, I sent interview requests and IRB-approved questions to ten individuals. I ultimately conducted interviews with four organizers, which I recorded and had transcribed. See appendix 2 for the full interview questionnaire.

3. Wides-Muñoz, "Youth Trek."

spread news coverage while confronting steep constraints circumscribing their rhetorical agency.

The Trail of Dreams was an early and significant contribution to the outpouring of undocumented youth activism in 2010,[4] building what communication scholars Claudia Anguiano and Karma Chávez have identified as an "exceptional communicative moment in social movement mobilizing."[5] The profound risk that attended this activism makes it a particularly significant site for understanding how young people navigate the rhetorical possibilities that childhood facilitates and how they cultivate rhetorical agency through reflection on their experiences as activists. Across an extraordinary number of coordinated actions, undertaken through grassroots organizing by an emergent coalition of youth-led im/migrant-justice organizations, young undocumented activists labored collectively to bring attention to exclusions that strongly shape their lives and communities.[6] Thrusting an ostensibly private, stigmatized status into the public sphere, these activists insisted upon public discussion of im/migration exclusions—at great risk to themselves and to their families and communities, who faced family separation, detention, and deportation by "coming out" publicly as undocumented while pushing for legislative action. As another of my interview participants underscored when she spoke to me about her work to prevent deportations, the consequences of separation, detention, and deportation are extensive and enduring: "the negative

---

4. In this chapter I primarily use the term *youth* rather than *children* to reflect the fact that many of the prominent activists I spoke with and whose strategies I discuss were in their early and midtwenties during their most intense organizing. Many were older teens (eighteen and nineteen) when they became involved in this burgeoning movement. This language reflects the fact that federal legal protections granting access to education end after high school. As undocumented teens seek driver's licenses, college funding, and employment, many experience the exclusions and constraints of that status more acutely as they grow older. At times I use *students* to refer to activists who are in high school or college, but status-based exclusions mean that only 5–10 percent of the 98,000 undocumented high school students who graduate each year enroll in college. See Zong and Batalova, "How Many Unauthorized Immigrants"; and Immigrants Rising, "Overview of Undocumented Students."

5. Anguiano and Chávez, "DREAMers' Discourse," 81.

6. I follow the usage of other scholars in adopting *im/migrant* rather than *immigrant*, which suggests an inappropriate teleology of a migrant's destination and orients analysis toward the so-called receiving country. I likewise use the appellation *DREAMer* only when that term is used by speakers or texts I am quoting, following the revised usage of many undocumented activists who have challenged the narrowness of "DREAMer" narratives. See Abrego and Negrón-Gonzales, *We Are Not Dreamers*, 8–10. On the ostensibly humanizing import of *undocumented* as a label for subverting and critiquing the power of bureaucracy, see Hartelius, "Undocumented and Unafraid?"

effects of this—of somebody being deported or somebody being detained—I mean, that family is never the same again."[7]

Confronting such risks directly was a key tactic of undocumented youth activism throughout 2010. For instance, when five students (including three who were undocumented) staged a sit-in in Senator John McCain's offices that spring, they performed the "first known act of civil disobedience by undocumented immigrants," in an "escalation of protest tactics" that marked "the first time students have directly risked deportation in an effort to prompt Congress to take up a bill that would benefit illegal immigrant youths."[8] The goal of their action was to be taken into deportation proceedings but, through media attention and public support, to avoid deportation, in order to publicly undermine the authority of Immigration and Customs Enforcement (ICE).[9] By successfully highlighting the discretion of ICE agents to elect *not* to deport when public opinion was marshalled loudly in opposition, this action laid the groundwork for numerous other acts of civil disobedience throughout 2010, including rallies, marches, sit-ins, mock graduations, hunger strikes, teach-ins, bus tours, and art- and social media–based campaigns.[10] Many of these actions highlighted activists' thwarted educational aspirations and centered their protest in their embodied experiences as undocumented youth.[11]

Not only the risks assumed by these activists but also the variety and quantity of actions they organized position this case as a key opportunity to consider how young people have navigated the constraints and possibilities that childhood affords, in particular as a racialized category linked with (white)

---

7. As Karma Chávez has emphasized, if undocumented people heed calls to come "out of the shadows" but "there is no move to provide them with legitimate access to a pathway to citizenship, they are increasingly vulnerable to detention and deportation, and numerous DREAMers have been detained, subjected to deportation proceedings, and then deported." See Chávez, *Queer Migration Politics*, 100.

8. Prerna Lal, "How Queer Undocumented Youth Built the Immigrant Rights Movement," *Huffington Post*, March 28, 2013, last modified February 2, 2016, https://www.huffpost.com/entry/how-queer-undocumented_b_2973670; Julia Preston, "Illegal Immigrant Students Protest at McCain Office," *New York Times*, May 17, 2010, 15, https://www.nytimes.com/2010/05/18/us/18dream.html.

9. See Unzueta Carrasco and Seif, "Disrupting the Dream," about the aims of this action. ICE replaced the Immigration and Naturalization Service (INS) in 2003 in the post-9/11 reorganization that created the Department of Homeland Security. See "History of ICE," US Immigration and Customs Enforcement, https://www.ice.gov/history; and, on the formation of the Bureau in 2003, see Ron Nixon and Linda Qiu, "What Is ICE and Why Do Critics Want to Abolish It?," *New York Times*, July 3, 2018, https://www.nytimes.com/2018/07/03/us/politics/fact-check-ice-immigration-abolish.html.

10. See Hogan, *On the Freedom Side*, 89–120; and Nicholls, *DREAMers*.

11. See Tara Bahrampour, "Students Disclose Illegal Status as Part of Push for Immigration Law Reform," *Washington Post*, July 21, 2010.

innocence and protection. Consequently, this chapter revisits the widespread undocumented im/migrant activism of this period in relation to the book's central questions: How do young activists leverage their symbolic power to address deeply constrained rhetorical situations? How does age facilitate and constrain these activists' efforts to challenge racialized exclusions from the protections of citizenship, and how, in turn, does the experience of aging—an embodied, situated phenomenon—contribute to the specific forms of rhetorical agency formulated through their retrospections? As in each chapter, here I aim to uncover how collectives of young people build rhetorical agency through embodied experiences and how they reflect on the significance of their activism in their own terms. By considering not only what undocumented youth activists *did* during their years of intense mobilization but also what they identify upon reflection as significant about that activism within their lives and communities, this chapter investigates how embodiment, vulnerability, and urgency are threaded together in strategic im/migrant activism in this era, tracing how activists deploy vulnerability as a (constrained) assertion of rhetorical agency and how they affirm agency as perspectival—rooted in partial perspectives that change over time.

Throughout the early 2000s, undocumented activists confronted enduring racialized exclusions from citizenship.[12] They thus inhabit a status commonly understood as legal and bureaucratic—or "administrative," as Tania Unzueta Carrasco and Hinda Seif explain—but in fact constituted along racialized lines of exclusion; as Unzueta Carrasco and others have argued, "the reason people come here undocumented is because there's no way for them to come documented."[13] In the words of education researcher Mónica González Ybarra, "although 'illegal' status is produced by and contingent on immigration law, it is also constructed socially through racist nativist discourses that strategically frame immigrants as criminal and thus justify their exclusion" from the United States.[14] As rhetorician Lisa A. Flores has argued in her historical examination of how "illegal" im/migrants are created through rhetorics that accumulate, "contemporary discourses of vulnerability, deportability, disposability, and 'illegality'" are co-constitutive, performative, and layered into ontological stability; these discourses expand and contract to meet changing

---

12. *Citizenship* embeds its own racialized, partial protections; see Brandzel, *Against Citizenship*; Flores, *Deportable and Disposable*; and Yam, *Inconvenient Strangers*, 3.

13. Unzueta Carrasco and Seif, "Disrupting the Dream," 282; and Marie Landau, "Out of the Shadows, into the Spotlight," *In These Times*, July 5, 2010, https://inthesetimes.com/article/out-of-the-shadows-into-the-spotlight.

14. González Ybarra, "Since When," 506. On the exclusionary logics that are reinforced at the "fraught nexus between the protectable child and the deportable migrant," see Chávez and Masri, "Rhetoric of Family," 211.

state needs while maintaining the whiteness of the US citizen ideal.[15] This makes the exclusions from civic participation experienced by undocumented youth different from those experienced by citizen minors who engaged in activism for peace and gun reform; those child and teen activists largely expected to become voters and to exercise conventional civic power through their vote, even though they spoke with urgency as nonvoters, unwilling to wait to exercise collective power only when they reach the official age of adulthood. In contrast, undocumented teen and youth activists are not only positioned by age as outside of formal electoral politics but also rendered stateless by racialized policies upheld by pervasive anti-im/migrant rhetorics. Undocumented youth address oppositional audiences who often resist the notion that they could become citizens at all.

The activists I interviewed recalled acute, embodied experiences of vulnerability that generated urgency for the work they and others undertook. One participant had been organizing to provide financial support for undocumented students on his campus for several years before he was detained and placed in deportation proceedings; another first organized a public campaign to prevent the deportation of a close family friend who had been detained following a traffic stop. These experiences catalyzed, in one participant's words, "the idealism . . . that fuels that risk-taking at the beginning." Cultivating urgency was a tactic for conveying otherwise misunderstood (or overlooked) experiences of racialized vulnerability that make mundane activity, such as driving to work or school, fraught with risk for undocumented people. Because racialized exclusion from citizenship protections does not dissolve over time, contesting the "ontological security" of the "illegal" im/migrant," to return to Flores's term, requires active, persistent, and creative efforts.

Across the groundswell of im/migrant activism in 2010, activists worked to translate their embodied experiences of vulnerability into an acute and shared crisis, one that would be felt by those—citizens, members of Congress, white people in general, as one of my participants emphasized—protected by privilege and status from the pervasive exposure to vulnerability of the undocumented. The strategies adopted in youth im/migrant activism, then, foster urgency beyond common conceptions of timeliness. Certainly, timing motivated some of the strategies of these collectives; for instance, 2010 was a midterm election year, and far from seeing any concrete gains during Obama's presidency, im/migrant communities witnessed increased deportations instead. Yet activists cultivated and sustained attention to their embodied experiences of vulnerability, to accumulate intensity among a

---

15. Flores, *Deportable and Disposable*, 159.

broader collective working toward change. This deep connection between embodiment, vulnerability, and urgency is reflected in my interviews with participants, who recall how they felt urgency as a form of intensification, an exigence that mounted and became more acute over time, across years of experiences of exclusion and precarity. The strategies developed by activist collectives throughout 2010 attempt to translate this exposure to risk as a mounting sense of pressure, with different events, actions, and campaigns layering exigence on top of exigence. Risk and embodied vulnerability were threaded through these events, creating a sense of escalation, functioning to generate and sustain intensity.

Embodied vulnerability—as evidenced in the Trail of Dreams demonstration and numerous other actions—offers a tactic for confronting rhetorical and material constraints. Whether narrated in first-person accounts or performed publicly, embodied vulnerability offers a powerful rhetorical resource for converting private experiences of vulnerability into public address. As disability scholar Renuka Uthappa has argued, disclosure of stigmatized—but not necessarily visible—status can be a viable tactic for rhetors who "seek from [their] audiences the full measure of dignity accorded to" valorized and normative speakers.[16] Uthappa suggests that acts of disclosure, while risky, also carry important benefits that lead speakers to use disclosure "to help audience members reach through the barrier thrown up by stigma and draw closer to us as human beings."[17] Drawing audiences into such relations became urgent for many undocumented activists during 2010, when opportunities for comprehensive immigration reform appeared to be waning and virulent anti-im/migrant legislation gained ground. In such a context, undocumented youth attempted to draw public attention to the exclusions, inadequacies, and contradictions of the im/migration enforcement system, confronting this system with the specificity and complexity of their lived experiences. I argue that young activists rely upon disclosure not primarily to position themselves as deserving—a critique of the "DREAMer narrative" that has been voiced by numerous scholars and activists—but instead to invite audiences to "draw closer" to their experiences and perspectives.[18] If the children peace activists of the previous chapter sought to constitute a vast, global collective by sharing

---

16. Uthappa, "Moving Closer," 164.

17. Uthappa, 165.

18. Many scholars and activists have rightly identified the way in which personal narratives associated with DREAMer activism often reify normative definitions of citizens (as productive workers, dutiful consumers, and diligent contributors to "American" values). See Abrego and Negrón-Gonzales, *We Are Not Dreamers*; Anguiano and Chávez, "DREAMers' Discourse"; Anguiano and Nájera, "Paradox of Performing Exceptionalism"; Rodriguez, "Supreme Court Case"; and Sirriyeh, "'Dreamers.'"

the names of tens of thousands of supporters with the County Council, such a relatively disembodied tactic of petition was unlikely to overcome the deep and racialized resistance faced by undocumented activists. Instead, these activists used embodied vulnerability to foster a shared sense of urgency, to prompt identification that would draw audiences closer to their experiences.

ADDRESSING OPPOSITIONAL AUDIENCES IN YOUTH IM/MIGRATION ACTIVISM

The Trail of Dreams was one of dozens of actions to garner national attention throughout the burgeoning movement that spring. Yet the flourishing activism among undocumented youth that marked 2010 did not emerge out of a vacuum. Instead, it represented a further development of earlier activism toward which im/migrant youth had already made vital contributions. As J. David Cisneros has argued, the demonstrations and actions of the immigrant rights movement in 2010 can be seen as "extensions or continuations of the immigrant activism of 2006," the year of La Gran Marcha, one of the largest public demonstrations ever seen in the US; millions of im/migrants and allies took to the streets across weeks of mass protests that year.[19] Young people and their organizing across media platforms, as media scholar Sasha Costanza-Chock has shown, played a vital role in the massive high school walkouts that drew tens of thousands of young people into the streets throughout the spring of 2006.[20]

These walkouts and marches were part of a burgeoning im/migrant political mobilization that paralleled the intensifying state-based denial of im/migrant rights. Across the first decade of the twenty-first century, an

---

19. Cisneros, *Border Crossed Us*, 111. See also Costanza-Chock, *Out of the Shadows*, 22–24. Cisneros notes several parallels between the 2006 and 2010 mobilizations, including that demonstrations in 2010 were "once more ignited in the most immediate sense by the passage of restrictive, nativist immigration legislation—Arizona's SB1070" (112). Signed into law in April 2010, SB1070 was at the time one of the most restrictive anti-immigration laws in the country, and notably included a provision that allowed law enforcement to demand residency documentation of anyone they deemed, on "reasonable suspicion," a possibly undocumented im/migrant (Cisneros, "Looking Illegal"). The passage of the bill prompted noncompliance actions, such as a day of support when allies were called upon not to carry documentation like drivers' licenses or IDs (see Puente AZ, "SB1070"). The 2006 mobilization itself built from the "rhetorical legacy of Chicana/o and Latina/o political mobilization, including the Chicano movement of the 1960s and 1970s, the agricultural and labor mobilization of groups like the UFW, and opposition to anti-Latino initiatives of the late 1980s and early 1990s (such as Proposition 187 and English Only)" (see Cisneros, "(Re)Bordering the Civic Imaginary," 29).

20. Costanza-Chock, *Out of the Shadows*, 25–27.

"intensification of immigration policing, surveillance, detention and removal . . . both altered the stakes involved in immigration struggles and generated a countervailing proliferation of activism and resistance by immigrants, their loved ones, and allies."[21] These opposing forces—the push and pull of political mobilization and backlash—formed a backdrop for the growth of organizations, coalitions, and direct actions in 2010. For instance, United We Dream, which would become an organizing hub connecting local and regional groups across the country, began in 2008, and Chicago's Immigrant Youth Justice League (IYJL) was formed in 2009; both organizations would plan, undertake, and support numerous direct actions throughout 2010. Alongside these organizations, state-based "Dream Teams," the art- and media-focused collective Dreamers Adrift, and other groups, such as Massachusetts's Student Immigrant Movement (SIM), provided organizational structures that enabled the intense activism of 2010.[22]

The youth-organized nature of the burgeoning activism of this period generated enormous public attention, underscoring these activists' savvy work to leverage their age as a resource. Media commentary from both national and local publications drew attention to the age—and often the vulnerability, thwarted opportunity, and contingent belonging—of the im/migrant activists who organized and participated in direct actions, at senators' offices, in major cities, at the nation's capital, and elsewhere.[23] The *Christian Science Monitor*, for instance, opened one feature story with an anecdote about a current college student who was brought to the US by her parents as a toddler; the same feature profiled other undocumented students who struggled to pay for community college, who were steered away from career paths such as nursing because of the certifications required, and who expressed frustration as "year after year, every year passes on, and nothing happens" to enable them to adjust their status.[24] Such coverage foregrounds the potent symbolic power of age as a key rhetorical resource activists sought to convert into media attention, creating what Kevin DeLuca has called "image events," which "'buy' air time

---

21. Boyce, Launius, and Aguirre, "Drawing the Line," 188.

22. See https://unitedwedream.org/who-we-are/our-story/; https://dreamactivist.org/; and https://www.youtube.com/user/dreamersadrift. The Immigrant Youth Justice League became Organized Communities Against Deportation; see https://www.organizedcommunities.org/.

23. "Chicago Immigrant Youth Are Undocumented and Unafraid," *Solidarity*, March 11, 2010, https://solidarity-us.org/march10/; Julia Preston, "Students Spell Out Messages on Immigration," *New York Times* May 18, 2010, https://www.nytimes.com/2010/09/21/us/politics/21immig.html; and Elizabeth M. Nunez, "Students Risk Dreams," CNN, Mary 23, 2010, http://www.cnn.com/2010/US/03/22/dream.act.education/index.html.

24. Richard Mertens, "College-Educated and Illegal: Immigrants Pin Job Hopes on DREAM Act," *Christian Science Monitor*, December 15, 2010.

through using their bodies to create compelling images that attract media attention."[25]

Even as activists leveraged their age to generate media coverage and marshal public attention, they confronted a daunting array of material realities circumscribing their political, social, and economic possibilities. An extensive body of cross-disciplinary scholarship has examined material effects of being undocumented or being in mixed-status families on matters such as educational aspirations and attainment, social mobility, romantic partnerships and family formation, and mental health measures such as depression and anxiety.[26] Some of this scholarship highlights the effects of age and timing on such experiences, emphasizing the deep disillusionment many undocumented youth experience just before and after high school graduation, when, as sociologist Leisy J. Abrego argues, "undocumented status may be particularly consequential."[27] The transition out of high school—marked for white, middle-class youth as a rite of passage into a range of potential pathways—is experienced by many undocumented teens as a foreclosure of opportunity. As Abrego and Negrón-Gonzales explain, as undocumented youth "approached the end of high school and were required to supply a social security number to apply for jobs or to college, many were forced to confront the . . . stark contradiction between full participation in school on the one hand, but inability to be legally present in the country, on the other hand. . . . It was the deep unfairness of this transition that compelled students to collectively demand changes to the system."[28] In these ways, undocumented youth were (and are) caught between access to education while minors versus deeply constrained opportunities for employment, travel, higher education, voting rights, and other forms of public participation beyond high school—rendering *age* as a complex limitation and affordance for undocumented activists.

The liminality many undocumented youth articulated was shaped as well by a larger historical shift in which im/migration in the US became reframed from a matter of *labor* to a matter of *security*.[29] The last major federal immigration legislation to pass, the 1986 Immigration Reform and Control Act (IRCA), provided legal permanent status to 2.7 million undocumented long-

---

25. DeLuca, "Unruly Arguments," 10.

26. See Abrego, "'I Can't Go to College'"; Enriquez, Morales Hernandez, and Ro, "Deconstructing Immigrant Illegality"; Sigona, "'I Have Too Much Baggage'"; Enriquez, *Of Love and Papers*; Valentín-Cortés et al. "Application of the Minority Stress Theory."

27. Abrego, "'I Can't Go to College,'" 217.

28. Abrego and Negrón-Gonzales, *We Are Not Dreamers*, 5.

29. For instance, Quinsaat shows the marked shift toward a security framing and away from a labor framing in media coverage of Arizona's SB 1070 in 2010, as compared with coverage of the 2006 Sensenbrenner bill. See Quinsaat, "Competing News Frames," 581.

term residents while instituting worker verification requirements, establishing financial penalties for employers who hire undocumented workers, and increasing enforcement measures. And because, as Abrego and Negrón-Gonzales explain, "every legalization is also an illegalization . . . migrants young and old who arrived after the dates of eligibility [for IRCA] faced much stricter policies and blocked access to legalization."[30] In the absence of federal legislation, local and state laws have largely enacted the intensification of policing and punishment that has characterized the last several decades of immigration policy. Thus while many im/migrant children and youth migrated with parents who were pursuing employment, punitive state and local laws position young people now within a framework of security. This intensification of policing accompanied other strategies designed to make seasonal migration back and forth across the border far more dangerous than previously; as a result, undocumented youth from the early 2000s onward have experienced severely limited opportunities to travel outside the US.[31] As many young activists argued, this has left them in a state of limbo, caught between nation-states and, to varying degrees, stateless.[32]

The vulnerability experienced by many im/migrants in the US, it must be recognized, is a cultivated policy, not an accidental byproduct of liminal circumstances. The punitive im/migration policy known as "attrition through enforcement" (ATE) seeks to increase im/migrant vulnerability, curtails collective support, and imperils im/migrants and their communities by design. ATE has been promulgated since 2005 by the Center for Immigration Studies, an anti-immigrant think tank designated a hate group by the Southern Poverty Law Center, and "aims explicitly at destabilizing the mechanisms for social reproduction of noncitizens in order to encourage their 'self-deportation.'"[33] Attrition-based strategies "include curtailing access to key institutions and services—such as education, employment, housing, and public benefits— criminalizing acts of assistance to unauthorized immigrants, and including

---

30. Abrego and Negrón-Gonzales, *We Are Not Dreamers*, 5.

31. In the 1990s, when the vast majority of border crossings took place in El Paso and San Diego, the US adopted a strategy known as "funneling" by tightening security at these two sites, a strategy that is "premised on the belief that concentrating enforcement resources in urban areas would force unauthorized migration out into remote desert areas 'less suited for crossing and more suited for enforcement'" (Immigration and Naturalization Service, 1994, p. 7). As a result, individuals would 'find themselves in mortal danger' (INS, 1994, p. 2), and it was believed that the resulting hardship would eventually lead would-be unauthorized migrants to simply abandon the effort." See Boyce, "Neoliberal Underpinnings," 193. See also the Undocumented Migration Project, at www.undocumentedmigrationproject.org, which documents the deadly effects of the "prevention through deterrence" strategy.

32. See, for instance, Wong et al., *Undocumented and Unafraid*.

33. Boyce, Launius, and Aguirre, "Drawing the Line," 188.

local police in federal immigration enforcement."[34] The psychological, social, and material costs of these practices have been abundantly demonstrated.[35] The cruelties of attrition through enforcement and the daily realities of living in undocumented and mixed-status families accumulate, intensify, and ensnare more and more people in ever-broadening nets of consequence. Sociologist Laura Enriquez has theorized this accumulation of harms as "multigenerational punishment," as "the sanctions intended for a specific population spill over to harm individuals who are not targeted by immigration policies" but whose racialized family and kinship connections with targeted individuals nevertheless generate lasting punitive effects—or in Enriquez's words, "family-level inequalities that endure."[36] Punitive policies designed to limit the mobility and safety of undocumented people reach into many millions of people's lives.

Activism has aimed to convert that experience of vulnerability into political power. Judith Butler has theorized vulnerability "as a deliberate exposure to power," used to "oppose . . . precarious conditions."[37] As Butler argues, "bodily vulnerability" can be "mobilize[d] . . . for the purposes of asserting existence, claiming the right to public space, equality, and opposing violent police, security, and military actions."[38] Pervasive experiences of embodied vulnerability were foregrounded in many of the direct actions undertaken by youth activists throughout 2010. As Unzueta Carrasco and Seif have argued, the movement's most prominent strategies, including "first person testimony and civil disobedience place[d] the undocumented body at the forefront of the national dialog on immigration."[39] These strategies located the bodies of young people in positions of visibility that exposed—and demanded that audiences confront—the absence of legal protections surrounding that exposure. Through strategic public actions, undocumented youth aimed to build support through "images of students peacefully submitting to arrest, handcuffed and arrested while wearing graduation caps and gowns, [which] blasted out across the country on mainstream media and social networking sites."[40] Direct action of this kind operates as a necessity when traditional avenues of influence are denied. As the Trail of Dreams walkers explained, they "needed to show with

---

34. García, "Return to Sender?," 1850.
35. See Briggs, *Taking Children*.
36. Enriquez, *Of Love and Papers*, 136.
37. Butler, "Rethinking Vulnerability and Resistance," 22, 12.
38. Butler, 26.
39. Unzueta Carrasco and Seif, "Disrupting the Dream," 279.
40. Hogan, *On the Freedom Side*, 110.

[their] bodies" how urgently change was needed. And as Matias, another of my interview participants, explained in response to my query about what he had gained or valued through his organizing, this work directly "saved [him] from deportation." It was, he felt, the only recourse available to contest his and others' deep, intense, and pervasive vulnerability to state violence.

Undocumented youth planned, organized, and staged dozens of high-profile direct actions throughout 2010. The Immigrant Youth Justice League staged the first National Coming Out of the Shadows Day on March 10; this rally garnered widespread uptake among activists in grassroots organizations around the US, serving, as Chávez notes, "as a catalyst to make 'coming out' a central strategy of the migrant youth movement."[41] Enormous nationwide demonstrations took place again on May Day "in over eighty cities and forty states," including a march of some sixty thousand in Los Angeles.[42] In July, twenty-one undocumented immigrants occupied the US Capitol building.[43] In September, undocumented students performed military drills in front of some senators' offices after Harry Reid announced his plan to bring the DREAM Act—with its provisions permitting a path to citizenship through military service or college—to a vote along with a defense bill.[44] Young activists performed hunger strikes outside of John McCain's office that fall, pushing senators to bring the DREAM Act to a vote during the lame-duck session following the 2010 midterm elections; in this action, Dulce Juarez, Celso Mireles, and other Arizona State University students fasted for nine days, reflecting each year the DREAM Act had not been passed in Congress since its initial introduction in 2001. As Mireles explained, "If we can't persuade [McCain] through logical means . . . maybe we can persuade him through the spiritual sacrifice and physical sacrifice."[45] As historian Wesley Hogan argues, these urgent efforts—which included both nonviolent direct action and electoral work through lobbying and traditional channels—were attempts to "forc[e] a way forward out of a dire limbo."[46]

---

41. Chávez, *Queer Migration Politics*, 81. Many of the leaders in the im/migrant activist movement in this period identified publicly as queer and drew links between their experiences as undocumented and their queer experiences and identities.

42. Cisneros, *Border Crossed Us*, 119.

43. Julia Preston, "Students Spared Amid an Increase in Deportations," *New York Times*, August 8, 2010, https://www.nytimes.com/2010/08/09/us/09students.html.

44. Preston, "Students Spell Out."

45. Uriel J. Garcia, "Students Fast to Pressure McCain for DREAM Act Support," [Arizona State University] *State Press*, November 29, 2010, https://www.statepress.com/article/2010/11/students-fast-to-pressure-mccain-for-dream-act-support.

46. Hogan, *On the Freedom Side*, 105.

DISCLOSURE AND THE RHETORICAL
POWER OF VULNERABILITY

Registering how these activists negotiated affordances and constraints to address the urgent rhetorical problems they confronted requires, as the previous chapter likewise did, holding open the possibility of their success. In this analytical section, then, I examine the widespread tactic of disclosure, or "coming out" as undocumented, as it relates to rhetorical agency. I do so by attending carefully to activists' strategic agency, that is, the tactics they adopted, as well as their reflexive agency, or the sense-making they undertook through reflection. Certainly embracing vulnerability is a tactic born from severe rhetorical constraints; it is an effort to convert the "dire limbo" of undocumented status into a rhetorical resource. Such a response often characterizes speakers and writers who lack access to formal avenues of power. The young undocumented activists who disclosed their lack of legal status demonstrated their willingness to expose themselves to risk to seek structural change. And the risk that attends the disclosure of stigmatized identities contributes to its political and rhetorical power. Yet the relationship between disclosure and exposure bears consideration: although the act of public disclosure puts the self more visibly in a position of exposure to harm, the vulnerability to severe risks—criminalization, family separation, detention, forced removal to another country—is perpetual, pervasive, and inescapable for these activists; consequently, the tactic of exposure seeks to direct audiences' attention toward the vulnerability experienced by im/migrants not as "periodic crises," as one of my interview participants put it, but as a daily grind. In Judith Butler's words, "political resistance relies fundamentally on the mobilization of vulnerability, which means that vulnerability can be a way of being exposed and being agentic at the same time."[47] The vulnerabilities of undocumented status are amplified by youth; at the same time, the age of these activists could be converted into a vital rhetorical resource when other resources were limited. I seek in the analysis that follows to help my readers recognize disclosure as a strategy for, in Butler's words, "being exposed and being agentic at the same time." Activists throughout 2010 used embodied vulnerability to foster urgency, prompt identification, and draw audiences closer to their experiences.

Proliferating first-person stories of undocumented youth were shared widely by activists. As one Associated Press article suggested, "the public disclosure tactic" of coming out as undocumented was demonstrably "on the rise,

---

47. Butler, "Rethinking Vulnerability and Resistance," 24.

especially among younger activists."[48] Activists organized "coming out" rallies in Michigan, Massachusetts, New York, and Illinois and designated March 10, 2010, "National Coming Out Day" or "National Come Out of the Shadows Day."[49] Julia Preston, writing for the *New York Times,* explained that young undocumented activists "realized that encouraging young people to recount the stories of their lives in hiding and of their thwarted aspirations could be liberating for them and also compelling for skeptical Americans."[50] Local and national media recirculated activists' narratives, which often recounted being brought to the US by parents at a young age and their growing awareness of their undocumented status and its implications for work, education, travel, and safety. This tactic targeted public audiences while also enabling coordination among movement members, constructing "bonds of solidarity and collective identification while also mobilizing participants across geographies."[51]

In these strategic acts of self-disclosure, undocumented activists often narrate embodied experiences that link their age and immigration status to foreground the exclusion and vulnerability they are subject to. Instead of merely announcing that their educational opportunities are curtailed by their lack of status, for instance, many narrate moments of intense, embodied contradiction to emphasize the disjunction between meritocratic ideals and the realities of exclusion. Activist Renata Teodoro, for example, writes: "One day I was called out of my classroom and asked to go to the school auditorium. I was surrounded by my friends and classmates who were waiting for me, and I found out that I had won a prestigious scholarship. The scholarship would pay for my educational fees all through college. I was really excited. But my heart sank when I read the requirements, one of which was a social security number. While everyone else was celebrating, I wanted to cry as I sat through the long ceremony."[52] Her narrative involves her audience in the felt sensation of contradiction—others celebrate her accomplishments while she struggles not to cry—and the alienation and isolation that sensation generates. Another speaker, during the first "Coming Out of the Shadows" rally

---

48. Sophia Tareen, "Undocumented Immigrants Hold 'Coming Out' Rallies," *Chicago Daily Herald,* March 11, 2010, 8.

49. See Tareen, "Undocumented"; and Julia Preston, "Young Immigrants Say It's Obama's Time to Act," *New York Times,* November 30, 2012, https://www.nytimes.com/2012/12/01/us/dream-act-gives-young-immigrants-a-political-voice.html. Chávez, in *Queer Migration Politics,* notes that the original flyer for IYJL's first event in 2010 advertised the event as "Come Out of the Shadows" day, but subsequent language consistently referred to it as "Coming Out of the Shadows."

50. Preston, "Young Immigrants."

51. Zimmerman, "Transmedia Testimonio," 1887.

52. Teodoro, "Following the Civil Rights Trail," 60.

in Chicago, recounted what it felt like to live in a neighborhood targeted by ICE: "during the weeks the raids were going on, my sisters and I had to stay inside our apartment by ourselves, with the windows and doors locked and the light off, waiting and praying for my mother not to get caught by [ICE] and taken away from us. This is the [same] excruciating feeling that I felt every time I saw a police officer in my rearview mirror as I was driving to work to be able to help my family with the rent and food." Age and im/migration status together compound the vulnerability this speaker communicates; at the same time, his status also reverses the typical structure of parent/child concern, as he and his siblings wait at home, fearing what might befall their mother. In such tactics, activists narrate their embodied experience to communicate across the distance between stigmatized speakers and their audiences—in this case, to ask speakers to inhabit these sensations of frustration, fear, and exclusion.

Risking exposure aims to stimulate reciprocal risks of identification among audiences. As Uthappa explains, speakers "make ourselves vulnerable . . . [because] vulnerability can be something beneficial" in drawing audience members closer to speakers' concerns.[53] That is, speakers may risk the rejection disclosure often prompts when they aim to kindle a reciprocal act of vulnerability among their audience members. This tactic resonates with rhetorical scholar Shui-yin Sharon Yam's theorization of "deliberative empathy," a practice of storytelling that "moves subjects toward each other without the complete erasure of difference."[54] Although the vulnerabilities of exposure are far from equal, deliberative empathy recognizes that "it is uncomfortable for interlocutors in the dominant group" to experience the destabilization of their "subjectivity, perceived interests, privileges, and identities" that storytelling practices can insinuate.[55] As Yam's framework underscores, undocumented activists do more than announce a status when they recount their experiences to public audiences: they invite those audiences to share in the experience of vulnerability.

Ultimately, this disclosure tactic requires an audience who responds productively to the experience of discomfort these rhetors aim to generate. The discomfort stems from recognition of mutuality and from an audience's willingness to expose themselves to narratives that contest stable distinctions—producing the "self-modifying feelings" or "self-scrutiny" that Yam aligns with deliberative empathy.[56] Undocumented activists sometimes articulate

---

53. Uthappa, "Moving Closer," 165.
54. Yam, *Inconvenient Strangers,* 5.
55. Yam, 4.
56. Yam, 32.

the challenge of taking up such invitations directly, as when Tania Unzueta Carrasco invites the LGBTQ community in Chicago to "understand . . . that in the end we are not looking for empathy—we are looking for action that creates change," or when Ireri Unzueta Carrasco explains that coming out as undocumented "forces people to see us and to recognize that we're here."[57] The action and recognition these activists call for emphasize the effects sought by disclosure in relation to the self-understandings, knowledge, and behavior of dominant citizen-subjects. As Yam argues, recognition can be a vital "first step in combating historical and systematic dehumanization of racialized subjects by the mainstream citizenry."[58] Employing disclosure makes the exchange between speaker and audience central and reveals disclosure as a tactic for reaching across, in Uthappa's words, "the barrier thrown up by stigma" to ask others to draw closer to one's stigmatized experience. By shifting relations between speakers and audience members, disclosure lays claim to rhetorical agency and opens up rhetorical space in the immigration debates that marked this period of activism.

Furthermore, many activists articulate their exposure of vulnerability as a practice that changes their own sense of agency, leading them to argue that *owning* risk is a reclamation of rhetorical agency. Following the first Coming Out of the Shadows rally in March 2010, for instance, when many young im/migrants delivered speeches that revealed their immigration status publicly, organizer Tania Unzueta Carrasco explained, "It's scary on one hand, but it's also liberating. . . . I feel like I've been in hiding for so long."[59] As activists and protestors throughout 2010 wore shirts and held banners announcing "I'm Undocumented" or "Undocumented and Unafraid," many linked their disclosures to experiencing a changed sense of their political and rhetorical power. Yahaira Carrillo, for instance, describing her willingness to risk being arrested and deported, explained to reporters that taking ownership over the fear of deportation by deliberately revealing her status offered a way to claim agency; in her words, living as an undocumented immigrant involves perpetual negotiation of "You shouldn't go here; you shouldn't go there," knowing that she "can be deported any time a cop stops me for something." But, she explained, by revealing her status publicly, as part of a direct action, "at least I would have had some say in my life."[60] As Tania Unzueta Carrasco writes, engaging in civil disobedience as undocumented people "is not just about changing immigration law and deportation policies, [but is also] about owning the risk of deportation with the knowledge that we can challenge deportability. Perhaps this is the most powerful challenge to the power of the nation-state to control its populations through fear and the threat of criminalization and expulsion."[61] Owning risk, as she puts it, offers an avenue for claiming agency. This is echoed in a collectively authored essay by the "McCain Five," Lizbeth Mateo, Mohammad Abdollahi, Yahaira Carrillo, Tania Unzueta Carrasco, and Raúl Alcaraz. These activists argue that risking public exposure leads to collective security rather than a loss of power, as "the attention we generated in the national press prevented ICE from aggressively moving to deport us. This doesn't mean we are safe," they argue, but that their actions reflect their "capacity to organize and resist oppression."[62] Embodied actions that expose and mobilize vulnerability can enable activists to claim agency as rhetorical beings. That is, the acts of self-disclosure and practices of embodied vulnerability so widely taken up within the undocumented rights movement collectively constitute an assertion of speakers' rhetoricity—their voice, their inherent capacity for self-expression, their agency as speakers.

CLAIMING AGENCY THROUGH CHANGING PERSPECTIVES

Participants' reflections on their activism offer temporally situated, renegotiated perspectives on the long-term implications of their work. Affirming their earlier perspectives, my interview participants articulated the value of taking action even from perspectives that are necessarily incomplete. When these participants spoke with me in 2021 from a middle-range point of view—a little over a decade past their intense organizing in 2010, and having moved into and out of public leadership roles over the course of that intervening decade—their reflections articulated *agency as perspectival,* rooted in embodied experiences and perspectives that change over time. Their retrospective assessments of strategies and impacts affirmed the imperative they had labored to cultivate through their activism: the necessity of acting in response to urgent need, despite the unknowability of outcomes and in full awareness that later perspectives would alter their values, priorities, and tactics. In what follows,

---

60. Maggie Jones, "Coming Out Illegal," *New York Times Magazine,* October 21, 2010, 36, https://www.nytimes.com/2010/10/24/magazine/24DreamTeam-t.html.

61. Unzueta Carrasco and Seif, "Disrupting the Dream," 296.

62. Mateo et al., "McCain Five," 69.

I show how activists can claim rhetorical agency as they return to the strategies of their movement and reconsider—not reject, but think through—the impacts of those strategies. This backward-reaching rearticulation has given new shape and meaning to their experiences, as these participants dwell in the space between their tactics and the outcomes those tactics effected. Perhaps because of their position in time—no longer in the thick of their most intense organizing—they have reviewed their earlier strategies in light of changed political and personal circumstances. In reflection, they opened a space in which to revisit the urgency—the accumulated bodily intensity, as described above—that characterized their activism in 2010 and the years that followed, and they have appraised and negotiated that activism from the perspective of their current context, embodiment, and situation.

Participants' reflections affirm their partial perspectives as a source of rhetorical agency, capable of shifting over time as they age. In interviews, they reconsidered earlier strategic decisions in light of later experiences, grappled with anticipated and unexpected outcomes, and assessed the mingled successes and failures that attend any long-running, large-scale, justice-oriented effort. They reconsidered earlier perceptions, revisited priorities that shifted across periods of intense activism, and reaffirmed the value of their work even when their perspective on that work had altered with time. Through such acts of reflection, these participants layered multiple temporal perspectives together—or in the words of sociologists Nolas, Varvantakis, and Aruldoss, they crafted a "tapestry of overlaid narratives of self as those unfold in time and across it."[63] Their perspectives underscore agency as situated: grounded in a specific, embodied perspective and shifting along with changing circumstances and contexts. Situated or perspectival agency involves participants accepting limitations on their earlier knowledge, negotiating impacts of earlier practices, registering bodily limitations, linking altered circumstances to perspectival changes, and considering how their activist capacities may be both augmented and diminished over time. In connection with the public-facing activism through which these speakers asserted their rhetoricity, the perspectival agency charted here asserts rhetorical agency across changing contexts.

Negotiating Effects and Impacts

Perspectival agency involves re-viewing, from the stance of their current perspective, the outcomes and consequences they and others have attributed to

---

63. Nolas, Varvantakis, and Aruldoss, "(Im)possible Conversations," 260.

their actions. My participants revisited earlier strategic decisions to reevaluate their effects and make new meaning through this reconsideration. In this way, participants explicitly claim rhetorical agency when they identify rhetorical work they are proud of and feel was successful. For instance, Felipe, a co-leader of the Trail of Dreams walk, immediately identified "actually getting the whole walk done" as a key experience for him. Speaking to me more than a decade later, Felipe emphasized that the walk "was a huge undertaking and I still look back and think to myself, man, how did we even get that done?" Contextualizing the difficulty of what they attempted, he explained: "back in 2010 when things weren't the way they are now, [when] being an immigrant, being undocumented and being queer was . . . really frowned upon. And doing all of that, deciding to unapologetically talk about who we were *completely,* in the deep South, was very dangerous."[64] He emphasized as well that their undertaking "was a huge accomplishment because it really came from *us.* We didn't get big grants. We walked and asked for donations and that's how we got to the other places. We didn't even have [hiking] shoes when we started." Felipe reiterated the vulnerability of their sustained, embodied action as he and his activist partners walked through the South, openly queer and undocumented, relying only on themselves and the support they could build along the way. This recontextualization, recalling the danger they put their bodies in, lays claim to rhetorical agency as it asserts both that their strategy was deeply considered and that it generated specific effects. In Felipe's assessment, their walk from Miami to DC and the media attention they garnered "really truly made a humongous difference. I really truly believe that if that walk hadn't happened that DACA would not have been advanced in the way it did. We were the first group of people to actually put that out there that the President could actually do something in using his executive power to stop the deportation of a large group of people like that."

Some participants identified long-term consequences for their work by pointing to organizations they helped to form. Matias, for instance, a cofounder of the organization United We Dream, explained that "one good thing about the work" he contributed is that even "some of us who kind of moved on to other things left the structure behind for other people to pick up the mantle and give it their best shot and their best effort." Though he expressed discomfort with "being prideful" about his accomplishments, he emphasized that "IDEAS [an early organization for undocumented students] at UCLA is still an organization on campus that helps people," almost two

---

64. Felipe learned after the walk that the Department of Justice had been monitoring their progress during the walk because the activists received "so many death threats."

decades after it began, and that United We Dream remains "a large-scale, multi-state strategic actor with thousands, I don't know, maybe hundreds of thousands in this digital organization" that he helped to create. Matias noted that "sometimes now I log in to their text campaigns," or he might "show up on the Zooms sometimes" and find himself assigned a task like any other supporter, even though he is one of the organization's cofounders. "For me," he explained, what matters is "the fact that that exists and someone is doing that and a dude like me can just plug in. [That]'s really special. So I think the longevity of the projects that I had a hand in helping develop, independent of my own current contributions to it, is what brings me a little bit of pride." The longevity and ongoing significance of this organization is, he explained, surprising when considered from his perspective at the outset of his activism: "I never would have thought, you know, in 2010/2011, which is when I was actually detained and faced deportation, that United We Dream would actually achieve becoming as big or as relevant as some of those other organizations at the time that we felt were controlling the advocacy narrative." Noting this shift from an earlier period of his activism to his current perspective, he articulates the value of such organizations in their ability to coordinate activist work across long durations and across shifting political circumstances.

Other participants identified impacts that took place below the national-level radar, in spaces such as high schools and neighborhoods and in the circumstances of specific families facing deportation. For Ireri, an organizer who worked with the Immigrant Youth Justice League (IYJL) in Chicago and with subsequent groups such as Organized Communities Against Deportations (OCAD),[65] their highly visible national work was only part of the distributed, localized activism happening at multiple levels through the participation of immigrant youth. Ireri explained that in the early days of 2009 and 2010, they and other activists focused on "what we could do to shift resources, shift narratives and to create different kinds of changes, both . . . larger . . . around the federal DREAM Act, and also smaller in terms of geography, like citywide policies and changes within the neighborhood." For instance, several activist collectives, including OCAD, Mijente, and BYP100, organized against a "gang activity database" operated by the Chicago police department, highlighting the devastating impact of this database on im/migrant and BIPOC communities.[66] As Ireri explained, "a lot of the folks who were involved in IYJL were also doing a lot of work within their own schools, whether these were high schools or universities, to really try to push forth these positive

---

65. Ireri is gender nonconforming and uses *they/them* pronouns.

66. On the "gang database" and the community response against it, see http://erasethedatabase.com.

changes for undocumented students and undocumented young people and undocumented families in general." Though local campaigns of this sort often escape wide notice, their effects can be outsized within their local communities. Similarly, for families facing deportation, the impact of advocates who can forestall that outcome is enormous. As Viridiana,[67] who led a DREAM Team chapter in North Carolina and whose work to stop deportations continued into 2020, explained bluntly, "I did a lot. I mean, I did a lot, and I kind of risked a lot. Not kind of; I did." She persisted in this work "for ten years, and I wasn't just, you know, speaking about my experience as an undocumented person, but I was fighting deportations and getting people out of detention." The purpose of Viridiana's work shifted over time toward direct interventions to forestall deportation; likewise, as IYJL's work shifted toward mobilizing against deportations, the outcomes of Ireri's labors shifted, because they took on support and communication work to connect detained people with family members and other supporters with limited ability to interact with their loved ones—work of vital consequence to the families and communities they served.

Some participants articulated, from the vantage of their current experience, a sense that their actions contributed in perceptible ways toward large-scale shifts in discourse or public perception. Felipe, for instance, understands his work as having contributed to changing public perceptions around "the intersectionality of the LGBT movement with the immigrant rights movement," especially in advancing the visibility of queer undocumented people. When he was hired in 2012 by GetEQUAL, he "was the first undocumented immigrant to actually hold a national role in an LGBTQ organization, and I talked a lot about racial justice in an LGBTQ setting." "That isn't always welcomed," he noted, but he felt that being someone who "spoke so frequently and so openly and pushed so many to do the right thing—I think that opened up space for a lot of people to also exist." Ireri articulated that the specific form taken by their activist community demonstrated the collective agency and deliberative capacity of members who worked to constitute their community with intentionality. Speaking to me about the formation of IYJL, Ireri

---

67. Viridiana voiced a strong antagonism to the term *activism* that was present in the materials I sent her in advance of our conversation. At the outset of our interview, she explained, "I hate the word *activism* because to me, the work that I was involved in was really more of something I felt like I *had* to do. It wasn't something I felt like, oh, yay, this is a hobby or . . . this is some fun thing that I can do, or, oh, poor undocumented people. . . . *I am* the undocumented person, so I have to do this. If not me, then who? So that's why I feel like . . . activism just maybe has that connotation, at least to me, of . . . some fun hobby thing that college kids do, you know? But . . . to me it was my life." Consequently, I avoid referencing Viridiana's work as *activism* and instead reference it simply as her *work*. As she says, "lived experience itself is activism because you've got to fight for *everything*."

explained, "that was really the first time that I experienced a very intentional community where we were thinking about our experiences as immigrants, specifically as folks who were undocumented, that came in at a young age," and it was also "the first time that I experienced activism and organizing in that sense. And it was very beautiful. Despite all of the frustrations that came with not having a status in the US, finding other folks with similar experiences was a very healing process for me, I would say." Ireri here names the experience of participating in a deliberate, thoughtfully formed, justice-oriented community as its own significant outcome, even as the consequences they identify are largely personal ones, noting what it meant to form and collaborate with such a community. Although such examples—changing public perceptions, forwarding intersectional approaches, healing through participation in community—are more difficult to quantify, participants who lay claim to these consequences express them as significant outcomes of their rhetorical agency.

The perspectival agency these participants lay claim to emerges further in their efforts to negotiate, without disavowing, what they view as negative or mixed outcomes of their work. For instance, DACA—the Deferred Action for Childhood Arrivals program that Obama's administration announced in 2012—was identified by two of my participants as a mixed success.[68] Matias, for instance, expressed his conflicted range of responses when younger undocumented people tell him that "DACA sucks." As he elaborated,

> That's the one I feel the most when I hear it. . . . It's very humbling because somebody might comment, I have DACA and it sucks, and I cannot tell that young nineteen-year-old, "No, you have it good," because in their mind, they don't, and rightfully so. They don't. They're still way behind their peers. Now, I could compare it to undergraduate life in 2005 and say none of us had DACA. All of us were working under the table. But that won't help that young person who thinks DACA sucks and it rightfully does, because by now, they've probably forked out $700, $800, $1000 just to be able to work over the span of five, six years.

---

68. DACA provides short-term reprieve from deportation and a temporary work authorization but offers no path to citizenship, does not protect family members of those who are DACAmented, collects data on undocumented people without providing assurance that even the limited protections of DACA will be maintained beyond a particular administration, and is costly to attain. See Gonzalez, Brant, and Roth, "DACAmented"; Roth, "Double Bind of DACA"; and López and Krogstad, "Key Facts."

DACA can be understood, as media studies scholar Sasha Costanza-Chock argues, simultaneously as both "the smallest possible bone the Obama administration could have credibly thrown the immigrant rights movement in the run-up to the election" while also being, at the same time, "a hard-won victory: undocumented youth battled for more than a decade to gain even this temporary administrative reform [that] came through their dedication, creativity, and bravery."[69] Matias explicitly grapples with the multiple perspectives he holds in relation to the protections available through DACA, juxtaposing the limitations felt by "that young nineteen-year-old . . . in their mind" and the absence even of minimal protections he "could compare it to" from "undergraduate life in 2005." Through this reflection, he holds both perspectives in conjunction as he assesses movement strategies and effects.

In accounting for the effects of their activism, participants confronted the limits of their ability to disrupt fundamental formations of citizenship, formations that sharply constrain activist possibility. Articulating their rhetorical agency involved identifying when, where, and how to act, both against and alongside these constraints. In particular, they confronted the narrative of "deservingness" that many scholars have noted.[70] Tania Unzueta Carrasco, for instance, has reflected on the "binder" full of "diplomas, test scores, newspaper articles and other accomplishments that could be used to justify my right to return" and notes that her strategic narratives, oriented toward circulation by the media, often "emphasized the characteristics of my life that matched those deemed 'good' by the nation-state—strong test scores, civic engagement, 'talent' and hard work."[71] In his interview with me, Felipe explained that

> one of the biggest [strategies he would revisit] is definitely—I feel like I somehow contributed to the good-versus-bad immigrant narrative that I really don't like, because I was the perfect student, I was Best Community College Student in the state of Florida, I always got good grades, and it always came easy to me. . . . And that was sort of the first narrative; the first Dreamer narrative was, "Look at this perfect student who just wants to become a teacher and he can't." And then I realized that what I was doing was creating this narrative that if I am good and I made no mistake, then someone else *did*—instead of reframing that whole conversation around, well, we all deserve the right to exist, to thrive, to fulfill our dreams, but also

69. Costanza-Chock, *Out of the Shadows*, 130.

70. See De Fina, "What Is Your Dream?"; Cisneros, *Border Crossed Us*, 128; Ribero, "'Papá, Mamá'"; Anguiano and Chávez, "DREAMers' Discourse," 83; and Chávez, *Queer Migration Politics*, 81.

71. Unzueta Carrasco and Seif, "Disrupting the Dream," 280.

live in our full potential, whatever that looks like, and that shouldn't be limited just to kids who get good grades.

Felipe registers the limits of his impact: he did not originate this "first Dreamer narrative," but feels he contributed to that narrative of deservingness. He nevertheless articulates a shift in perspective—marked by the phrase "And then I realized"—that prompted further shifts in how he engaged with circulating narratives as an activist.

The impacts, regrets, and successes my participants mentioned were only part of their broader perspectival approach. Each participant offered their careful, thoughtful reassessment of the possibilities of their activist work with a clear-eyed view of the constraints they were facing. Viridiana, for instance, explained, "That's the thing, I guess. Now, going back and reflecting, I mean, there's so many things that I could say I would have done differently, but the reality is, when you have people coming at you asking you for help and you know that they are trying to look for help out there, but nobody wants to do anything," that any labor she could offer in response to such urgent requests was ultimately work she felt proud of. She emphasized the paucity of options available for people working to stop deportations: "at the end of the day, when somebody has a final order of deportation, all we can ask of ICE is to grant discretion, a favorable discretion. . . . They're not *canceling* out the order of deportation. They're just saying, 'Okay, we acknowledge it, but for the time being we're going to ignore it and allow you to stay. [We will] give you a formal allowance of time for you to stay here." Given that there are very few avenues for legally changing one's status once a person is in the US without authorization, often Viridiana's only option was "to get ICE's attention [by] doing some sort of public kind of plea," which is why "the public campaigns worked so well" compared to more complicated legal strategies, which were often misguided. What I hear in Viridiana's response is an unwillingness to disavow the public campaigns she embarked on—even knowing that they ultimately led to her experiencing serious mental and physical exhaustion—because she recognizes how severely limited the options were for effecting change in the situations of people facing deportation.

In fact, Viridiana's response foregrounds the consequences of disavowing one's agency. She represents *doing anything* in the face of the ongoing human rights crisis as rightfully recognizing the claims that the crisis *should* have on everyone, rather than avoiding responsibility to act. Viridiana noted at several points in our interview the likelihood that she could have operated differently—been more modulated in her interactions with mainstream organizations so they would have been willing to give her more resources, for instance—but she ultimately affirms the ways in which she responded to the injustice she recognized in her own and others' lives. After pausing to consider my question—are there any things you feel especially proud of when looking back at this work?—Viridiana expressed the impossibility, in retrospect, of taking a different approach. When she "analyze[s]" her work from "years ago" she concedes, "Okay, I could have done that different, but it's okay, you know? I did it like this, and here's what I can learn from that. And I think that makes me proud, too, and it makes me feel grateful, that I *do* have the opportunity to be able to reflect on work that I did, and I can now [express]: okay, if I could do that again, I would do it like this." In this, I hear Viridiana articulating her reflective capacity as itself a mechanism by which she asserts her rhetorical agency: she has the capacity to consider prior decisions and adjust in an ongoing process of work, reflection, and revision. Later in the interview, Viridiana expanded on this response, expressing her satisfaction that she *did something* regardless of how effectual or ineffectual some of her efforts may ultimately have been. She remarked that even though she can see ways she might have operated differently, she is proud of having done as much as she could:

> If I could go back and would be given the choice . . . to *do something* or not, I would still do something because I think that's the right thing to do. It was the right thing to do. And I wouldn't change that. I wouldn't change having opted to be involved, because the reality is that . . . my parents could have been detained or deported. I could have been detained or deported. I mean, literally anybody in my family [could have been]. So, you can't just stand by and not do anything. Now, would I have maybe chosen other [strategies or] been wiser? [shrugs] I mean, honestly, that comes with experience. There's no way of just *knowing* how to be wiser.

The agency Viridiana articulates here appears as a responsibility to take ownership of her capacity to intervene—an agency formed in contrast to the stifling lack of action undertaken by people and organizations with more power, resources, and security. She voices frustration not with the outcomes of her work but with organizations that are "swimming in" resources, whose "Facebook [pages are] blowing up with . . . content about immigration," but in response to which she asks, "What are they doing? . . . What are you doing? . . . What are you actually tangibly delivering?"

All my participants laid claim to rhetorical agency in affirming the value of their experience, whether that value was in its impact on federal policy or public opinion, the prevention of someone's deportation, or the significance in their own lives of the communities they have formed and the capacities they have developed. As they responded to my invitation to assess what their labors mean to them from the perspective of their current lives and selves, all four devised ways to negotiate between positive and negative impacts of that work. I view this negotiation itself as an articulation of agency as perspectival—that is, as rooted in circumstances that shift over time and as emerging through particular perspectives that enable retrospective reflection.

Even outcomes that might seem straightforwardly positive nevertheless prompted these activists to revisit them through the complex perspective of their present understandings. Matias, for instance, conceded with a laugh that his work benefited him in the sense of "enrich[ing] me" or enabling him to "learn all these skills, which I did, but it also saved [me] from deportation." Yet this acknowledgment is complex; he described stepping back from leadership within im/migrant rights organizations, taking some time to heal and move out of a state of perpetual crisis, but he noted that doing so involved for him "a bit of survivor's guilt that comes with" recognizing the arbitrariness of who is deported and who is permitted to regularize their status. He explained that he needs to "be grateful for" what his organizing work accomplished for him but "without saying, well, why couldn't [we] save everyone else?" while recognizing that "there's still work to be done." Ireri similarly identified the direct help of their network of support as crucial in 2016 when their DACA renewal was denied and these activist communities were mobilized in a public campaign to get their status reinstated. But from Ireri's current perspective, organizing through IYJL and OCAD "allowed me to figure out how to not just share my narrative but have a vision of where I wanted it to go . . . and the changes that I wanted to help support as part of a group." Forming a community through IYJL provided direction and valuable connection with other young undocumented people, and it was this connection to community that Ireri identified in the present as most valuable.

Connecting Time to Perspectival Change

Not only are perspectives limited, but bodily capacities are as well, and all of my participants discussed their experiences of burnout—a mark of bodily limitations that they represented as a constraint on their activist labors but not on their agency. Felipe, for instance, brought up burnout in response to my query about advice he would pass along to other young activists; his immediate response was to affirm that "burnout is horrible," but it "can be avoided if you take care." Elaborating on the "few times in [his] life that [he] actually felt . . . completely burnt out," he explained how difficult this sensation of bodily limitations can be for activists who are deeply connected to their work: "You just feel no motivation, and when you feel that your life's mission is so connected to activism and advocacy and you lose motivation in *that*, it feels like you're losing motivation in your overall life."

For other participants, responding to their experiences of burnout involved a kind of "stepping back" from what Matias called "the heat of a campaign" and taking the necessary "personal space and time to build space to heal, to reflect." He recounted stepping back from his formal roles—for instance, on the board of United We Dream and the Massachusetts-based organization Student Immigrant Movement (SIM)—as a response to the "real experience [of] burnout and the mental health struggles" that he recognized after having spent many years pushing for im/migration policy changes. Even articulating what he was experiencing *as* burnout involved a struggle, as he reflected that during his most intense years of activism "there was a lot of courage, but sometimes it could be bravado [or] defiance; we had defiance, but that takes a toll on your spirit." After working more than four years with United We Dream, Matias labored to recognize and respond to the mental health struggles he had accumulated, which took "a toll." He framed his need to step back and reflect in connection with the very different forms of stress experienced by undocumented people in contrast to those who hold a more secure status:

> There still are a lot of deportations [and] a lot of periodic crises, where I think for the American public, a lot of the time, these things flare up, right? Like a couple of weeks ago with the Haitian migrants at the border, the consciousness of the country refocuses momentarily once again on the issue of migration. But for somebody like myself or those others who have grown up in that movement, it never really ends. It might be just little random things throughout the day that remind you of the struggle that so many people are facing.

I hear Matias in this discussion emphasizing an embodied experience of enduring strain—a strain both strongly felt and sustained rather than periodic. Stress that can be endured periodically becomes unbearable when it is unrelenting; enduring that stress required Matias to acknowledge, as he put it, that "even if I make it to eighty or however long, there's still going to be fights for migrant rights afterwards." This realization, which "gives pause to a lot of the idealism or the defiance that . . . kind of fuels that risk-taking at the beginning," generated a perspectival shift for Matias; he described how it felt when the reality set in for him of how long the fight would continue: "it's a struggle because . . . it just kind of changes your outlook on things." In reflection, Matias articulates a space apart from the intensity of "risk-taking" and "the heat of a campaign," a space in which his perspective shifts and his work takes a different form. He experiences this shift as resituating but not forestalling his ongoing activism. He articulated how he has come to value leadership that takes the form of support, mentoring, encouragement, and emotional labor, for instance, rather than viewing, as he did when he was younger, the most visible movement leader as necessarily the one doing the most vital work toward change.

The perspectival shift that Matias articulates—in which grappling with the enormity of the struggle for im/migrant justice "changes [his] outlook"—also emerges for other participants, who likewise reflect on the accumulated toll their work takes on their bodies. Viridiana, for instance, explained that she had "kind of known" that she was "emotionally and mentally burned out" but didn't "realize how bad it was" until she experienced a panic attack: she "started freaking out, . . . I felt like I couldn't breathe. I felt like my heart was racing . . . and I realized, oh my gosh, I need to get out of here. . . . I mean, I knew that I wasn't *okay,* but I didn't realize how bad it [the burnout] was until" that experience. She articulated this experience as her body forcing her to register her limitations and reckon with "how much your body just *absorbs,* you know?" She elaborated on this sense of inescapable responsibility as both a strength and a detriment: "generally . . . I would argue, if you're an activist it's because you really care about something. You really care about people. And so you're an empath. And so I'm sitting here, hearing all these devastating stories. But I don't understand how much I am actually absorbing [others' pain and stress] until I'm freaking out, my body is having this reaction. And in my mind, I'm fine, but my body is freaking out." The embodied experience of having panic attacks forced her to register, as she puts it, how much pain she absorbs through her work to stop deportations, activating a perspectival shift that altered her relationship with her antideportation work. Though she explained to me that she cannot readily "step back" from the needs that are brought to her, she nevertheless developed and clarified for herself an altered perspective on her work.

Participants link their changing roles to the shifting perspectives from which they undertake their work. In particular, they articulate ways that their changing self-understandings and circumstances have prompted revisions to their activist roles. For instance, several participants explained that their calculation of risk had shifted as they aged. As Felipe explained,

Each phase of your life determines what's important. When I was twenty-two, I didn't really have a lot to do—that's how I felt about it, even though I had a lot. But I felt that way. I was like, well, life is already messed up. It may get worse, but it could also get better. If I just stay here, it's not going to get better. . . . Nowadays, there are so many other things [that] are so important to me, like my family, my husband, other things that are so, so dear . . . which also means that I have a different focus now.

He found himself unable to say retroactively what was most important to him about his activism, because at "each time, *that* was the most critical thing for me at the moment." Matias articulated how aging, accompanied by other personal changes in relation to his family and his documentation status, ultimately led him to shift to a role where he supports other young activists while maintaining "a degree of separation now from the heat of a campaign that rests on my shoulders." Explaining this shift in his perspective, Matias pointed out that the difference in "risk measurement from being twenty-three to being thirty-five changes a lot." When he looks back on his actions as a young undocumented person, "what's surprising—and it's kind of a feeling that I don't have anymore—is how much we were willing to risk." Participants also charted how their emotional and attitudinal changes created a different perspective on their work; Matias, for instance, referred to his earlier activism as connected to pride and bravado. Viridiana articulated shifting away from the anger that motivated her initially. She explained that she has been "kept from going to college and pursuing my dreams all because of my immigration status and [I have] all this pent-up anger and resentment and all these emotions—it was almost like I was dealing with them through my activism. And so, it was healthy and it wasn't. I was doing something with those emotions, right? But it wasn't healthy in that *that* was the foundation. The foundation [of her work] was anger. And love, yeah, sure, but it was also anger." Viridiana links these motives to both the burnout she experienced and her newly emerging perspective on antideportation work.

Changes to their situations likewise prompted participants to articulate revised perspectives and approaches. Some participants noted that the urgency they brought to their activism changed when family members left the US, for instance; others identified changes to their motivations or priorities as a consequence of reflection, sometimes prompted by burnout or by taking space to reconsider their involvement. Viridiana, for example, identified a significant disconnect between her earlier and her present antideportation work, brought about by a change in her religious faith. Discussing this change during her interview, she was careful to articulate her belief that although her concrete actions would not likely have been different, undertaking them from within her current religious practice would have changed how she felt about the burdens of responsibility that she carried. As she put it,

> If I would have been walking with the Lord, then I wouldn't have felt like, Oh, this is just on *me*. It's all on me. Me, me, me. If I don't get this right then, you know, this family is going to get deported. If I don't answer this right away . . . I better word that press release correctly, and I better dot my Is and cross my Ts and make sure I got the press release ready and make sure I got the emails to the correctional office ready and make sure I have this and this and it's just like "ah!" [with] all this stuff going on.

Her speed and the mounting intensity expressed here show her returning in an embodied way to the mental and emotional space she was in during her most intense work against deportation. Although Viridiana had communicated how exhausted she was from ten years of working to stop deportations and get people out of detention, as she turned toward the future, she articulated her hope that her new perspective might enable her to pursue antideportation work again, but in a framework in which she shares responsibility with others rather than centering it entirely on herself. She related, for instance, an experience of disclosing to her pastor that she is undocumented, which led to her church's incipient intervention at the detention center in her county, offering a way for Viridiana to move forward with this work.

As these participants formed links between their changing perspectives and the roles they have taken in the im/migration justice movement over time, several articulated their current role as a form of mentoring in which they develop and support other activists from positions of expertise, experience, or greater power than they held previously. Felipe, for instance, who worked as a city official at the time of our interview, discussed his new focus on cultivating other leaders to take on key positions; the difference, as he explained, "is that it's not about what I think needs to happen; it's really about what they want and what they think, their vision. And then I play more of a consulting position, a mentor, someone who helps them think through their strategy, think about how they can create shape to their efforts." Matias described a similar shift occurring as he moved into higher education, where his role is to support folks who are planning campaigns and actions, "with a listening ear and with just my experience of what worked and what didn't and how things can feel at any point." Matias described the translation involved in articulating his experience alongside those of the young people he now supports, explaining,

I can say, I relate to you because I was there. I've been to actions. I've helped plan actions that were not that successful. I've struggled with teammates in the same organization and had to figure it out. And sometimes we failed to figure it out. . . . It happens. It's actually, like, sometimes the problems that student activists or student organizers think are unique to their moment in time, they're actually very common occurrences in organizing. So I could . . . sometimes provide examples of how those same dynamics were present in my work as a student activist.

The perspectival form of agency participants articulated was situated in forms of change that have taken place not only inexorably over time but also in relation to concerted efforts to develop their activist capacities. Ireri articulated this most clearly through the Spanish verb *capacitarse,* explaining that through IYJL, participants undertook explicitly to prepare themselves in ways that developed their capacities: "Sometimes we would try to shift roles. Like if you hadn't had this role before, try to sort of shift [into] it and talk to some of the folks that had done those roles." IYJL invited the support of a fellow community organizer, who shared a public storytelling framework before staging the first Coming Out of the Shadows Day, for instance, and engaged in another training focused on language justice in order to make the second Coming Out of the Shadows Day more bilingual and accessible. IYJL also drew directly on "support from folks that had been part of direct actions in other movements," who "would come in and share their experiences and work with us to learn how to be a police liaison" or

> how . . . you make these things where you can stick your hand in the lock boxes, where it's harder to take you out, so I would say that a lot of those skills were learned from watching and learning from other folks who had done this in different movements who were willing to come and share their skills. And some[times] . . . we were like, okay, we tried something, this didn't work; let's try something else. That didn't work, maybe we should ask for different opinions, you know? And then the folks that were coming into the group were also coming with lots of different kinds of experiences. And so we were able to draw from everybody's expertise or everybody's experiences and adapt some of the things that we were doing.

These practices underscore complex relations among rhetorical agency, time, and collective capacity. Deliberately seeking to incorporate varied experiences and expertise into their efforts, and engaging in reflection along the way as

well as after the fact, the participants in this collective worked toward—cultivated—increased capacities.

CONCLUSION: PERSPECTIVAL AGENCY IN RETROSPECT

As this chapter has argued, perspectival agency is attuned to time, accumulation, and shifting intensities and social locations, asserting agency across contexts of perpetual change. If accumulated intensity—as experiences of "legal
violence" accrue and anti-im/migrant exclusions mount—contributed to the
urgency of undocumented activism throughout 2010 and afterward, perspectival agency traces activists' adjustment to change over time.[72] Intensities shift,
relationships alter, and reflection reframes the significance they see in their
work. As Felipe explained, "It's kind of like seeing yourself in a spectrum of
change. Also knowing that you are not the same as the person before you,
even the previous version of yourself, and being sure that the current version
of yourself is not the future version of yourself. And being open to that." The
felt experience of vulnerability is not static but shifting; consequently, its role
as a rhetorical resource requires ongoing rearticulation. For instance, Felipe
noted how his perspective has changed as he has achieved an insider position
working for the city government to support inclusion and diversity efforts; no
longer the undocumented community college student who felt he had nothing to lose, Felipe reflects, he is now the person being petitioned, and the
resources he oversees are being sought by others. As he put it, this move to
a position as an insider in systems of power "really drastically changed" his
"relationship to movements," because "now I am the person being lobbied at
instead of the person doing the lobbying." Yet the agency Felipe claims stems
not from having resources but from his openness to "seeing [him]self in a
spectrum of change," including revising his aims to encompass "support[ing]
others . . . in their journey [and] in their advocacy."

Such a perspectival shift resonates with Kefaya Diab's conceptualization
of an embodied "sense of agency," which she defines as "an affect or affective power that emerges from within historical, cultural, and lived fluxes."[73]
This sense of agency changes moment by moment, making possibility in the
world. Reflecting on their experiences, the im/migration activists and workers
I spoke with confronted the extent to which agency, in Diab's words, "was con-

72. On "legal violence," see Menjívar and Abrego, "Legal Violence."
73. Diab, "Rise of the Arab Spring," 263.

strained and incongruent with the final results" of their efforts; nevertheless, Diab writes, "the sense of agency that passed through protestors' bodies was effective in keeping them moving forward."[74] While Diab focuses on the physical movement of bodies advancing toward the Jordanian-Israeli border before being turned aside by tear gas, the reflections of activists in this chapter also chart paths forward into ongoing, if altered, forms of advocacy. Perspectival agency ultimately offers a mechanism by which activists incorporate into their "sense of agency" their experiences of incessant change, curtailed possibility, and outcomes that are "incongruent" with the social and legal transformations they sought. It allows activists to grapple with the reality that, in Matias's words, "even if I make it to eighty or however long, there's still going to be fights for migrant rights afterwards." In this way, perspectival agency embraces perpetually altering circumstances and thereby recuperates them into a form of rhetorical agency.

Ultimately, interview participants, by revisiting their strategies, challenged the common binary trajectory from childhood *feeling* to adult *reason*. Against ubiquitous admonitions leveled at those taking countercultural stances, that they will "grow out" of them or "see things differently," the reflections of undocumented activists affirm that we will always see things differently but must operate *now* to work toward, rather than wait for, future change. These activists' reflections validate sustained activism as an activity of mutability and persistence, in which shifting perspectives generate new strategies amid acceptance of a lifelong struggle.

---

74. Diab, 262.

CHAPTER 3

Agency as Capacity

Disruptive Activism for Gun Reform

After weeks spent giving interviews to television, print, and other news media and being followed by news crews and documentary teams, survivors of the Parkland, Florida, school shooting took the stage during the 2018 March For Our Lives demonstration in Washington, DC. As one of the most prominent public faces among the survivors, X González was the final speaker in the day's lineup.[1] In their opening words—"Six minutes and about twenty seconds"—González identified the length of time it took a shooter to take the lives of seventeen people and injure fifteen others. González furrowed their brow, wiped away tears, and recalled the names of these classmates, then stopped speaking and stared into the camera. This moment stretched on and on. Members of the crowd, which numbered in the hundreds of thousands, whispered to each other, repeatedly began chants and cheers, and struggled to wait as the seconds stretched into minutes. Because major television news networks continued to broadcast the silent figure on stage, millions of people watched the event as it aired. Ultimately, González remained silent for nearly four and a half minutes, speaking again only when a timer went off to indicate that they had been on stage for six minutes and twenty seconds. González briefly informed the audience of the meaning of the silence they had just experienced, and quickly closed their remarks and left the stage.

---

1. González changed their name in 2021 and uses *they/them* pronouns. See González, "The Education."

Although a brief moment of silence is a routine and conventional feature of memorial events, vigils, and protest activities related to violence, grief, or loss, the duration of González's silence was extraordinary, challenging audience expectations in ways that register even in recorded video of the speech, as the gathered crowd grew noticeably unsettled as the silence continued. Media commentators immediately afterward called González's extended silence "powerful," "defiant," "profound," "remarkable," "incredible," and "chilling."[2] It was not the act of silence but its duration that prompted such a response; Peter Marks, theatre critic for the *Washington Post,* noted that "a moment of silence is the ritualized form of respect we employ on many occasions to mark tragedy, but it's usually only a moment. González's silence was an act that felt, in its way, radical."[3] Sociologists Mary Bernstein, Jordan McMillan, and Elizabeth Charash recounted from their field notes taken at the march that participants around them whispered and wondered aloud if the silence would last for seventeen minutes to mark the seventeen lives lost[4]—indicative of how long the experience felt to those present at the time.

These responses indicate the extent to which González's performance disrupted expectations. Media studies scholar Emily Bent interprets González's long period of silence as a strategy that "elucidated young people's frustrations with the political system."[5] Theater scholar Meredith Conti characterizes those four and a half minutes of silence as a "collaborative, unscripted composi-

2. See Sonam Sheth, "'Fight for Your Lives Before It's Someone Else's Job': Parkland Student Emma González Sends a Powerful Message at the 'March for Our Lives' Rally," *Business Insider,* March 24, 2018, https://www.businessinsider.com/emma-gonzalez-six-minutes-speech-march-for-our-lives-rally-2018-3; Kayleigh Roberts, "Emma González Spoke Volumes in Her Powerful Moment of Silence at the March for Our Lives," *Harper's Bazaar,* March 24, 2018, https://www.harpersbazaar.com/culture/politics/a19583877/emma-gonzalez-march-for-our-lives-speech/; Lisa Ryan, "Emma González's March for Our Lives Speech Lasted As Long as the Parkland Shooting," *The Cut,* March 24, 2018; Dave McNary, "Steven Spielberg Praises Emma González's 'Profound' Speech at March for Our Lives: 'Everybody Was Crying,'" *Variety,* March 27, 2018, https://variety.com/2018/film/news/steven-spielberg-lena-waite-ready-player-one-premiere-1202737241/; Michael Livingston, "Emma González Leads Remarkable Moment of Silence at Washington March," *Los Angeles Times,* March 24, 2018, https://www.latimes.com/local/california/la-me-saturday-walkouts-liveupdates-march24-2018-htmlstory.html; German Lopez, "Emma González's Incredible Moment of Silence at March for Our Lives," *Vox,* March 25, 2018, https://www.vox.com/policy-and-politics/2018/3/24/17159916/march-for-our-lives-emma-gonzalez-silence; and Ari Berman, "Emma González Is Responsible," *Mother Jones,* March 24, 2018, https://www.motherjones.com/politics/2018/03/emma-gonzalez-is-responsible-for-the-loudest-silence-in-the-history-of-us-social-protest/.

3. Peter Marks, "Emma González and the Wordless Act That Moved a Nation," *Washington Post,* March 25, 2018, https://www.washingtonpost.com/news/arts-and-entertainment/wp/2018/03/25/emma-gonzalez-and-the-wordless-act-that-moved-a-nation/.

4. Bernstein, McMillan, and Charash, "Once in Parkland," 1164.

5. Bent, "This Is Not Another," 803.

tion between performer and audience," arguing that because González "leaves unspoken the purpose of [their] prolonged silence, [they] guide spectators into temporary states of confusion and/or apprehension, gesturing toward (albeit in a low-stakes, nonviolent way) the Parkland students' disorienting lockdown experience."[6] Situated in the speech-making context of the march and in "a political environment that is overwhelmingly, relentlessly noisy," Conti argues, González's prolonged silence is "bold" and "capacious."[7] Journalist Megan Garber emphasizes the power González wielded during these minutes in which they "stared at the crowd—and at the cable-news camera, transmitting it all to the world," knowing that they were "giving them dead air" and that nevertheless, "the cameras would not turn away."[8] I especially want to draw attention to Garber's interpretation that standing in silence in this context is a forceful act of disruption—a refusal to provide what watching media expect and an exercise of power in knowing that the spectacle of the march, culminating in this speech and viewed voraciously in real time, would not permit this silence to be interrupted. Such power can be seen as something the Parkland survivors, and González in particular, had garnered during their previous weeks of organizing, which included widespread use of the hashtags #MarchForOurLives and #NeverAgain and a national school walkout ten days earlier.

If silence in such a moment is disruptive, it fits within the broader strategy of disruption that characterized March For Our Lives activism from mid-February through the 2018 march. A primary effect of the social media campaigns, national school walkout, and DC rally organized by Parkland survivors was that they "managed to keep the tragedy that their school experienced—and their plan to stop such shootings from happening elsewhere—in the news for weeks, long after past mass shootings have faded from the headlines."[9] That is, they disrupted the widely acknowledged "predictable cycle" of media coverage following mass shootings in the US.[10] Rhetoric scholar Craig Rood has characterized this cycle as "cast blame, pick sides, move on," and Robert Spitzer has described "the political pattern typifying the gun debate" as "one in which repetitive political scenarios play themselves out with great fury but astonishingly little effect."[11] Many journalists have identified the same repeti-

---

6. Conti, "Sound of Silence," E10–E11.

7. Conti, E8.

8. Garber, "Powerful Silence."

9. Jonah Bromwich, "How the Parkland Students Got So Good at Social Media," *New York Times,* March 7, 2018, https://www.nytimes.com/2018/03/07/us/parkland-students-social-media.html.

10. Zoller and Casteel, "#March for Our Lives."

11. Rood, *After Gun Violence,* 5; and Spitzer, quoted in Rood, 5.

tive quality in discourse about gun violence, pointing out that "mass shootings typically are followed by outrage, cries for gun reform, heavy media coverage—and reactionary anger from pro-gun activists—before fading."[12] Consequently, between the shooting at Parkland and the March For Our Lives in DC, commentators observed that even maintaining public attention for six weeks was a significant disruption to the fleeting cycle of media attention. The tactic of sustaining attention through disruption is mirrored in the prolonged silence in González's speech: resisting the pull back to normalcy and the resumption of prior patterns, and marshaling (material and rhetorical) resources to hold an audience captive for longer than expected.

March For Our Lives activism offers further demonstration that childhood both facilitates and constrains rhetorical possibility. The age and rhetorical savvy of survivors of the Parkland shooting made their efforts to organize large-scale calls for gun reform newsworthy, as they leveraged *youth* to forward a coordinated call for policy change that involved hundreds of thousands of young people. Associations of youth with emotionality, impulse, and lack of consideration for decorum functioned as constraints that activists navigated, as I detail below; young activists employed tactics of disruption to resist routine patterns of media coverage and to leverage media attention toward racialized impacts of gun violence in the US. Yet those same associations also structured media responses, which returned obsessively to the question of young activists' success or failure, determined along narrow measures such as outcomes of the 2018 midterm elections. Teen activists' reflections counter such narrow framings of their rhetorical impacts. Against the push-and-pull of *repetition* and *disruption*, this chapter employs interviews with young organizers conducted in both an immediate (three to six months after the march) and longer retrospective frame (more than two years later). Drawing on these interviews I argue that young people develop embodied capacities through their activist commitments—and in reflection, they articulate those capacities as forms of rhetorical agency.

CONTENDING WITH A RACIALIZED TOPOGRAPHY OF VIOLENCE

The disruption González enacted at the march—and the additional strategies I analyze below—contends with a national context of everyday gun violence

---

12. Andrew Wong, "The NRA Faces a New Kind of Opponent: Kids Who Understand Social Media," CNBC, March 5, 2018, https://www.cnbc.com/2018/03/05/neveragain-gun-control-debate-pits-nra-against-kids-on-twitter.html.

that is simultaneously astonishingly pervasive and deeply normalized. From 2018 to 2021, the United States averaged more than 43,000 gun deaths each year.[13] Sixty percent of these annual deaths—roughly 25,000—were suicides, and the United States has a gun suicide rate nearly twelve times higher than other high-income countries. Each day, "120 Americans are killed with guns, and more than 200 are shot and wounded."[14] Although mass shootings represent only "the tip of the iceberg" of the pervasiveness of gun violence in the United States—representing approximately 1 percent of gun deaths each year—they nevertheless occur with far more frequency in the United States than in other countries.[15] Different thresholds for defining mass shootings, such as whether victims whose wounds are nonfatal are included, and determining the public or private context of a shooting, result in different accounts of how rare or common mass shootings are. When nonfatal injuries are included, mass shootings become visible as "a far more serious problem: there were 253 mass shootings in the United States in 2013, 270 in 2014, 335 in 2015, and 382 in 2016."[16] Even when calculated according to more narrow criteria, "there is evidence that mass shootings have increased in the United States: Between 1982 and 2010, mass shootings occurred every 200 days on average. Between 2011 and 2013, mass shootings occurred every 64 days on average."[17] Attempting to assemble trustworthy information from varied sources in the absence of federal research, Everytown's research efforts have found that more than 19,000 people have been killed or wounded in mass shooting events since 2015. Since 2020, there have been more than 600 mass shooting events each year.[18] Among those injured and killed in mass shootings, a quarter of victims were children or teens, and in more than half of all mass shooting incidents, a family member or intimate partner of the shooter was among those killed.[19]

Within what sociologists Mary Bernstein, Jordan McMillan, and Elizabeth Charash have described as this country's "topography of violence," media coverage and public attention operate along racialized and gendered lines, obscuring the extent to which vulnerability to gun violence is unevenly distributed.[20] From 2018 to 2021, Black Americans were twelve times more likely than white

---

13. Everytown, *Gun Violence in America*, May 19, 2020, last updated February 13, 2023, https://everytownresearch.org/report/gun-violence-in-america/.

14. Everytown.

15. Everytown, "Mass Shootings in America," last updated March 2023, https://everytown-research.org/mass-shootings-in-america/.

16. Rood, *After Gun Violence*, 3.

17. Squires, *Dangerous Discourses*, xviii.

18. Everytown, "Mass Shootings in America."

19. Everytown.

20. Bernstein, McMillan, and Charash, "Once in Parkland," 1158.

Americans to die by gun homicide,[21] yet white and suburban victims elicit far more media attention and expressions of public sympathy and outrage than Black and urban victims of gun violence. Communication scholar Catherine Squires notes that public discussions occur largely "in the wake of horrifying mass shooting incidents, despite the fact that guns are used more often in domestic violence situations than mass shootings, and suicides and police shootings kill many more people each year in daily doses of oppression and intimidation."[22] Gun ownership is itself an uneven and racialized phenomenon; as Daniel Cryer notes, "the vast majority of licensed US carriers are white men in 'small towns and rural areas' (Cook and Goss 22), who are among the least physically threatened people in the nation"—though these men are at elevated risk of death by suicide.[23] More than seventy percent of the 25,000 gun suicides every year are white men.[24] Widespread gun ownership by men is costly for women; on average, "five women are murdered with guns" every day in the US, with Black women "twice as likely to be victims of gun violence as white women."[25] The relationship between guns and intimate partner violence is profound. Guns are "used with alarming frequency by abusers to injure victims or attempt to do so," resulting in a context in which "nearly 1 million women in the US alive today have reported being shot or shot at by an intimate partner," and 4.5 million women in the US have reported being threatened with a gun by a partner or family member.[26] Although disparities and biases in reporting make data on queer, trans, and gender nonconforming victims of gun violence difficult to assemble, the highest lifetime rates of intimate partner violence are reported for bisexual women (61%), transgender people (54%), and lesbian women (43%).[27] Alongside these pervasive daily vulnerabilities, mass shootings are closely linked with expressions of misogyny and patterns of masculine domination: "men using firearms to inflict public terror often share histories of violence against women,"[28] though such linkages are rarely identified in news coverage. Rhetoric scholars Carol Stabile and Bryce Peake argue that a "still largely male news force" fails to recognize

---

21. Everytown, "Gun Violence in America."

22. Squires, *Dangerous Discourses*, xvi.

23. Cryer, "Good Man Shooting Well," 255. See also Rood, "Protection Narratives."

24. Everytown, "Gun Violence in America."

25. Squires, *Dangerous Discourses*, xviii.

26. Everytown, *Guns and Violence against Women: America's Uniquely Lethal Intimate Partner Violence Problem*, October 17, 2019, last updated April 10, 2023, https://everytownresearch.org/report/guns-and-violence-against-women-americas-uniquely-lethal-intimate-partner-violence-problem/.

27. Everytown, *Guns and Violence*.

28. Everytown.

and contextualize the patterns of masculine domination that contribute to the shooting events they recount; they argue that journalists rely on "the logic of 'the snap,'" which treats suicide-mass shootings as "disconnected incidents of misogyny gone wild," when "it is more accurate to consider them as amplifications of widespread and far from marginal misogynistic discourses."[29]

If such statistics outline the extent to which racial identity, gender, sexuality, and other characteristics strongly shape one's exposure to gun violence, such characteristics likewise filter public assessments of victims' value. Put bluntly, "gunshot deaths of black and brown bodies in urban settings are viewed as normal while gunshot deaths in suburban settings are extraordinary and worthy of outrage."[30] By comparing the tactics of urban and suburban gun violence prevention advocates, Bernstein, McMillan, and Charash reveal material and rhetorical contrasts that distinguish activism within urban communities of color from that of largely white suburban communities responding to a mass shooting; ultimately, they argue, the most salient distinction between urban and suburban gun violence activism is that the "worthiness of victims" is "fundamentally racialized."[31]

DISRUPTING AN AMERICAN RITUAL

The context outlined above indicates patterns of violence, media response, and congressional inaction that have ossified over the first two decades of the twentieth century, solidified into "a distinctly American ritual."[32] Two additional rhetorical strategies adopted by national March For Our Lives activists aimed to disrupt ritualized media coverage following mass shootings. These strategies anticipated and addressed opponents' rearticulations of their arguments. Though earlier chapters have shown the susceptibility of young activists' arguments to adult rearticulations, this chapter highlights how such maneuvers can be anticipated and partially forestalled. These two strategies— breaching decorum and leveraging privilege as mostly white, affluent, suburban victims—contributed to the efforts of March For Our Lives activists to resist the rapid movement of the news cycle and counteract the resumption of routine media coverage.

---

29. Stabile and Peake, "Coverage That Kills," 12.

30. Bernstein, McMillan, and Charash, "Once in Parkland," 1154.

31. Bernstein, McMillan, and Charash, 1165.

32. Natalie Reneau, "A Unique American Ritual: The School Shooting," *New York Times*, February 23, 2018, https://www.nytimes.com/video/us/100000005743519/school-shooting-images.html.

Breaching Decorum

Publicly grieving people are expected to show emotions—particularly sadness, pain, and the kind of controlled anguish noted in President Obama's many national eulogies in the aftermath of mass shootings.[33] The emotionality displayed by teen activists in the weeks leading up to the march differed, however, in their embrace of emotions typically prohibited, namely anger, impatience, and disgust. For instance, González delivered their "We Call BS" speech at the Rally to Support Firearm Safety Legislation in Fort Lauderdale, Florida, on February 17, 2018, only a few days after the shooting at their high school. The transcript of the speech circulated widely, and a reader can register their anger in phrases such as "Shame on you!" and a lack of decorum in the repeated phrase "We call BS." Video shows González positively vibrating with anger, as they shout, "You didn't know him," about the shooter. This intense display of anger, coupled with its informal (or uncivil) language, led commentators to identify the "We Call BS" speech as "emblematic of a potentially new strain of furious advocacy" in relation to gun control legislation.[34] The incivility of "angry and frustrated" teens drew commentary again at a televised town hall hosted by CNN on February 21, when González insisted that NRA Spokesperson Dana Loesch answer their questions more directly, and members of the crowd shouted angrily in response to evasions by Loesch and Marco Rubio.[35] In an interview with the online periodical *The Outline*, David Hogg described inactive politicians as "sick fuckers" and asked "what type of shitty person" cares more about campaign contributions than children's lives.[36]

We can see how age operates as both a resource and a liability in this case, in audience responses to these disruptions of decorum. Young people's expressions of anger and incivility often lead media to emphasize activists' age, as when they are characterized as "typical" teenagers who are "impervious to the etiquette expected from adults."[37] Yet their confrontational strategies can also be seen in connection with their broader effort to sustain attention and inter-

33. Rood, *After Gun Violence*.

34. Alex Horton, "Advice from a Survivor of the Florida School Shooting: It's Time to Start Ignoring Trump," *Washington Post*, February 18, 2018, https://www.washingtonpost.com/news/post-nation/wp/2018/02/18/advice-from-a-survivor-of-the-florida-school-shooting-its-time-to-start-ignoring-trump/.

35. Emanuella Grinberg and Steve Almasy, "Students at Town Hall to Washington, NRA: Guns Are the Problem, Do Something," CNN, February 22, 2018, https://www.wral.com/story/cnn-to-hold-town-hall-with-students-and-florida-s-politicians/17358970/.

36. George Zornick, "How the #NeverAgain Movement Is Disrupting Gun Politics," *The Nation*, April 3, 2018, https://www.thenation.com/article/archive/how-the-neveragain-movement-is-disrupting-gun-politics/.

37. Charlotte Alter, "The School Shooting Generation Has Had Enough," *Time*, March 22, 2018, https://time.com/longform/never-again-movement/.

rupt the cycle of media coverage that settles quickly back into routine patterns following mass shootings. Such displays of anger and impatience contrast with the tactics adopted by several of the well-funded, national, adult-organized gun violence groups that emerged after Sandy Hook and that have worked incrementally toward improved gun legislation since 2012, organizations that embrace "an inside game of slow consensus-building with lawmakers and taking small legislative wins where they can."[38] Some adult activists involved in those groups have voiced appreciation for the potential of emotional, disruptive teen activists to "close the passion gap" that has long advantaged gun supporters over those working on behalf of limiting gun violence.[39] Yet as activists over time have shown, speaking from a rhetorically disadvantaged position can make such an emotionally laden strategy particularly risky; incivility in the form of impatience, exasperation, or expressions of anger, particularly when voiced by people of color, can provide opponents with further ground for dismissing arguments, shifting to tone policing, and sidestepping good faith engagement. Conversative commentators characterized Hogg's profanity-laced expressions of anger as evidence that young people in general lack the capacity for nuance or for considering others' perspectives; one wrote, for instance, that Hogg's "profane, immature, and crass" interview shows that "we should not be giving children the microphone and platform to dictate politics and policy."[40] When applied to a high school senior, *children* is clearly meant here as a disparagement, signaling unreasonable outbursts, lack of restraint, and inadequate knowledge of adult complexities of "politics and policy." Indecorous displays of emotionality, then, simultaneously breach decorum and disrupt media routines, yet allow opponents to rearticulate young activists' arguments—by diverting attention from gun legislation toward critique of activists' tactics.

Leveraging Privilege

In the weeks immediately after the Parkland shooting, many media outlets drew attention to the fact that the most prominent survivors were largely white and that the outrage sparked by mass shootings in affluent and suburban areas continues to give these events outsized importance relative to the daily

38. Zornick, "How the #NeverAgain Movement."

39. Randi Kaye, "Sandy Hook Survivor Joins Parkland Students to Say 'Enough,'" CNN, March 23, 2018, https://www.cnn.com/2018/03/23/us/sandy-hook-survivor-joins-parkland-students/index.html.

40. Stirling Preston, "David Hogg Claims NRA Would Be OK with Children's Blood on Their Faces," *Minority Report* (blog), March 23, 2018.

exposure to gun violence experienced in many communities of color. One approach adopted by Parkland activists was to acknowledge their position of affluence and privilege, addressing the inequities of media coverage head-on. Speaking at Thurgood Marshall Academy in Washington, DC, just before the march, for instance, David Hogg explained, "We've seen again and again the media focus on school shootings, and oftentimes be biased toward white, privileged students. . . . Many [other] communities are disproportionately affected by gun violence, but they don't get the same share of media attention that we do."[41] Another white Parkland survivor, Delaney Tarr, explained to a reporter for *Time,* "We came from an affluent area, and we're mostly white, and we have to use that privilege."[42] The whiteness and affluence of their suburban community was noted repeatedly in speeches by survivors during the March 24 event in Washington, DC, where survivors of the suburban mass shooting in Parkland spoke in alternating sequence with speakers from communities where gun violence is far more pervasive and where exposures to gun violence typically happen in neighborhoods, grocery stores, and on the way to and from school. Non-Parkland speakers at the DC march included survivors of gun violence from Los Angeles, Chicago, Baltimore, Alexandria, and Brooklyn who recounted friends and relatives being killed or wounded by guns. Zion Kelly, a student at Thurgood Marshall Academy, spoke onstage about his twin brother, Zaire Kelly, who was shot and killed returning home from a college prep class, and Edna Chávez recalled her older brother's death and the trauma and anxiety of daily exposure to gun violence, explaining that her community "has become accustomed to this violence. It is normal to see candles. It is normal to see posters. It is normal to see balloons. It is normal to see flowers honoring the lives of black and brown youth that have lost their lives to a bullet."[43] These speakers and others confronted the stark differentials in media attention that overlook the shooting deaths of people of color and instead lavish attention on the mostly white student survivors of a suburban school shooting.

Activist survivors of the Parkland shooting also emphasized their role as coalitional throughout their summer 2018 Road To Change bus tour: they organized events that would highlight the concerns of young people already organizing in the communities they visited, and they combined public-facing events with opportunities for conversation with local activists working on the

---

41. George Zornick, "The Adults Have Failed, So Students are Leading the Way," *The Nation,* March 24, 2018, https://www.thenation.com/article/archive/the-adults-have-failed-so-students-are-leading-the-way/.

42. Alter, "School Shooting Generation."

43. Zornick, "Adults Have Failed."

solutions that are most important to them.[44] As some coverage noted, the activists were "aiming to build a movement that's multiracial and inclusive— one that addresses gun violence everywhere, not just in suburban schools and movie theaters."[45] The amicus brief submitted by the March For Our Lives organizers to the Supreme Court in August 2018 likewise situates vulnerability to violence in intersectional terms, linking race, class, and gender. As Rachel Gilmer, codirector of the Florida-based racial justice group Dream Defenders, which is part of the Movement for Black Lives coalition, explained: "What has created the condition for the Parkland movement to happen is the fact that they've grown up in the age of Black Lives Matter," she said. "So, it's not like this movement is happening in a silo. They're actually joining our movement and that should be something that's seen as progress and not in competition with the other."[46] This particular tactic of leveraging privilege operates, then, as both an overt strategy adopted by the Parkland teens and as a savvy antici- pation of adult rearticulations they expect; they are going to be described, especially by opponents of gun control, as coddled, affluent, and protected, and thus they anticipate such critiques by incorporating them into arguments for more comprehensive change.

MEDIA FRAMINGS OF SUCCESS AND FAILURE

As the conspiracy theories, death threats, and online harassment directed at national March For Our Lives activists has shown, merely being the recipi- ents of media attention does not counteract the compromised rhetoricity of young people.[47] What sociologist Jessica Taft has identified as "the passivity

---

44. Maggie Astor, "'Let Us Have a Childhood': On the Road with the Parkland Activists," *New York Times,* August 15, 2018, https://www.nytimes.com/2018/08/15/us/politics/parkland- students-voting.html.

45. Zornick, "Adults Have Failed."

46. Aaron Morrison, "Racial Justice Groups Are Sending Thousands of Black and Brown Kids to the March for Our Lives Rally," *Mic,* March 23, 2018, https://www.mic.com/ articles/188560/racial-justice-groups-are-sending-thousands-of-black-and-brown-kids-to-the- march-for-our-lives-rally.

47. See Bent, "This Is Not Another"; Applegarth, "News That Isn't New"; Jonah E. Brom- wich, "Parkland Students Find Themselves Targets of Lies and Personal Attacks," *New York Times,* March 27, 2018, https://www.nytimes.com/2018/03/27/us/parkland-students-hogg-gon- zalez.html?action=click; Michael Kranz, "'No One Would Know Your Names': NRA TV Host Slammed the Parkland Kids Ahead of the March for Our Lives Rallies," *Business Insider,* March 25, 2018, https://www.businessinsider.com/nratv-host-colion-noir-said-parkland-kids-wouldnt- matter-if-classmates-were-still-alive-2018-3; Mica Soellner, "No, the March for Our Lives Was Not Prepared Several Months in Advance of Its Date," *PolitiFact,* April 3, 2018, https://www. politifact.com/factchecks/2018/apr/03/fellowship-minds/no-march-our-lives-demonstration- was-not-prepared-/; Michael M. Grynbaum, "Right-Wing Media Uses Parkland Shooting as

assumption," or the "assumption that children are uncritical sponges who absorb the perspectives of adults," circumscribes attributions of agency for young activists.[48] As Taft explains, "many people assume that children who are involved in social movements or who engage in political speech are merely pawns of adult activists. Children who are politicized are frequently described as manipulated, with their political education being depicted as brainwashing and their claims dismissed as mimicry."[49] Such was clearly the case among the conspiracy theorists who promoted the idea that the Parkland survivors were "crisis actors" and who described the teens as manipulated by larger gun-control organizations. Yet even appreciative news coverage that found young activists "savvy" and "passionate" wondered whether their activism would have any effect, implicitly questioning their capacity as rhetorical agents. Young activists were admonished to heed the lessons of adult leaders and prior movements; the efficacy of their strategies was scrutinized, their understanding of political change was interrogated, and dire warnings about the difficulty of achieving social movement success were reiterated. In this way, even ostensibly supportive media coverage reinscribed authority within adult contexts and circumscribed the rhetorical potential of young speakers and organizers.

This discursive context is shaped by pervasive understandings of youth as distractible, lacking in commitment, and more focused on their peers than on political change. Assessments of activist strategies and discussions of their successes and failures invite attention to temporal concepts such as *momentum, timing,* and *endurance.* Media coverage of MFOL activism throughout 2018 reiterated narrow temporal framings as it asked adult audiences to consider whether the disruptions young activists were creating would endure. Many framed this uncertainty through the evocative binary contrasting a "moment" and a "movement." For instance, Erica Evans's headline asks, "Is Saturday's 'March for Our Lives' a Moment or a Movement?" Evans notes that "the teenagers who are front and center in these protests have already proved they are able to attract media attention. . . . But will they be successful in creating lasting change?"[50] The concept of "lasting change" is likewise reiter-

Conspiracy Fodder," *New York Times,* February 20, 2018, https://www.nytimes.com/2018/02/20/business/media/parkland-shooting-media-conspiracy.html; and Daniel Victor and Matthew Haag, "'Swatting' Prank Sends Police to Home of David Hogg, Parkland Survivor," *New York Times,* June 5, 2018, https://www.nytimes.com/2018/06/05/us/david-hogg-swatting.html.

48. Taft, *Kids Are In Charge,* 4.

49. Taft, 6.

50. Erica Evans, "Is Saturday's 'March for Our Lives' a Moment or a Movement?," *Deseret News,* March 22, 2018, https://www.deseret.com/2018/3/22/20642222/is-saturday-s-march-for-our-lives-a-moment-or-a-movement.

ated across media coverage, which often announces concern about whether teen activists truly comprehend the "long road ahead."[51] For instance, a story in the *New York Times* poses the familiar "moment or movement" question in its title and reminds student activists that they face the challenging task of "translating sound and fury into the long, slow work of lasting change."[52] An NPR interview with older civil rights activists warns young activists that they face "a long struggle," one best understood as "a marathon, not a sprint"— another pairing frequently reiterated by commentators.[53] The suggestion that the period leading up to and including the march represents "sound and fury" highlights a further repeated contrast, between *fleeting attention* and *sustained impact.* A widely reprinted story from the Associated Press asks in its headline whether young voters constitute a "Political Force or Fad?" Its author speaks to political organizations about their youth engagement efforts and concludes that it is "far from certain" that all the marching, speaking, and walkouts among youth will result in "a political force at the ballot box this fall."[54] Political strategists caution that "motivation is fleeting" and warn young activists that "it takes a lot to keep up this enthusiasm."[55] Numerous journalists adopt a similar approach, seeking out academics, political experts, and adult activists to consider whether "these young people" will "fade into the background."[56] Though they currently hold "the attention of millions," will they be, like "most [movements,] unable to sustain the effort?"[57]

These repeated temporal framings sharply narrow the parameters of success and failure, suggesting that it will quickly be evident whether "anything of significance" has resulted from hundreds of walkouts and marches, or

51. Julian E. Zelizer, "What Gun-Control Activists Can Learn from the Civil-Rights Movement," *The Atlantic,* March 23, 2018, https://www.theatlantic.com/politics/archive/2018/03/civil-rights-and-parkland/556244/.

52. Matt Flegenheimer and Jess Bidgood, "Gun Control and Fall Elections: Moment or Movement?," *New York Times,* April 2, 2018.

53. Erin B. Logan, "Advice for Student Activists: It's a Marathon, Not a Sprint," NPR, March 23, 2018, https://www.npr.org/sections/ed/2018/03/23/590274332/advice-for-student-activists-its-a-marathon-not-a-sprint; and Martin Vassolo, "Marathon, Not a Sprint: March for Our Lives Just the Beginning of Long Fight," *Tampa Bay Times,* March 25, 2018, https://www.tampabay.com/florida-politics/buzz/2018/03/25/marathon-not-a-sprint-march-for-our-lives-just-the-beginning-of-long-fight/.

54. Steve Peoples, "Political Force or Fad? Young US Voters Clout Uncertain," AP News, March 26, 2018, https://apnews.com/article/85e10b9ea5f54b8cb6680620fc621fcf.

55. Peoples, "Political Force or Fad?"

56. Christal Hayes, "After March for Our Lives, What's Next for Students?: Young Protesters Vow to Press On, While Veterans See a Long Road Ahead," *USA Today,* March 24, 2018, https://www.usatoday.com/story/news/2018/03/24/thousands-students-staged-walkout-and-marched-across-u-s-whats-next/443755002/.

57. Hayes, "After March for Our Lives"; and Evans, "Is Saturday's 'March'?"

millions of individual expressions of public support, represented by the diffuse activity swirling around the 2018 marches and extending through subsequent months—now years—of organizing.[58] In short, taking up March For Our Lives activism as "a moment or a movement" rearticulates youth activism in terms that diminish the rhetoricity of these activists. In contrast to the question of whether anything of significance will result, we might listen to Marilyn Cooper, who reminds us that "agency is simply action and the emergence of something new" and that "agency always has effects."[59] Actions, explains Cooper, "always make a difference in lives, not by determining an outcome but by opening up 'a whole field of responses, reactions, results, and possible inventions.'"[60]

Reflection is one response that my interview participants engaged in readily, generating and laying claim to a form of agency that exceeds the narrow time frames above. Instead of centering adult rearticulations, with their tenor of advice and admonishment, in the rest of this chapter I demonstrate the value of engaging directly with young activists' own understandings of their work. My interviews with youth participants reveal relationships between their acts of contemplation and their acts of organizing. Inquiring into the significance of their activism within their lives and in their own words enriches my formulation of reflexive agency, as it foregrounds the embodied, literate capacities these activists have cultivated through their organizing work—capacities that operate in complex ways across present and future contexts.

DEVELOPING ACTIVIST CAPACITIES ACROSS TIME

Fundamentally, by reclaiming their activist experiences as forms of literate capacity-building, the teen activists I interview contest widespread claims that their work is a fad, momentary and unsustainable. Because their activism cultivates embodied capacities, its effects linger and reverberate. This chapter mirrors the findings of my interviews with peace activists in chapter 1, where even two decades later their embodied experiences remained memorable and available for ongoing contemplation and rearticulation. Analyzing the motivations, experiences, priorities, and reflections of teen March For Our Lives organizers within local communities in North Carolina, here I explore how

---

58. Applegarth, "News That Isn't New."
59. Cooper, *Animal Who Writes*, 137.
60. Cooper, 137.

their activist work cultivates and asserts their rhetorical agency.[61] Although the young activists I spoke with for this chapter began their work from a state of unfamiliarity and discomfort with many of the practices they adopted, they developed contingent and kairotic capacities to enable ongoing activism and reflection.

Teen activists develop embodied capacities for activism through the practice of engaging in this work. That is, they learn how to do something by doing it. I call this *learning-by-doing*, to invoke community organizer Ella Baker's approach to developing leadership capacities among the young people she mentored, which is a long-term legacy of Baker's influence in twentieth-century freedom movements.[62] The teens I spoke with recounted experiences organizing, forming new networks, and communicating in new situations; they elaborated in detail on the ways in which they converted prior unfamiliarity to new forms of competency and capacity. In their accounts, learning-by-doing is visceral, taking place in and through the body and converting experiences into new sources of rhetorical power. My interviewees made frequent reference to their development over time. They recollected periods of disorganization that they attributed to their inexperience; they recounted high-stakes speaking and writing situations that they initially found intimidating but grew comfortable with through repeated experience; they noted tasks they had no prior experience with but nevertheless needed to accomplish. For instance, one participant I spoke with, Cameron,[63] explained that she had primarily taken on financial tasks for the organization because she "wanted to stay behind the scenes," explaining that she had not spoken at the march or given any interviews to news media in the weeks before it. She then explained, "a few months ago, I would have not been inclined to do this [her interview with me] at all. But I just had to develop the necessary social skills over these past six months, and so now I am comfortable with public speaking. But at

---

61. Directly contacting individuals who were named in the news coverage, I sent interview requests and IRB-approved interview questions to approximately ten individuals. I also sent recruitment materials directly to the organizational email addresses of some March For Our Lives chapters in North Carolina, and at the end of each interview I asked new participants if they would be willing to share my recruitment materials with other possible participants. I ultimately conducted individual interviews with six youth involved in local activism related to gun violence, which I recorded and had transcribed. See appendix 3 for the full interview questionnaire. I also conducted a follow-up focus group discussion in which five members of a single local chapter participated, including two who had not completed individual interviews with me previously. Individual interviews took place between July and September 2018, and the focus group discussion took place in June 2020. See appendix 4 for the full focus group questionnaire.

62. Hogan, *On the Freedom Side*.

63. Participants chose names for me to use in referencing their interviews for this chapter.

the time [of the march], I was just very shy and inexperienced." Other participants reflected on their growth over time, noticing how their capacities were altered by their experiences. Such narratives suggest that learning-by-doing offers insight into forms of significance and consequence for teen activism that exceed the success-or-failure framings I noted above.

By highlighting the development of new capacities through embodied experience, learning-by-doing resonates with scholarship on literacy and with accounts of how people acquire, develop, and repurpose literacies across time. Literacies are incredibly varied, including not only the traditionally literate practices of reading and writing but an encompassing array of "acts of interpretation and communication."[64] Literacies are sponsored by economic interests, civic imperatives, and educational institutions, yet they also proliferate across activist and social contexts and garner support from community stewards in ways that exceed and upend corporate imperatives.[65] Activist literacies within Black freedom struggles, as scholars such as Carmen Kynard, Rhea Lathan, and Elaine Richardson and Alice Ragland have shown, develop from fierce need and move toward undetermined ends; though activist literacies sometimes intersect with practices privileged in schools, they are not oriented toward or confined within schooling contexts, and they often directly confront the white supremacist literacies that schools privilege.[66] The literacies developed by the participants I spoke with are likewise unsettled; they are spurred in response to keenly felt exigencies, and they mark embodied capacities that may be put to unpredictable uses across diverse future contexts.

Organizing

Engaging in activism transforms the self in an ongoing way. One of the primary areas in which my participants developed new capacities through their activist experiences was in the broad category of organizing. Tasks related to organizing are broad, involving logistical matters as well as the allocation of resources such as time, attention, money, and people. As organizers of March For Our Lives events, the participants I spoke with learned how to organize

---

64. Ríos, "Cultivating Land-Based Literacies," 60.

65. Brandt, *Literacy in American Lives*; Wan, *Producing Good Citizens*; Kynard, *Vernacular Insurrections*; Jackson and Whitehorse DeLaune, "Decolonizing Community Writing"; Richardson and Ragland, "#StayWoke"; Ríos, "Cultivating Land-Based Literacies"; Pritchard, *Fashioning Lives*; and Frost, "Literacy Stewardship."

66. Kynard, *Vernacular Insurrections*; Lathan, *Freedom Writing*; and Richardson and Ragland, "#StayWoke."

by engaging in the work of staging events: they determined what kind of event to hold, when and where it should take place, which stakeholders should be included in the planning, what permissions or sanctions from elected officials or city employees were required. They allocated responsibilities among members and volunteers. Behind the scenes, they developed bureaucratic and procedural literacies, including budgeting and management of funds and familiarity with the laws or procedures that govern an organization's financial responsibilities and insurance requirements.

Many of the initial tasks these participants took up related to making decisions. For instance, they decided collectively "to have very few adult mentors involved" and to try to operate "100 percent student-led." They consulted on a couple of occasions with a community organizer from a neighboring town who was a young adult—in his midtwenties—but they determined to limit the organizing team to teenagers. The one or two activists in that team who were eighteen were asked to take on all tasks requiring a legal adult. This decision meant that authority for decision-making remained with teens, despite their unfamiliarity with the tasks required. As one organizer, Anne Joy, explained to me, because they chose to be entirely student-led, "no one was standing there telling us what to do. We had to figure it out on our own, which is one of the crazy things about it for me. . . . There isn't a list of rules that tell you steps." Another organizer, Jonah, emphasized the consequences of this decision to remain student-led with pride, nothing that "a lot of . . . other marches had, you know, adult helpers or three or four adults that were involved, and this was one of the few that was all students. We didn't have any forty-year-olds or anything that would have [had prior organizing] experience or people who have worked in business or politics. It was just us."

As a consequence, their early labor focused on determining tasks and assigning responsibility for those tasks, an iterative process in which each job they accomplished seemed to generate additional, unfamiliar ones. Anne Joy explained that early in their planning, they learned, "oh, you need insurance. We had to deal with an insurance company and call them and get insurance and get quotes and pay that. Oh, we probably need sound and a stage and flyers and buttons and all this kind of stuff that you deal with that was just heat of the moment. You figure it out and you do it."

The "heat of the moment" nature of these proliferating jobs contributed to an organizational structure of diffuse responsibility, characterized to me as everyone "work[ing] together" with minimal specialization. As Jonah explained, "We kind of just went together to get it done," with "no one [in] the whole circle . . . in charge of anyone else." Nick, another organizer, explained, "when we started, basically until after the march, the team wasn't divided into categories. Now, I am the director of planning . . . but there wasn't any of that at the start. It was just, 'Hey, can someone do this? Can someone do this?'" One organizer, who described herself as having "a little bit of a control freak mindset," characterized her primary tasks as coordinating "volunteers for the day of the event" as well as taking on some work to arrange food trucks, some work with permitting, a lot of "phone calls and interviews and that kind of stuff . . . and outreach as well"—a list that hints at the lack of boundaries around domains of work in the weeks leading up to the march. When I asked a follow-up question to try to get clearer insight into the processes by which the team determined and allocated tasks, Nick laughed and exclaimed, "Oh, God. You think we were more organized than we were!" He emphasized the lack of specialization within the team, clarifying that "we really had no idea what we were doing. It was like the first few days were a hot mess." Because, he explained, the national March For Our Lives organizers were not providing guidance—they "came out with their march toolkits way late, like ten days before the march"—the organizers and volunteers within their local group "were just kind of like, okay, we'll just do this. And we just kind of fumbled our way around it," even though it was "a whirlwind of news interviews and events and all of this stuff." By the time I began my interviews, a few months after the march, many of these activists had assumed specific roles and titles, but they recalled little division of responsibilities until after the march had taken place.

Despite their inexperience with bureaucratic dimensions of protest, these organizers had to discover and follow numerous bureaucratic processes, leading to the development of additional literacies. This introduction to bureaucratic requirements began as soon as Anne Joy first announced a plan to hold a march and requested support from others in her social networks. As she explained, "someone mentioned to me, oh, you have to get a permit, you know that, right? I was like, that sounds fancy." The organizers navigated city websites and numerous forms to follow the permitting process; at stake was the relationship between the march and the city and whether that relationship would be supportive or antagonistic. As Jonah explained, because the mayor was supportive, they still would have been able to hold the march without a permit; "the police would have let us do it, but instead of protecting us, they would have been waiting to arrest us if we did anything wrong. We would have had fines to pay." Seeking a permit for the march also led to their realization that they would have to arrange and pay for insurance for the event, an extremely unfamiliar procedure that was made far more difficult by having only one or two legal adults among their team. Although they were eventually able to secure insurance shortly before the deadline, several participants commented on this as an especially stressful and difficult process, one in which their status as nonadults allowed insurance companies to ignore their phone calls and delay processing their forms. One participant recounted having to push repeatedly to get the insurance requirements completed, calling and calling their contracted insurance company to get the final documentation the city required for the permit, culminating in "a not very nice voice mail" that finally generated the response they needed.

Similarly, they gained financial literacies related to fundraising, holding funds collectively, and documenting expenditures. They launched a GoFundMe, which one participant "never expected in a million years to work at all, but within the first day . . . we got $1200 in donations, which was crazy suddenly." Their sudden need to develop financial literacies was a particular challenge. With only a few weeks between announcing and holding the march, they committed to courses of action before fully having the capacity to follow through on those plans. For instance, they "raised [money] so fast," but "didn't know how to set up a . . . business bank account," which meant one person in their group was temporarily holding the money in her personal bank account. Jonah explained, "We had raised all of that money in the course of a week. . . . And then we were buying stuff. We didn't know what to do with the receipts." Cameron took the lead in developing these financial literacies, explaining, "my parents . . . were always very open about . . . all of the financial aspects of being an adult, so I just retained that, I suppose, and was able to utilize it." She created the GoFundMe and "set up a bank account," tasks that required not only knowledge but also rhetorical savvy to navigate them as a teen. For instance, she explained that "part of [setting up a] GoFundMe is describing why you're raising money, and at the time, because there were so many GoFundMes related to March For Our Lives, GoFundMe themselves did not think we were a legitimate organization and did not want to let us access the money that people had donated. So I had to go back and rewrite that paragraph multiple times, adding more information" in order to establish sufficient authority. Likewise, in setting up accounts and managing the group's finances, she adjusted her "terminology" to sound "professional" over the phone, explaining that she developed this capacity because "most people don't want to give insurance to a fifteen-year-old." Relatedly, the group had to develop a capacity to budget, deciding collectively what expenditures they could afford and what was beyond their means. As Nick explained, "learning how to budget is a huge thing, because there are so many things we could do if we had a million dollars, but we don't. So, you know, we have to learn: What corners can we cut? Can we even do this event? Do we have the money to do this event?" Participants noted that they wound up spending "almost half the money we raised just for insurance," and some felt in retrospect that they had been charged far more than they should have. Their lack of familiarity with that aspect of organizing, combined with their short time frame for completing the permitting process, led them to accept terms that they later came to understand as excessive.

Gaining familiarity with a range of bureaucratic literacies gave these activists experience not merely with following procedures but also pushing back at times against constraints. Their dogged efforts to gain insurance, for instance, showed them that they might need to be less neutral and "professional" at times when confronting bureaucratic hesitation. Anne Joy recounted the barrier she encountered when first seeking a permit for the march: "I looked it up on the website for the city, and the special events permit—which is what we use for all of our events—actually has to be submitted sixty days in advance, and we only had thirty days because we had a month to plan this march. My first reaction was like, we missed it. That's it. We can't do it. It's legally not possible. But I decided to email the special events guy anyway just to [say], we never had two months. . . . And he actually [said], we'll waive the deadline and . . . we'll waive the fee." Her comment not only foregrounds her current familiarity with the permit they "use for all [their] events" but also the perspective gained by successfully working around a bureaucratic barrier .

These organizers also navigated the demands associated with operating alongside the material constraints associated with being in high school. This often involved translating those constraints for adult audiences who overlooked the extent to which being in school structured their daily lives. As Anne Joy explained, "working with companies" was particularly difficult "because I think it's hard for people to comprehend that you are in school," a constraint that limited the organizers' ability to make phone calls to vendors, insurance providers, city offices, and so on. She explained that often, journalists would "reach out for interviews" and try to schedule them at impossible times. They might suggest ten o'clock a.m., to which she would respond, "No, I'm in high school. Okay, so lunch. We'll meet somewhere for lunch. No, I can't drive. I'm really still in high school. You know, three o'clock, no, four o'clock. I get out right at four o'clock." The intensity of this period meant that organizers committed enormous amounts of time to making arrangements and decisions. She elaborated that most leaders were spending "several hours after school every day" on "a lot of phone calls and emails and tons and tons and tons of meetings between everyone who was working there. We'd get together all the time, because there was always another thing to do." The variety and number of tasks meant many "did [this work] during school. I did interviews during gym when we didn't have anything to do. I did interviews during lunch. People were calling sound companies during lunch. We were calling insurance companies during lunch. . . . We had thirty minutes in the middle of the day, so we did everything there that we could." She recalled "walking between class" with another organizer, and though "we have six minutes in between class . . . he was calling a food truck, because we just didn't have the time to wait."

In recounting these experiences, my participants repeatedly foregrounded their development of new capacities through these tasks. They often emphasized the contrast they saw between their initial efforts and what they became capable of over time. For instance, Nick recounted an early opportunity, when the group was invited to "table" at a local voting organization's event for democratic primary candidates. As he explained, they accepted the invitation even though they were not at all certain what such an event would require or make possible for them: "we were like okay, wait, a table? We don't know anything about a table. [But] I had some sticker paper lying around, because I used to have an Etsy shop where I made stickers. So, [I] quickly printed out some stickers of our logo and you know, cut them and got some flyers. . . . We didn't even have a donation jar." No one in their group initially saw "tabling" as an opportunity for fundraising, and as a consequence "we didn't really get any donations from that, but you know, that was not even our first thought." Later in our interview, Nick returned to this anecdote, explaining that at a similar event only a week later, "we had a table there. It was much more professional [and] we got like $500 from the donation jar." Tabling is one of many capacities for organizing actions, coordinating people, raising funds, staging events, navigating bureaucratic procedures, and more that these activists developed by tackling them as the need arose in the intense weeks of preparation leading up to the march.

Communicating

Like those related to organizing, communication tasks were numerous, varied, and distributed and taken up in an ad hoc way as they arose. As Nick explained to me late in the summer after the march, "Now we have people on the outreach team that are good at writing and we're *categorized* as that. But at the beginning, we were pretty much like, 'Hey, we need a press release. Can someone . . . ? It just wasn't as organized as it is now" because of the short time frame they faced.

As they prepared for and staged events, their work included communicating their decisions to numerous audiences, including what events would happen, where they would take place, who could participate, and in what ways. This meant writing numerous press releases; Jonah indicated that he wrote press releases "announcing our march location, the route, announcing our speakers. We had some members of the General Assembly that had stepped up to support us, [so he wrote press releases] announcing that." He similarly wrote "social media posts" communicating this information as well. When I asked Nick how the organizers decided what to write in genres such as press releases that were unfamiliar, he explained, "we'd go on [the] Women's March or the National March For Our Lives website [to] look at press releases they'd done" and would mimic those formats while "add[ing] our own language, obviously."

In addition to promotional writing, they engaged in direct communication behind the scenes: contacting vendors, persuading vendors to donate, negotiating prices, and coordinating volunteers, all of which required not just logistical knowledge but also significant awareness of audience and purpose. As one explained with a touch of humor, "I obviously had to learn to write a formal email"—a literate capacity acquired early in this process and then deployed extensively over the ensuing months. Communication work was necessary to coordinate the core team of organizers as well as a much larger group of volunteers. Participants coordinated with city police and communicated with city councilors, the mayor, and candidates running for office; they interacted with representatives from numerous supporting organizations and addressed questions submitted through their website.

Speeches, which these participants wrote and delivered in numerous venues, represented a high-stakes and high-profile mode of communication. They delivered speeches at a town hall event for Democratic candidates a few weeks before the march, and numerous teens delivered speeches both at the initial gathering and at the final destination of their march, where the audience was largest. As Jonah explained, it was important to this group that each individual wrote their own speeches, though they also "worked together as a team to make sure that we weren't all saying the same thing." Some participants gave feedback to each other and worked to "coordinate" and give advice about "what can be said better," with the goal of "making sure that we stayed on message."

The overwhelming publicity generated by the national March For Our Lives organizers and in relation to eight hundred sister marches held on the same day meant that the teen organizers were called upon repeatedly to give interviews to the media. This was understood as a significant opportunity for communicating in relation to their activism. Nick, for instance, described seeking guidance from the national organization to navigate this new genre:

"I talked to their communication director to get tips for news interviews," which included advice such as "after every question, you say 'yeah, so,' because . . . not only does it make it seem like you're engaged, but it also gives you a moment to think of your answer." Likewise, he shared the advice, "Don't be afraid to take a breath, take a second to think about what you're going to say. Speak slowly, and if you don't want to answer the question or don't know how to, if it's a live interview, answer the question with a question or answer it with a call to action, or if it's not a live interview, then just say I don't want to answer that question." The scope of this advice, which Nick rattled off readily months later, highlights the communicative capacities required to capitalize artfully on these opportunities.

Public-facing communication also took place through their website, which developed in an ad hoc way, related to the prior interests of those who contributed. Nick explained that website-building skills he had developed through his hobbies were repurposed quickly in the crunch time before the march. Describing himself as "that odd child that would go on Weebly, make a free account, and make a website about whatever just because," Nick used that prior experience and created their local organization's website initially as a Weebly page, saying to himself, "I'll just do what I've been doing." After the march, he looked around actively for further tools: "At the start, our website was basically just text and pictures and a contact form. Now it has progressed and there is a donation page and you can write a letter to your representative straight from our website."

Ongoing communication tasks in response to inquiries through the website remained distributed, as the whole group continued to "pitch in" to respond to emails. As Anne Joy explained,

> Because we have forms on our website where you can send a message, whether it's volunteering or advice or whatever you want, you can just send it in and we have a bunch of people sending questions or just emailing our account. . . . Oftentimes if we get an email with a specific question, who-ever sees it first will screenshot it and send it to the group chat, and then whoever has been working on that or would be able to answer that question [answers]. If it's about volunteers, it goes to me. If it's about any kind of money stuff, it goes to [another participant] because she's our treasurer. If it's about any kind of planning stuff, it goes to whoever has been planning that specific sector.

This process suggests shared responsibility as well as trust in others to respond appropriately; she explains, "We don't have a template [for responses]. . . . We want to be professional and definitely not be sloppy but we also want to [show that] there are real people who are answering you and we are just kids. We don't copy and paste our response. We really get back to you in the way we feel is most helpful."

Akin to their development of organizational literacies, my participants reflected frequently on the ways in which tackling such a range of unfamiliar communication tasks led to growth and increased capacities in this domain. They expressed pride in the way that the communication literacies of individuals and the collective improved over time. For instance, they were not uniformly savvy in relation to social media at the outset of this work; one participant explained that a team member had been given the task of making a Snapchat geofilter for the march, and no one realized until the day of the march that this had been done badly: "it [was] just the logo right in the middle of the screen with the orange around it, and we're like, oh, that's nice. It was just right in the middle. So nobody used it." This participant found this failure laughable in retrospect—not a crucial dimension of their overall success in planning and staging the march—but nevertheless expressed pride that the organization, several months after the march, presented a more polished appearance through social media platforms. By August, "for our rally with the [Marjory Stoneman Douglas] kids" who visited their community as part of the Road to Change tour, "we had a geofilter, but it was much [better]; the text was, you know, not in the middle of the screen." As he explained:

> Something that really stands out to me when I see an organization is branding, and when I see a good brand around an organization, I'm like, "That is an established organization." So, as one of the main people who do graphic design [within their chapter], that is one of my goals. And so, *now*, we have a set brand. I mean, in my notebook, in my bag, I have the color code for the colors that we use and so, I know . . . all of these graphics match and our website matches the graphics, the same font. . . . In my opinion, graphic design is one of the last things you focus on when you're starting an organization. So, if you have time to be able to do that, and if you have the capacity to be able to do that, you have most of the other stuff down. . . . for the march, we had no brand at all because we were just like, we need permits. We need a stage and sound and all of this kind of stuff.

As this explanation makes clear, visual design is connected to a broader communication strategy; through its ethos-building, audience-focused dimension, it can support the group's long-term efforts to develop a trustworthy public presence.

Alongside narratives of collective growth, my participants reflected on their own development of greater capacities in relation to a range of communication practices. In response to a question about what she finds important about her involvement in this activism, Cameron explained, "I am now more comfortable speaking to people because of all of the numerous phone calls I've had to make. I am now aware of . . . how to plan stuff and the best way to go about a professional situation. I also just learned a lot personally [about] how to work with other people, how to deal with . . . disagreements that will inevitably come up." For her, these developments are connected to repeatedly pushing beyond her comfort zone. Although she initially took on the role of treasurer so she could remain "behind the scenes," even that role demanded that she stretch beyond her comfort level as a speaker: "I have had to make a lot of phone calls that I just didn't want to. You know, I was tired after getting out of school and any extracurriculars that I had that day, and I had to get into the mindset of, 'I'm too tired to do this but I still need to,' so over time I have developed the social skills to be very professional when needed." This development happened not because she was determined to become a more proficient public speaker, but because her commitment to staging the march created a sense of responsibility. Making a professional phone call is an embodied practice, something this writer has grown capable of doing, despite her disinclination, because she has made herself perform that task again and again.

Other participants also highlighted their embodied readiness as a capacity they developed by practicing despite their initial feelings of discomfort. One organizer who spoke both at the march and at a school walkout ten days earlier explained that her anxiety made speeches and interviews initially harrowing: "I think interviews especially were something I had to get used to . . . There are always nerves beforehand, and [worry, thinking] am I saying the right things?" But, she continued, "At this point, I think I've gotten over it a lot. . . . I just try to be as honest and as open as I can be. . . . It's definitely hard for me. It's not necessarily my kind of thing. But I think it's because I'm so passionate about this that I always want to do it. I always volunteer myself to do it." Repeated practice has led to growth over time, to developing a new capacity beyond her former strengths and skills. Another participant recounted a similar narrative of moving from discomfort—even aversion—to eventually develop a capacity that mitigated her initial feelings of avoidance around public speaking, explaining, "I have just had to, you know, put myself in a position that I normally would not do. I did my first interview the night before the rally. Because I needed to." When I asked how it went, this participant minimized the challenge of that experience, finding it wasn't as uncomfortable as she expected, "because they were questions that I had been asked at certain points along the planning process. I knew how to answer them and it was okay."

Others who started with more initial comfort with public speaking nevertheless reflected that through activism they had developed new communication capacities. One expressed wonder at how much he saw his writing and speaking "grow over that time." He described giving his "first stump speech" at a countywide event for Democratic women shortly after the march was announced, comparing this early speech with a far more accomplished one he had delivered the day of the march: "I have videos of both of those speeches and they are just so different. The first one, I started with, 'I don't remember the last time I was this nervous in a room full of women. It was probably prom.' I mean, that got a laugh but that wasn't on message." In his earliest speech, he "barely had notes, like probably this long [*gestures*] on my paper," while his later speech for the March even included "when I was going to pause and say um and all of that."

The growth in capacity that participants experienced came about through repeated practice. Jonah, for instance, explained that he initially prepared a great deal for interviews, "researching . . . what we want done, how we can make change, researching that so I can articulate that clearly." He also developed close familiarity with details, "knowing things like when is the march, what is the route, what if you want to volunteer, what is the security going to be like, where can you park . . . because especially beforehand, . . . an important part of the interviews was spreading the word and getting people involved." Even without knowing the interview questions beforehand, he "kind of knew in my head if they ask me this, what I would say." Reflecting further on the relationship between preparation and repeated practice, this participant explained, "I probably did the most [interviews] of everybody involved," because "after I did one or two . . . they wanted to interview me again. So, it just kind of snowballed." As a result of this preparation and practice, he developed a kind of embodied readiness, which he characterized as, "after a while, I started saying my talking points in my sleep to the point where it was kind of second nature. You could wake me up and I could do an interview and I'd be fine." He returned again to this point later, reflecting further on the growth he had experienced, saying, "I can see myself get better with [interviewing] too, . . . because I am pretty long-winded, but I could see myself get better as I went along, because I kind of knew what questions they would ask and I kind of knew what I would say. . . . Since [the beginning,] it [has become] kind of like 'What's the interview about? Okay, let's go.'" These reflections emphasize a capacity for responsive communication, a capacity developed through extensive preparation but that has become almost automatic over time. It is embodied deeply enough that "you could wake me up and I could do an interview," echoing what Debra Hawhee has called "the corporeal acquisition of rhetorical movements through rhythm, repetition, and response" that was a hallmark of sophistic pedagogy.[67] Repeated experience with interviewing has led Jonah to a form of embodied expertise that is not routine but flexible, responsive to individual situations because it has been developed through intensive research, practice, and revision in high-stakes contexts.

Both of these areas of increased embodied capacity—organizing and communicating—were spurred by the exigence of staging a large public event. Staged by teens, the march functioned as a moment when teen efficacy would be assessed by outside audiences, which motivated enormous activity in many forms that my interview participants had not performed before. The intensity of their preparation impelled the growth of their communication capacities and organizational literacies. For Anne Joy, having reached out to others through social media to ask for help staging the march, "that was kind of my first motivation, I think. I've told people that I'm doing this. I've made promises to the people I'm working with that this is going to happen, so I need to do everything I can to make it happen." Receiving funding likewise committed them to action; Anne Joy recalled thinking, "now I have people's money, and now I have to really, really do something, because you can't return it to them. It's GoFundMe. You can't take it back." There were moments leading up to the march when these participants were unsure if they would complete everything demanded—there was uncertainty about whether insurance would come through, whether permitting requirements would be met, whether they would have sound. Several participants expressed their worry beforehand that there would be more counterprotesters than supporters at the march, and one expressed the modest hope that at least four people who were not parents of the organizers would attend. They keenly felt their age as a constraint. Nick reflected that "no matter how much people say that they are with the youth and they trust the youth, there is always going to be that small little drop of distrust, which [is] understandable," but it means "we have to be on our A game. We cannot make mistakes." Referencing both the necessity of research and the incongruity of staging large public events without prior know-how, he explained, "when we *don't* make mistakes and we produce something really cool, it renews faith in the community, because then they're like, these kids planned this."

---

67. Hawhee, "Bodily Pedagogies," 160.

The intensity of compressed time led to these participants' rapid development as organizers and communicators; one characterized the change over the month leading up to the march as akin to "freshman year compared to senior year." Another expressed a similar sense of wonder at how quickly their collective gained experience and expertise:

> Looking back at it, the progression of not only the march but the organization is really incredible, how week to week it's a completely different and completely evolved organization and that kind of progress is still—you can still see it today. I mean, obviously, it's slowed down because we're established but . . . it's kind of incredible to see a month before, how we were, and then just, month to month, the progression is really insane.

This intense "progression" can be viewed as a consequence of the learning-by-doing that these young activists engaged in, which motivated intense collaboration, repeated practice, and determination to learn how to do the numerous, proliferating tasks the march generated.

Creating and Maintaining an Organization

The narrow concern with March For Our Lives activism as a "moment or movement" is countered not only through participants' embodied capacities but also through their efforts to create lasting organizations. If the organizational and communication literacies above reflect enduring capacities developed through the exigence of staging a march, those below emerge out of activists' determination to "keep going" beyond the march. As one organizer explained, "directly after the march, all of us were kind of like, yeah, we're not going to stop here." The timing of my interviews—in summer and early fall of 2018—captured their transition from staging initial events to creating and maintaining an organization. These participants devised structures to enable continuity and developed processes of evaluation and reflection that they emphasized in interview and focus group discussions.

Although the march generated an extraordinary development of activist literacies among my participants, it was also an ephemeral event. It created an opportunity for the gathered crowd to communicate their collective will and support, and that is no small feat; Anne Joy recalled seeing thousands of people spilling out from the downtown plaza where the march began and realizing that the march was a space "where people can really send a message, and you've kind of created that way for them to do that." The march itself was "the big event," however, and "it wasn't necessarily obvious to us that we were going to continue, because we didn't necessarily have to." Yet their feelings of accomplishment and satisfaction generated a sense of momentum. Anne Joy explained that they continued organizing events "because we were in that mindset and we were like, what do we do with the time that we have now?" This sense of momentum also counteracted concerns that they would disperse or disappear; as she explained, they did a lot of "promotion and posting and making sure to stay involved" over the summer after the march, "so that everyone knew that we were still a set thing and that we were still going to be working." Another participant, who had organized two walkouts demanding improved counseling and guidance services at his majority-Black high school, explained that he felt ongoing momentum for activism and "just love[d] the organizing" dimension of activist work, even as that led him to focus his activism on issues beyond gun reform that concerned him more directly. For instance, he had followed his March For Our Lives leadership with an internship with a local Black Lives Matter group, and at the time of our interview he was working intensively to create a youth ball in his community; he noted that in his city, "there are not a lot of places for LGBT youth to come together and meet other than the club, and everybody is not over eighteen. So I want to create that space . . . for youth." His larger activist goals centered on creating spaces for queer community-building, as well as educational opportunities to help queer teens feel more informed and less isolated throughout their adolescence and teen years, explaining that his community needs access to better information about sex and sexuality, because "we're not hetero. We're not cis men and women. We're not straight. . . . We go through different things . . . [and] need the information *now*." The momentum he experienced after organizing multiple school walkouts spurred him to ongoing action; as he explained, afterward he felt "well, what can I do next?" But he explained that as a Black teen, "the school shooting thing is not really my problem. . . . I need to work on things that are my issue. . . . LGBT, that is my issue because that is my community. So . . . that is what I started to work on." In recounting how he repurposed his activist experience toward racial justice organizing and toward improved sexual health information for queer youth, this participant underscores the enduring significance of flexible activist capacities that can be used toward undetermined ends.

Those who remained focused on gun reform staged additional events related to gun violence and described their desire to continue using the capacities they had developed—capacities for coordinating people, communicating, garnering publicity, and so on—and the literacies they had gained. But working to maintain an organization also fostered additional capacities. As one explained, "we did realize we want this to be a lasting thing . . . hopefully [for] years to come," which meant they needed to "sit down and organize this group and organize *us* as an organization."

The transition into creating an organizational structure signaled further new terrain for the group to navigate. As Anne Joy explained, "the thing about being in a movement" is that "no one is going to tell you what to do. No one is going to sit there and [say], all right, next step, here's what we're doing next, because *you* have to make that next step. That's kind of what we did afterwards." This "structural work," focused inwardly, took place after the intensity of staging events faded; they understood that "*during* the march-planning process" their focus had to remain on immediate tasks, and they recognized that "we can't work on structure right now." Only afterward did they turn their attention to processes for creating stability and continuity, such as "hiring interns, getting more people involved," and "making sure we have processes to get people in and out, because eventually we'll go off to college and then you have to hope that people continue behind you, and you want to leave a system."

Experiences across this transition taught these activists the importance of developing capacities for addressing interpersonal challenges and intergroup dynamics. For instance, several participants commented on dynamics that create struggles for many activist organizations: differential levels of commitment, participation, and responsibility among their members. As Nick explained, because "we are at our core a local grassroots organization . . . we don't have the money to pay everyone. When you're operating off of a volunteer basis . . . it's hard to keep people engaged. A lot of times, there's a core group of individuals doing the bulk of the work." In a volunteer community marked by varying levels of commitment, "having everybody do their jobs" is a challenge. Consequently, many participants experienced discomfort connected to teen leaders telling other teens what to do. Although you "have to have some structure for an organization to function," one explained, it is nevertheless "weird for both parties" to navigate leadership roles and responsibilities; he recounted that "a lot of times, I felt uncomfortable [saying], 'Hey, can you do this?' It can seem condescending to the other side." As another organizer, Elliot, explained, "it's still nerve-racking to [say], I told you to do this, why didn't you do it?" Though the group developed a formal description of responsibilities associated with different positions, these formal measures did not entirely dispel tension over the distribution of tasks and responsibilities. Corinne elaborated on this challenge, explaining that "high school students . . . telling other high school students what to do . . . gets a little muddy." By characterizing these interpersonal dynamics as "nerve-racking" and "condescending," these participants foreground the challenge of navigating power within a horizontal organization; nevertheless, as with other dimensions of activist capacity-building, many expressed that they have developed greater comfort navigating intergroup dynamics over time.

To create stability for their organization over time, these activists developed a formal document of responsibilities they termed a social contract, as an explicit tool to create a sustainable group structure. As a "contract," it aimed to govern relations and outline responsibilities for members, following from the inefficiencies of everyone "fumbling around and doing our best to make sure everything got done." As Anne Joy explained, the contract "covers everything, the structure of the group, all the positions," with the goal of creating greater stability and clarity through "a more official document so that we had something to go by and we had jobs that were outlined for each of us." When the social contract didn't fully mitigate issues related to participation and responsibility, they devised an interview practice that communicated strategically to potential members about their commitment. When I asked during a June 2020 focus group discussion about challenges they had experienced over their first couple of years as an organization, Elliot described the difficulty of having a lot of participants with only shallow commitments: "originally, when [this chapter] was so big and everyone was talking about March For Our Lives, there were a lot of people that came in just because they wanted to be part of this giant thing that everyone was hearing about, but they didn't quite know what they were signing up for. There was a lot of work to be done interpersonally when people . . . tried to back out of a lot of responsibilities." Another explained that the social contract only helped a little in managing these commitment issues; she felt their more important strategy involved "creat[ing] a better system of how people enter the organization." Though they initially welcomed "anyone who wanted to join," they gradually adopted a "system of interviews," which they use not so much to limit membership, but instead to communicate about the commitment they expect:

> There are very few people that we would say no to, but [interviewing] allows us to effectively communicate the responsibility that comes with being a part of this organization, that it's not just kind of a fun thing to do with your friends. Hopefully, it is fun. Obviously, we hope that and we try to make it a nice environment, but it does come with work. If you're not interested in being a part of that, then you can always support us, and there are so many other ways to be involved, but organizing might not be what you enjoy the most.

Together, these strategies for managing intergroup issues have generated a smaller core of organizers with stronger commitments to their work; Elliot explained that as some have drifted away and others have developed a stronger sense of responsibility, "we've truly been able to create a team that's based more on what they want to do [and people who are] willing to make the changes and take on the responsibilities."

While seeking to develop an organization that can be sustained over time, participants grappled with collective decision-making and coalitional alliances with other organizations. They evaluated opportunities, strategies, and collaborations, with an eye toward how these would advance their collective purposes. As Nick explained, "who are we willing to work with" is a "huge" question for the group. He elaborated that "some of our team members were unwilling originally to . . . have this co-branded tour with Everytown" leading into the November 2018 midterm elections. Their conversations ultimately underscored that "we aren't going to be able to do this tour [otherwise], and you know, we're working [toward a] common goal." Some concerns about such partnerships related to their efforts to remain nonpartisan and in particular to keep communicating with Republicans, who are "vital to the conversations" they want supporters to have. For instance, Nick discussed their decision to support Pride events in their town and to adopt "a rainbow logo for Pride Month," but even these expressions of support required negotiation within the group. As he explained, "we have to be very careful about how we approach things like that, because we need to make sure that we aren't pushing [Republicans] away," since the goal is to have "Republicans be able to say to their fellow Republicans, why aren't you supporting them?" Collective decision-making about partnerships and affiliations with other organizations foregrounds fundamental concerns of audience and purpose and requires members of the group to negotiate between individual and collective commitments to concrete action and intersectional approaches to social justice.

In addition to their strategic reflection about coalitional decisions, participants also discussed transformative experiences of reflection that revised how they understood social justice as interrelated and intersectional. Nick, for instance, characterized how he now views gun violence, after more than two years of activism in this area, as deeply interwoven with structural forces: gun violence, he explained, is a "canary-in-the-coal-mine issue, where a healthy society doesn't have a gun violence problem. That's just not something that happens. And so if you look at gun violence, you see how nuanced the issue is and also how intertwined it is with other issues like health care and income inequality. And even how a city is built can have a huge effect on gun violence, so [my involvement] has definitely broadened my horizons as to different issues" that are deeply interconnected. This has involved reflection and revision of prior understandings, including conversations and research, that have "enlightened me to things that I thought were good measures that . . . aren't." Elliot elaborates on this response, explaining that though he "always thought I was politically aware," he found through his activism an opportunity

> to do more research and to step outside of my tiny box, my little bubble, and see what was going on with the rest of the world and really try to speak out and find my voice. I think that was really big for me, because I just didn't really understand what was going on. I just wanted to help, but only on the general scale, so learning more about everything really helped me improve knowing *what* I want to help and knowing what I want to change with the world.

Such expressions of transformative learning were common among my participants; they not only engaged in practices of self-education but also connected with larger networks of activists who pooled resources toward the end of becoming more informed and effective activists. One mentioned participating in a Discord channel with scores of other activists from the "most active marches in the country," where members contribute to "a toolkit channel where we write toolkits and publish them. We [create] bill briefs where people volunteer to write briefs on different bills related to gun control and mental health, stuff like that, and then publish them there for everyone to use." Sharing resources, experiences, and expertise through genres such as tool kits and bill briefs provides further concrete opportunities for learning-by-doing in relation to expanding horizons of social justice activism.

GROWTH, VULNERABILITY, AND ENTANGLEMENT

Among the changes actuated by sustained organizing are activists' own self-understandings. For instance, Anne Joy marveled at having pulled off the march when the skills demanded initially lay outside her understanding of herself. She reflected that what she valued most about her experience was "kind of proving to myself . . . my own capability . . . how much I was capable of, which is really an emotional thing, for me." She doubted this capacity initially; when her mom mentioned to her that there was no march planned for her town, she responded, "I could never actually do a march. Like, that's funny. I have no experience with any of that. That's way too big. You know? . . . But then . . . I kept thinking about it for a few days and I was like, yeah, yeah, I could just try. I could see what happens if I see if people want to get involved." Later in our conversation, she elaborated on how her self-understanding was changed by this experience, emphasizing the importance of

> learning my own capabilities and learning what I can do and learning the power that not just I have but that everyone has. . . . I don't know why I threw myself into it, because I knew there were so many places where I could fail. It doesn't make any sense to me why I ever did that. Obviously I'm so happy I did. It's made me a person who is more likely to kind of throw myself into situations where . . . I may fail, I may make a mistake.

Jonah emphasized that the "lesson" he would take from his experience was "to focus yourself on what you're trying to accomplish. Sometimes there can be a lot going on or a lot of distractions, but . . . if you focus on the goal, the end goal, it is a lot easier to do effective work." After the march, Jonah had begun working for the campaign of a candidate for the US House of Representatives who was running for election in 2018, and he saw parallels between his March For Our Lives organizing and this political work, explaining,

> If we're at an event or walking in to an event with protesters yelling at us, you know, that is kind of discouraging. Or if we're like, oh, this is so much work, we have to get six months' work done in two weeks, you know, that is kind of discouraging. But at the end of the day, we thought, we want to have thousands of people out marching for our lives, and that is what happened. It's the same with the campaign. Things can be discouraging, . . . [for example] we have two hundred phone calls to make today. That sucks for us. But if we focus on the end goal, which is [this candidate] getting sworn in to Congress, it makes that work a lot easier. I think that is a lesson. I didn't think about it that way before, but I think that is really important.

The "lesson" that united Jonah's March For Our Lives activism and his subsequent political organizing echoes other insights from participants who found the experience of working intensely and collaboratively toward a common goal to be transformative.

Experiences that altered their self-understandings and perspectives also generated among these participants a remarkable attitude of openness to others' ideas and arguments. Receptivity to cross-partisan exchange was identified by several participants as a significant outcome of their activism. Cameron, for instance, addressing a question about her interest in continuing to be involved in activism, responded, "It's startling to me that people are always like, oh, you don't want to pursue politics, because it's such a contro-versial issue. I really want to change that narrative, because if you're not open to having these discussions, then nothing will ever change. . . . I will always be in support of having those tough conversations with your friends and your family and then working your way up to lawmakers and political officials." Her embrace of "tough conversations" and her concern with widespread tropes about politics being too "controversial" to engage in reveals the importance she places on exchange. Even though difficult conversations make one vul-nerable, she argued, refusing such exchanges means that "nothing will ever change." Many other participants emphasized their desire to speak and lis-ten across partisan lines, and they shared meaningful experiences of learning and growing through conversations with others who hold differing political perspectives. For instance, Nick particularly valued "connecting with people" and "learning how to have conversations and find a common goal," a value he situated in "youth organizations" and their greater desire to "push for . . . tol-erance, compromising, finding common goals." He elaborated that "blaming" political opponents "is not how we're going to work together, and we need to work across party lines," and he found significance in everyday efforts to find "something in common, even if that's a TV show, [because] it makes it so much harder to hate someone or to be bigoted towards them if you have a personal connection with them." This desire for cross-partisan exchange is not merely aspirational but grounded in the concrete practices of political engagement and lobbying that he experienced. To illustrate the importance of conversing with people who disagree with you, he recounted an experience in which he was

> in Raleigh at the State House talking with a person who actually cospon-sored a bill for permitless carry in North Carolina. . . . I was with another organizer from Wilmington. At first, this man was yelling at us. It actually took me aback, because we had had conversations with plenty of people who didn't agree with us that day, but he was the first person to yell at us. But we kind of refused to leave. I basically told him that we're not going to leave until you actually have a conversation with us about this, because he was just there to yell at us and close the door. . . . I actually want to have a conversation, because I want to get your perspective on why you think per-mitless carry is such a necessary thing to have in North Carolina. We had a long conversation. It was probably half an hour long. We left the room with him going to the clerk's office to take his name off the bill. . . . It was not so much that we were able to change his opinion, but we were able to show him a different perspective.

Reflecting further on this experience, he explained, "having conversations is so important. Because I never go into a political conversation expecting to change my belief, and neither does anyone else, but I think showing a different perspective and at least sparking some thought and some reflection is really important." This episode, which demonstrates his capacity to refrain from villainizing political opponents, also foregrounds a key practice advocated by the teen activists I spoke with: embracing vulnerability to others' perspectives, promoting a stance of learning and growth through conversation.

This embrace of vulnerability contrasts strongly with what recent rhetorical research has argued regarding the embodied habits cultivated by the practice of carrying a weapon. Daniel Cryer's investigation of the US Concealed Carry Association highlights the learned, embodied habits that users associate with concealed carrying, one of the benefits of which, he argues, is an experience of *un*freedom that offers protection from vulnerability. Cryer argues that concealed carrying demands particular forms of attentive embodiment oriented around the presence of a gun, which "stifles . . . the freedom to become entangled with others, which is the freedom that comes from vulnerability[,] . . . or a capacity to be affected or persuaded." As Cryer explains, carry culture develops embodied habits of "vulnerability toward an object that forecloses vulnerability to people."[68]

Such a disinclination to entanglement runs counter to the embodied capacities cultivated among the teen activists I spoke with. These young people both advocated and practiced interpersonal vulnerability, emphasizing the necessity of direct conversations with elected officials and of direct actions that reach out to embrace those who think differently from them. For instance, participants in the focus group discussion recalled a specific individual who had attended several events only to later post on social media about her objections to their activism. What they found remarkable was her repeated decision to attend events, to be present with people she disagreed with, while being unwilling to voice her stance in person; they found this a strange, closed-off refusal to engage in direct or open exchange. Their reflections on the importance of engaging in dialogue across difference echo the insights of rhetorical scholar Renuka Uthappa, who reminds readers that while empathy "involves an openness to the influence of the other," vulnerability "involves greater risk, a risk to our sense of our self—our integrity or our own views."[69] Despite the well-known gaps between proponents of gun ownership and advocates of gun reform, the young activists I spoke with cultivated a stance of openness and a

68. Cryer, "Good Man Shooting Well," 265.
69. Uthappa, "Moving Closer," 171.

determination to engage with perspectives and arguments from those on the other side of this divide.[70]

Certainly, being openly armed is an embodied strategy that successfully closes off entanglement and exchange.[71] Armed counterprotesters create a feeling of embodied vulnerability for their opponents; as Nick reflected, "when the counterprotesters have AR-15s on their backs . . . it's definitely intimidating. It worked. [Intimidation is] the whole point of what they're doing." Several participants recalled their feeling of vulnerability when they had to walk past an armed counterprotester after the march had ended. One recounted all of the organizers "in our bright orange March For Our Lives shirts" walking back to the central plaza, past a man "standing around [wearing a] 'Black Rifles Matter' shirt" and open-carrying: "We just walked by as fast as we could because, . . . I'm sure nothing would have happened, but it was still like, ah . . ." Another, in a separate interview, recalled the same moment as the "one time where I've been nervous around a protester." She, too, recalled wearing "our bright orange" and noticing his gun and his "Black Rifles Matter" shirt. She was nervous, "because we did have to walk directly past him," and she felt worried, thinking, "there aren't police here, there aren't our parents here, adults here, and we are very clearly offending him." Being visibly armed in public operates not just to discourage dialogue but to ensure opponents register their own bodily vulnerability. As Nick explained, "at some level, when you see someone [armed] like that, even if they're willing to have a conversation, sometimes it's best for us to just step away, because we don't—I mean, again, like I said, I'm sure they would never use it on another person, but we honestly don't have a way of knowing."

CONCLUSION: ACTIVIST CAPACITIES IN RETROSPECT

This chapter has demonstrated that embodied experiences of activism, and the activist literacies that young people develop in a learning-by-doing approach, matter in enduring ways. They matter in individual lives and in local communities. As one organizer recalled, just before the march began in her

---

70. For further rhetorical scholarship that addresses the intractability of this divide, see Wilkes, Kreuter, and Skinnell, *Rhetoric and Guns*; and Williams, "Gun Control and Gun Rights."

71. Laura Collins has argued that among proponents of "unrestricted" interpretations of the Second Amendment, carrying a firearm is represented as an "inscribed, inarguable, and unshakeable part" of their identities; consequently, any action that restricts their behaviors—such as any prohibition against openly carrying a firearm in a public location—reinforces that identity as "vulnerable to marginalization and discrimination." See Laura Collins, "Second Amendment as Demanding Subject," 746.

community, "we walked up [to] this spot overlooking the whole crowd" and saw "just a sea" of people. Before this moment, she "had no idea how many people were there," so "to look out and literally see all of Government Plaza out and to the sidewalks and spilling out. We really filled the full space out and there wasn't any question of, oh, four people came." The realization that the space was entirely full of supporters caused this organizer to, in her words, "melt to the ground and start crying" because she found this experience so overwhelming: "it's insane to me that you do this and you put in the work . . . your friends and you have been through this and you look out and people have come and people are excited." As my interviews with peace activists in chapter 1 showed, such embodied experiences remain memorable and vivid across long spans of time. For this activist, the experience of having created a public opportunity for thousands of people from her community to speak in support of gun violence prevention had already prompted ongoing and sustained activist work over the years since this event.

Such experiences are connected to transformations in identity and capacity, and although the participants I spoke with should not be taken as representative, it is no stretch to say that the experiences they recounted have likely been enacted, to differing degrees, in hundreds of towns and cities across the United States. Furthermore, the activist experiences that my participants recounted center on *creating embodied experiences* for others. That is, organizing a march differs from marching; registering others to vote differs from voting, requiring different commitments and developing different capacities. Instead, the organizing, communicating, and organization-building strategies recounted above operate across longer durations. These practices aim to create embodied experiences for others, amplifying others' capacities and working to create sustainable structures over the long term that will enable others to experience similar transformations.

The enduring, embodied capacities for communicating and organizing that my participants' experiences generated belie the constrained framing of "success" and "failure" that so obsessed media coverage of the 2018 march. Perhaps a focus on the success or failure of any social movement or protest is typical. Nevertheless, media preoccupation with diagnosing whether this particular activism represented a "moment" or a "movement" has likely been heightened by pervasive attitudes about youth as in need of guidance, as focused on momentary feelings rather than invested in the long work of social change, and as unlikely to maintain focus long enough to be effective.[72] In framing youth activism along these overdetermined lines, media predict,

---

72. Applegarth, "News That Isn't New."

for instance, that young people will fail to vote in midterm elections and thus fail to engage in the most recognizable form of civic behavior, which is treated reductively as *the* mark of political agency.[73] These dismissive attitudes toward young people's activism make it even more crucial that we develop alternative frameworks for considering activism's impacts and effects. The learning-by-doing approach that my participants emphasized highlights ongoing, unpredictable uses and flexible, embodied capacities, rather than overdetermined narratives that frame teens as passionate but too focused on their short-term feelings to sustain a movement over the long haul.

Considering reflection as a site of agency allows scholars to attend more carefully to the embodied and enduring experiences recounted by those who have undertaken this organizing work. Activists' reflections—their efforts to make sense of their collective labors, both in the near and long term—counteract narrow assessments of success or failure. Reflexive agency designates embodied capacities, rooted in shifting perspectives and oriented toward undetermined future uses; in reflection, the activists I spoke with have expanded their strategy of disruption, extending it across months and years in which they labor to cultivate new ways of being. By considering what these participants understand as most significant about their activism, researchers can take steps toward treating young people as agents—assuming their rhetorical agency rather than searching relentlessly for signs of their success or failure—and can thus, in Taft's words, "engage kids as citizens-in-the-present rather than citizens-in-the-making."[74] As Marilyn Cooper has argued, agency is not a characteristic but a relationship among agents, broadly construed. Because change is a given—it is the perpetual state of the universe, in which "everything is made new in every moment"—writers, speakers, and activists can direct change by seeking transformations that enable shared responsibility, counteract injustice, and pursue possibility.[75] Cooper's notion of an entangled mode of transformation offers an apt way of characterizing the experiences my participants recounted, in which their commitments to each other prompted them to develop new capacities, their commitments to self-education and vulnerability prompted them to strive toward meaningful cross-partisan exchange, and their commitments to action on gun violence prompted them to labor together toward creating durable institutions capable of sustaining activist work over time.

---

73. Flegenheimer and Bidgood, "Gun Control and Fall Elections"; and Peoples, "Political Force or Fad?"

74. Taft, *Kids Are In Charge*, 11.

75. Cooper, *Animal Who Writes*, 9.

CONCLUSION

Reflecting on Activism and Age

Throughout this book I have argued that childhood operates as a constraint, both facilitating and limiting rhetorical possibility for young people. *Child, adolescent, teen, youth*—these designate discursive formations that materially impact rhetors' available means; these terms likewise impose stability across widely varied, intersecting embodiments and shore up the crucial binary of child/adult. As a constraint in Keith Grant-Davie's sense—not merely an obstacle, but a feature of the rhetorical landscape that might be leveraged, mitigated, or otherwise managed—childhood is frequently rhetorically salient, impacting how audiences respond to or resist young rhetors' arguments and agency. Despite being rhetorically salient, both *childhood* as a construct and children as rhetors remain only minimally recognized in rhetorical scholarship and—more importantly—in the rhetorical landscape of public life.

It might seem that we are presently in a moment when young people are taken more seriously as rhetors than ever before: Greta Thunberg, for instance, was *Time* magazine's Person of the Year in 2019, and while young protestors filled the streets during the COP26 UN Climate Change Conference in Scotland in 2021 and the COP27 conference in Egypt in 2022, young people were not only outsiders but were invited observers and delegates as well. As childhood studies scholar Spyros Spyrou argues, "children's political intervention in the climate debate illustrates to the world what childhood studies has been arguing for years, most notably that children, far from being passive and naïve, are knowledgeable social actors who can, on occasion, also act as agents of change."[1] The case studies in this book both substantiate and belie Spyrou's affirmation. The pervasive associations that impact young people's rhetorical agency also leave their arguments vulnerable to adult rearticulations—as when post–Cold War child peace activists were dismissed as dupes and puppets manipulated by adults or when teens organizing in the aftermath of a deadly shooting were disparaged as "crisis actors" or depicted as engaging in a momentary outburst of passion rather than the measured, long-term strategy characteristic of adults. When the demands of young protestors are disdained as naïve or, as in the encounter between Dianne Feinstein and the Sunrise activists, dismissed on the grounds that "you didn't vote for me," the constraints that childhood poses for young people seeking to "act as agents of change," in Spyrou's phrase, are glaring.

Working against such forms of dismissal, the young activists whose rhetorics I have examined in the previous chapters operated strategically, employing the form of agency Krista Ratcliffe and Kyle Jensen describe as *personal*—a "capacity and willingness . . . to act, which creates an opportunity to be heard."[2] Their capacity and willingness to act should be evident, even as the assumptions and associations of *childhood* as a discursive formation limit many adults' willingness to listen when young people are speaking. Young activists made strategic use of amplification, spatial linkages, disclosure, and disruption as they sought to address resistant audiences and to influence public matters. Through amplification and spatial linkages, young peace activists formed a transnational collective and tried to use the strength of their tens of thousands of supporters to petition a resistant audience that did not recognize their standing—an audience that instead reframed their transnational reach as a mark of their outsider status. Through the practice of disclosure, young undocumented activists sought to transform their vulnerability to state violence into a matter of public concern, using storytelling to draw audiences closer to the embodied experiences of vulnerability that shaped their lives, families, and communities. And addressing the repetitive and racialized patterns in media coverage of gun violence and its victims, young gun reform advocates anticipated audience critiques and sought to disrupt routine patterns of response by staging events that would keep public attention trained on gun violence beyond the duration of a typical news cycle.

Young activists adopted these strategies to address the constraints shaping their rhetorical situations, including the limitations and affordances, both

---

1. Spyrou, "Children as Future-Makers," 3.
2. Ratcliffe and Jensen, *Rhetorical Listening in Action*, 55.

symbolic and material, that *childhood* conferred. The rhetorical activity I have traced in prior chapters simultaneously addresses and belies the widespread perception that children and youth lack rhetorical agency. As a discursive formation, a material barrier, and an embodied state, *childhood* impacts available means for these individuals and collectives—but the strategic activity they undertake to navigate around and through *childhood* underscores their fundamental rhetorical capacity. Taken together, these case studies should leave my readers convinced that age is consequential for rhetorical activity—not as a barrier to rhetorical analysis but as a discursively constituted form of embodied difference that, like race, gender, disability, and other dimensions of embodiment, impinge upon rhetorical situations broadly, not only when difference is glaring but when it is normalized and submerged as well. Like other forms of embodied difference, age is both a limitation and a resource for people using their capacity to think and act together to "address rhetorical problems," in Ratcliffe and Jensen's phrase.[3]

The case studies in this book offer a beginning, but further analysis is needed to consider the myriad ways in which childhood operates as a rhetorical constraint, and to investigate the strategic activity of collectives of young people who maneuver around and through childhood. In this conclusion, through brief consideration of additional contemporary examples of youth and child activism, I connect my arguments with potential directions for further research. My core argument—that *childhood* constrains and facilitates rhetorical possibility—leads me to further discussion of activism among Black youth, whose maneuverings around and through childhood require exceptional rhetorical dexterity. My methodological commitment—that scholars should seek young people's perspectives and analyses of their own rhetorical practices wherever possible—leads to further consideration of how scholars can operate conscientiously through the tropes of *listening* and *exchange*. And my theoretical contention—that reflection is a form of rhetorical agency rooted in embodied perspectives and oriented toward contingent future contexts—leads me to consider ways that scholars might anticipate reflexivity and the perspectival changes reflection generates. Pursuing intergenerational collaboration—a hard-won deviation from normalized practices of age-based dismissal—offers a challenging but potentially generative path through the thickets of contemporary rhetorical problems.

---

3. Ratcliffe and Jensen, *Rhetorical Listening in Action*, 14.

NAVIGATING INNOCENCE AND AGENCY
IN BLACK YOUTH ACTIVISM

As I outlined in the introduction, *childhood* is a deeply racialized construct, conferring to white children the protections of innocence while denying the status of "innocent" to Black children and other children of color. In the contemporary US, "the image of childhood as a time of safe, protected, and responsibility-free play is," as Jessica Taft reminds us, "a racialized and class-specific myth," one played out repeatedly with the direst of consequences in classrooms, public spaces, police encounters, juvenile courts, and elsewhere.[4] For Black families, who "dread the day when children go from innocents to threats in the eyes of a historically racist society," the stakes of Black youths' exclusion from "innocence" could not be higher—motivating, for instance, "the Talk" as a rhetorical commonplace and an intergenerational survival strategy.[5]

Navigating the racialized contours of "innocence" and "threat" has required young Black activists to operate with extraordinary rhetorical dexterity. The unequal vulnerabilities experienced by Black youth have sparked coordinated and multifaceted activism over the past decade. Although not all the activism coordinated through the framework of Black Lives Matter has been youth-led, numerous organizations and campaigns have emerged from or centered on young people's experiences. For instance, the Florida-based Dream Defenders began organizing youth in 2012 in response to the murder of seventeen-year-old Trayvon Martin. Their name echoing both Martin Luther King Jr.'s "I Have a Dream" speech and Langston Hughes's "Dream Deferred," they targeted the legal protections that shielded deadly racism from prosecution while endangering Black youth. They organized students to undertake a forty-mile march to Sanford, Florida, to mark the forty days that had passed without George Zimmerman being indicted; when Zimmerman was acquitted of Martin's murder in 2013, the Dream Defenders staged a high-profile occupation of the Florida State Capitol for thirty-one days in an effort to pressure then-Governor Rick Scott to convene a legislative session to pass

---

4. Taft, *Kids Are In Charge*, 11.

5. See Plourde and Thompson, "The Talk." As a "rite of passage" for many Black children, "the Talk" explains "how to behave in the presence of police to mitigate potential harm." Though the practice spans generations, racial justice protests in 2020 prompted renewed attention to "the Talk" as evidence not only of the disparate dangers of routine encounters with police but also of the emotional toll of such unequal vulnerabilities within Black families. As one parent explained, "Am I going to have a conversation with [my young son]? Does it upset me? Yes. But I want my kid to come home! If this is about whether [he] winds up in the hospital or winds up in the morgue, that is real. He has got to come home to me."

Trayvon's Law, which would rescind the state's stand-your-ground law and address the school-to-prison pipeline.[6] These young activists drew attention to the way that Zimmerman's actions—an adult white male pursuing a Black teenager and murdering him—cruelly invert the "protection" children are meant to be granted, and foregrounded how racial bias is enshrined in laws that instead "protect" Zimmerman from consequences. The Dream Defenders and other young activists drew on age as a rhetorical resource, affirming their identification with Trayvon—a regular kid, wearing a hoodie to get a snack in the rain—and translating that identification into action, refusing the conditions that imperil their lives.

In the decade since, many other collective actions have been spurred among Black youth through age-based identification and resistance. These actions contribute to the larger BLM strategy of "enact[ing] modes of freedom and equality that the dominant order . . . denies—above all, the freedom to engage in practices in which one steps outside of one's assigned roles," as political theorist Glenn Mackin has argued.[7] In the numerous high school walkouts that young people have coordinated—such as those that took place in 2014 after a grand jury declined to indict Darren Wilson in eighteen-year-old Michael Brown's murder, or in Minnesota following twenty-year-old Daunte Wright's murder in 2021—activists have leveraged the material constraints that require young people to attend school. Using the lever of compulsory attendance to generate media attention, school walkouts convert age-based constraints into opportunities for expressing their demands for change. Taking a knee during the National Anthem is another form of coordinated refusal that many young people have adopted as a strategy for registering dissent within the routine demands for compliance that students experience. When Colin Kaepernick's protest drew condemnation from then-President Trump in 2017, acts of solidarity among high school athletes and other youth garnered media attention. The action of taking a knee acquires different significance in relation to activists' age, as students are subject to locally varying policies that often curtail their rights to free speech and prohibit them from engaging in acts of protest.[8] And perceptions of young people as manipulated rather than agential—even when they face censure for their actions—persist. For instance, Naylah Williams, a seventeen-year-old Black cheerleader, described her motivations for

---

6. See Ransby, *Making All Black Lives Matter*, 34–37.

7. Mackin, "Black Lives Matter," 479.

8. See Valeriya Safronova and Joanna Nikas, "High School Students Explain Why They Protest Anthems and Pledges," *New York Times*, October 21, 2017, https://www.nytimes.com/2017/10/21/style/high-school-students-explain-why-they-protest-anthems-and-pledges.html.

kneeling (alone) during the national anthem at football games: she recounted learning about Kaepernick's protest and seeking to understand "Why did he do this? And what does it mean to him?" and having repeated conversations with her family about whether she should also take action to reflect her dissatisfaction with "social injustice, racial inequality, and police brutality."[9] Yet Williams's experiences of knowledge-formation and reasoned action are routinely disparaged as critics—including other teens—characterize young athletes who take a knee as "following a trend." As another teen explained, "the kids kneeling in high schools . . . probably don't really reason with what they're doing. They feel like it's cool to follow along."[10] Such instances foreground childhood and youth as simultaneously a source of rhetorical potential and a constraint that must be navigated; age may generate media attention but often shapes dismissive responses from audiences. Further research—in particular, more conversations with activists about their strategies—can help scholars grapple with the tactics young people adopt to leverage, mitigate, anticipate, forestall, and contest the age-based constraints they operate under.

LISTENING TO YOUTH CLIMATE ACTIVISTS

Instead of construing young activists as idealistic, naïve, or misguided, I suggest that audiences—including scholars—recognize the fundamental rhetoricity of young people. Following on such recognition, adults can seek forms of relation with young activists that counter the pervasive assumptions that childhood studies scholars have delineated, including the assumption that children should be excluded from both work and politics and the assumption that adults should hold more power than young people.[11] Recognizing the rhetoricity of young people is necessary if adult scholars and activists are to engage fruitfully with contemporary youth climate activism—a vibrant and dispersed global phenomenon that merits attention but also caution, as routine patterns of *speaking over* and *speaking for* imperil intergenerational coalition-building.

Associations between youth, climate, and activism have perhaps never been stronger or more frequently reiterated than they are at present. Yet responses to widespread climate activism continue to reveal adults' limited and limiting relations to children and young people. In particular, racialized and gendered constructs of age, innocence, threat, political power, and future

9. Safronova and Nikas.
10. Safronova and Nikas.
11. Taft, *Kids Are In Charge*, 4.

promise structure the ease with which white activists from the Global North are singled out as "leaders," "faces," and "voices" of global youth climate movements.[12] Contrary to such practices that elevate white activists to positions of outsized prominence, Black, Indigenous, and other young people of color represent the majority of youth climate activists globally, and their leadership contests the misrepresentations circulated through racialized (particularly Western and Global North-focused) media coverage. Youth climate activism is pervasive, expansively global, and deeply connected to local and regional circumstances, industries, and effects. Ugandan activist Vanessa Nakate, for instance, has worked to forestall biodiversity loss and deforestation in the Congo Basin rain forest, coordinating these efforts with other youth activists working to bring attention to drought-induced devastation within the Lake Chad basin; Nakate has leveraged her status as a highly visible activist to campaign against a proposed East African oil pipeline.[13] Mauritian activist Shaama Sandooyea held an underwater climate strike, circulating arresting underwater photographs to forward awareness of the effects of rising sea levels on "small island developing states" such as Mauritius.[14] Some activists work directly with corporations to create sustainability plans, trying to leverage their social media influence to change corporate behavior—a fraught endeavor, Mexican-Chilean activist Xiye Bastida explains, that creates a sense of "guilt" from the recognition that "everything is tied to fossil fuels in some way. . . . It's hard to be part of the solution without touching any of this."[15] Youth climate activism spans scales, from local tree-planting efforts to transnational collaborations that aim to establish climate policies; it takes the form of familiar street demonstrations and social media mobilizations as well as direct and disruptive action against industries. For instance, the Just Stop Oil campaign in the UK has used tactics such as activists gluing their hands to tanker trucks to prevent

---

12. For critiques of this practice, see Gaël Branchereau, "Greta Thunberg Puts Africa's Climate Activists in Media Spotlight," *Jakarta Post*, February 3, 2020, https://www.thejakartapost.com/life/2020/02/03/greta-thunberg-puts-africas-climate-activists-in-media-spotlight.html; Frazer-Carroll, "On Environmentalism"; and Taft, "Hopeful, Harmless, and Heroic." For instance, Ugandan activist Vanessa Nakate was cropped out of an Associated Press photograph of a climate summit in Davos, where Nakate was the only nonwhite and non-European representative among the five youth climate activists in the original photo. See Rafaely, "Cropped Out"; and Nakate, *Bigger Picture*.

13. See Nakate, *Bigger Picture*; and Vanessa Nakate, "This 900-Mile Crude Oil Pipeline Is a Bad Deal for My Country—and the World," *New York Times*, April 8, 2022, https://www.nytimes.com/2022/04/08/opinion/environment/east-africa-oil-pipeline.html.

14. Emily Chan, "'Listen to the Science': Mauritian Climate Activist Shaama Sandooyea on Why the Future of Her Island Is Under Threat," *Vogue*, March 8, 2022, https://www.vogue.com/article/mauritian-climate-activist-shaama-sandooyea.

15. Widdicombe, "How Xiye Bastida Became a Leader."

the distribution of oil—tactics that interviewers, speaking to twenty-year-old activist Miranda Whehelen, have called "childish" and "playground-ish."[16] As recent media studies scholars have shown, portrayals that focus on "perceived immature or childlike antics" help to "delegitimize" youth-led movements.[17] In a contemporary context where young people's urgent work to forestall climate catastrophe is everywhere in evidence, it is vital to engage young people's rhetorical agency differently—to avoid repeating the constraining, patronizing, and dismissive reactions of the past.

Young people's public arguments are also frequently minimized through forms of praise that eschew deep engagement with the substance of their ideas. Sociologist Jessica Taft has identified this phenomenon as "wowing"—a breathless wonder at the activism of young people that "effusively celebrate[s] the fact that youth are acting, but without meaningfully engaging with the content of young people's political ideas and actions."[18] As Taft argues, "wowing may celebrate children and youth, but it does not foster meaningful political and intellectual relationships across generations and thus impoverishes social movements themselves and limits our theoretical and empirical understanding of these movements."[19] Effusive but superficial engagement can be seen abundantly in media coverage of the Fridays for Future demonstrations, particularly when demonstrators are young, white, and polite.[20] As one of my interview participants reflected, the "rush to canonize" Greta Thunberg "so that she can be more quickly and thoroughly ignored" offers an example of this practice of evacuating and circumscribing young people's political and rhetorical power. "Wowing" lies on a continuum with related dismissals, as one among many "exceptionalizing" discourses.[21] For instance, scholars have noted how "young people's environmental activism becomes both spectacularized and compartmentalized—framed as inspiring leadership, but leadership whose impacts are ultimately hard to pin down."[22] Further exceptionalizing practices can be seen in media coverage and other adult responses that focus

---

16. Rebecca Cook, "GMB Hit with Ofcom Complaints after Richard Madeley Slammed 'Childish' Protester," *Mirror*, April 13, 2022, https://www.mirror.co.uk/tv/tv-news/gmb-hit-ofcom-complaints-after-26703271.

17. Mayes and Hartup, "News Coverage," 3; and Bergemann and Ossewaarde, "Youth Climate Activists," 267. See also Collins, "Great Games and Keeping It Cool."

18. Taft, "Is It Okay," 194.

19. Taft, 194.

20. Taft, "Hopeful, Harmless, and Heroic"; and Mayes and Hartup, "News Coverage." Of course, abundant media coverage of iconic figures such as Greta Thunberg has also been abusive and dismissive; for an overview of sexist, ageist, misogynistic, and ableist media coverage, see Murphy, "Speaking for the Youth," 201–3; and Keller, "This Is Oil Country."

21. Taft, "Hopeful, Harmless, and Heroic," 12.

22. Collins, "Great Games and Keeping It Cool," 336.

on the *fact* of young people engaging in activism, rather than the *substance* of their arguments and claims. Youth climate activists have responded strategically to coverage of their activism that frames it in exceptionalizing terms, responding to journalists' and politicians' praise by reiterating their demands for commitment to change; in the words of activist Sophie-Anne Read, "we're not asking for your admiration, we want your action."[23]

How can we operate differently? I offer *listening* and *exchange* as modes of scholarly response that build from our field's established practices and orient toward young people specifically. *Listening* in rhetorical studies largely references Krista Ratcliffe's transformative work in this area, where rhetorical listening names an orientation toward communicative exchange that strives to discern underlying logics that aid or impede communication across difference, operating from a location of "non-identification."[24] In line with her theorization of rhetorical listening, Ratcliffe articulates (and recuperates) the practice of "eavesdropping" as a trope that "may offer an effective rhetorical tactic: standing outside, in an uncomfortable spot, on the border of knowing and not knowing, granting others the inside position, listening to learn."[25] Alongside Ratcliffe's work, I draw from its uptakes in the form of queer rhetorical listening, which Timothy Oleksiak argues "embrace[s] the tension between this longing for kinship and the continuous transformations necessary for inventing meaningful responses."[26] Whether listening directly or, in Ratcliffe's formulation, practicing rhetorical eavesdropping by "purposely positioning oneself on the edge of one's own knowing so as to overhear and learn from others," adopting a stance of listening in relation to the rhetorical practices of children and young people diverges strongly from the postures adults typically assume. Indeed, instructing, advising, guiding, teaching, directing, informing, and ordering are far more typical rhetorical postures and practices for adults to take up in relation to the young people around them.

Listening to young people may take place when their rhetoricity is assumed rather than denied or held under suspicion. My thinking on the significance of listening to young people has been shaped not only by work within rhetorical studies but also by scholarship in childhood studies, where the political, world-making capacities of young people is largely taken as a given. In her recent essay, "Childhood Publics in Search of an Audience,"

23. Mayes and Hartup, "News Coverage," 18.

24. Oleksiak, "Queering Rhetorical Listening." See also Ratcliffe, *Rhetorical Listening*.

25. Ratcliffe, "Eavesdropping as Rhetorical Tactic," 90. See also Johnson, "From Rhetorical Eavesdropping to Rhetorical Foreplay," for a critique and queer uptake of Ratcliffe's formulation of eavesdropping.

26. Oleksiak, "Queering Rhetorical Listening."

Sevasti-Melissa Nolas contextualizes the attitude of surprise adopted by many adults in response to the urgency, organization, creativity, and intensity of young people's climate advocacy. This rhetorical activity can be met with surprise—itself another form of dismissal—largely because of adult practices of tuning out young people's expressions, denying that their worldviews are political, and casting their communication as *noise* rather than *discourse*. As she argues, "public reactions to the children's environmental movement . . . remind us that our practices of listening, both in person and when mediated, are rooted in the conditions of the present moment and continued figurations of children as both innocent and experienced, in need of protection and disciplining."[27] Listening, in Nolas's evocative framework, is a practice that makes demands on adults—in particular, the demand that adults reimagine ourselves as an audience.

Listening assumes the potential intelligibility of young people's sounds, seeks the political intelligibility of the visions they offer, and takes on the task of discerning meanings without overriding difference—aligning with the practices of deliberative empathy advocated by Shui-yin Sharon Yam.[28] Education scholar Carla Shalaby offers another example of listening in her ethnographic research on young children's experiences of disciplining and exclusion in elementary schools. Identifying "troublemakers" as those who act as their freedom demands within schooling situations that attempt to dehumanize them, Shalaby suggests that "the child who deviates, who refuses to behave like everybody else, may be telling us—loudly, visibly, and memorably—that the arrangements of our schools are harmful to human beings."[29] The noncompliance of young children can be understood, she argues, as "lessons in listening" that adults are largely not receptive to, because hearing these lessons disrupts the assumption of adult authority and the smooth operation of power.

As a secondary practice that follows upon listening, *exchange* denotes a form of reciprocal critical engagement that is, again, infrequently practiced between adults and young people. Jessica Taft models this practice in her essay, "Is It Okay to Critique Youth Activists?" Against the dismissive practice of "wowing," Taft advocates for generous and reciprocal critique between academic researchers and young people's movements. Critique, of course, does not always take reciprocal form, and certainly young activists are accustomed

---

27. Nolas, "Childhood Publics," 329. For an in-depth exploration of the disability implications of rhetoricity as it intersects with involuntarity, action, motion, and volition, see Yergeau, *Authoring Autism*.

28. Yam, *Inconvenient Strangers*.

29. Shalaby, *Troublemakers*, xxxix.

to adult responses that critique (or criticize) in order to reassert the superiority of adult experiences and perspectives. And dismissals operate in multiple ageist directions: young people, too, can disparage the experiences and perspectives of adults, as refrains such as "OK Boomer" foreground. But critique *can* be generative, generous, and reciprocal. By way of illustration, consider the contrast between two situations: on one hand, the feedback or critical response I offer to students in my writing class, which (however invitationally I might frame it) generally maintains rather than disrupts relations of power between student and professor; on the other hand, the feedback or critical response exchanged among members of my writing group positions multiple perspectives horizontally rather than hierarchically. When I provide critical response to a colleague, this is an act of generosity: of taking their work seriously, seeking to inhabit it, and offering my response to enable their further work. There is reciprocity built into our relationship, because members of my writing group in turn extend the generosity of their critique to my writing. Additionally, as anyone forming a new writing group has experienced, reciprocal exchange is not a given but an achievement, something cultivated over time through careful attention to relationships, through practices of listening, and through the development of mutuality in pursuit of shared ends.

This is the form of exchange that young activists deserve from adults—and indeed, that older activists deserve from their younger co-conspirators as well. But forms of intergenerational power-sharing must be laboriously cultivated, because they so fully counter assumptions of power. In the words of rhetorical scholar Jennifer Nish, "political and activist engagement are about more than public action; activism also involves building relationships. These relationships are part of how movements transform people and transform worlds."[30] The case studies in this book underscore how the formation of intergenerational relationships can contribute to the world-remaking possibilities of activism—and how those possibilities can be undermined by refusals to listen or engage in reciprocity across generational divides.

Cultivating opportunities for reciprocal exchange offers researchers an avenue for practicing a "kinship" model of children's agency, a model that foregrounds "negotiation, collaboration . . . and the scripted creation of space in between bodies and across perspectives of age."[31] Such an understanding of agency reaches across the binary separating *child* and *adult*: as Spyros Spyrou has argued, "children are not just beings but also becomings," which is to say, "they become different with time, and that realization does not and should

---

30. Nish, *Activist Literacies*, xiv.
31. Bernstein, "'You Do It!,'" 889. See also Gubar, "Hermeneutics of Recuperation."

not challenge their status as beings; they can be beings in their own right but beings who are in the process of change, not unlike the adults who are also in a constant process of becoming."[32] This fundamental orientation—that both adults and children are *beings* in a perpetual process of *becoming*—incorporates an awareness of time and its unfolding into our encounters across age. Operating from such an awareness, I argue in this project, expands our capacities for knowledge, action, reflection, and collaboration.

REFLECTING AGE AND AGENCY ACROSS TIME

Because *beings* are also *becomings,* researchers who speak directly with young activists should also resist instituting fixity and instead anticipate how reflection brings about perspectival changes. As Marilyn Cooper has argued, agents act, and by virtue of that action, they and their surrounding contexts undergo incessant change. Agency is not "scarce, rare" but "radically and inexorably common."[33] Reflexive agency, I suggest, represents an underresearched form of agency, a form that makes longer trajectories of influence visible, against the widespread insistence that activism reveal its impact in immediate and visible outcomes. If, as V. Jo Hsu has argued, reflection is fundamentally a practice of relationality, then reflexive agency foregrounds participants' efforts to generate new knowledge, narratives, explanations, and insights out of the relationships they articulate with their prior experiences.[34] Reflexive agency forms relations that reconfigure present and future possibilities. Developing this concept through interviews with activists twenty years, ten years, and a few months after their intense involvement in activism, the case study chapters reveal agency as enduring in embodied experiences, as rooted in changing perspectives, and as oriented toward uncertain future uses. Together, these chapters move between the enduring and the emerging: in reflection, participants formulate how past experiences endure, how urgency is generated in the present, and how capacities are developed for undetermined futures.

Further scholarship, by considering reflection and aging together, can foreground the intergenerational possibilities that reflexive agency generates. Reflexivity involves thinking about the self, revisiting prior experiences and understandings, contemplating the significance of actions and decisions, and

32. Spyrou, "Children as Future-Makers," 4.

33. Jeffrey Nealon, *Foucault beyond Foucault,* 105, 103, quoted in Cooper, *Animal Who Writes,* 128.

34. Hsu, "Reflection as Relationality."

anticipating future forms of significance and change—so I pause here to invite further engagement with the reflection undertaken by activists as they age.

One timely case for consideration can be seen through numerous interviews and essays published in 2022 by Kim Phuc Phan Thi,[35] an antiwar activist who, as a nine-year-old in 1972, was the subject of Nick Ut's Pulitzer Prize–winning photograph *The Terror of War*. On the fiftieth anniversary of the photo, Phan Thi participated in numerous media interviews, appeared on TV shows, published an opinion essay in the *New York Times*, and more. Across these events, Phan Thi recounts the loss of agency she experienced through becoming a symbol for others to use and exchange. In one interview, she explains that, as the image grew in fame, she "became a voice for propaganda . . . I [didn't] belong to me anymore" but was treated as a "war symbol for the state. . . . They did not want to listen to me."[36] Elsewhere she describes how she "sat through endless interviews with the press and meetings with royalty, prime ministers and other leaders, all of whom expected to find some meaning in that image and my experience. The child running down the street became a symbol of the horrors of war," while "the real person looked on from the shadows."[37] She recoiled from the exposure the photograph forced upon her—"I thought to myself, 'I am a little girl. I am naked. Why did he take that picture? Why didn't my parents protect me?'"—and felt that her role as a symbol of suffering overwhelmed her specificity as a person. Although the alienation Phan Thi describes is severe, her experience of being discounted as a speaker while being praised as a symbol is one likely to resonate with many young people launched into public life through activism or trauma in this way.

Through reflection, however, Phan Thi charts a transformation for herself from symbol to speaker. As she explains, she now gives media interviews because she wants to celebrate the transformations she has experienced: "I want everybody to celebrate my life, 50 years later. I am not a victim of war anymore. I am a survivor. I feel like 50 years ago, I was a victim of war but 50 years later, I [am now] a friend, a mother, a grandmother and a survivor

---

35. As she explains in her memoir, Kim Phuc is her given name, and Phan Thi is her surname. After years of living in the West, she now arranges her name Kim Phuc Phan Thi in accordance with Western naming conventions, though when she lived in Vietnam she went by Phan Thi Kim Phuc. See Phan Thi, *Fire Road*, 6.

36. Sylvia Thomson, "50 Years Later, 'Napalm Girl' Has Message for Children in Ukraine," CBC News, June 11, 2022, https://www.cbc.ca/news/world/50-napalm-girl-kim-phuc-ukraine-1.6484977.

37. Kim Phuc Phan Thi, "It's Been 50 Years: I Am Not 'Napalm Girl' Anymore," *New York Times*, June 6, 2022, https://www.nytimes.com/2022/06/06/opinion/kim-phuc-vietnam-napalm-girl-photograph.html.

calling out for peace."[38] In another interview, Phan Thi emphasizes the agency she has claimed for herself in relation to the image that circulated without her choosing when she was a child; determining to use her relationship to the photograph to forward her antiwar work, she explains, "that is *my choice*," to work with the image for peace.[39] Narrating shifts in her self-understanding over time, across multiple interviews, Phan Thi demonstrates how reflexive agency reaches into the past, carrying present and future orientations and implications. She writes that "photographs, by definition, capture a moment in time. But the surviving people in these photographs, especially the children, must somehow go on. We are not symbols. We are human. We must find work, people to love, communities to embrace, places to learn and to be nurtured."[40] Laying claim to her capacities for self-definition and action, Phan Thi's reflections extend my formulation of reflexive agency as embodied, perspectival, and future-oriented. The transformations she narrates across her interviews and essays are not, I would argue, merely the obligatory consequences of aging. Instead, these are outcomes of reflection, sponsored by public interest and undertaken through Phan Thi's determination to revisit and reconsider earlier experiences.

This project recuperates the significance of activism within the lives of those who undertake it, as they exercise strategic and reflexive agency across momentary contexts and longer durations. As activists age, they can be invited to reflect on earlier strategic decisions and to articulate how their strategic rhetorics reflect and transform self-understandings that also shift over time. The insights generated through case study analyses and retrospective interviews should reaffirm for both scholars and activists the value of diverse, embodied, and intergenerational perspectives as the grounds from which collectives can seek change.

---

38. Thomson, "50 Years Later."
39. "Kim Phuc Interview."
40. Phan Thi, "It's Been 50 Years."

Video Call and Face-to-Face Interview Questionnaire for Children's Peace Statue Project

SECTION 1: MEMORIES OF INVOLVEMENT WITH THE CHILDREN'S PEACE STATUE PROJECT

What are your strongest **memories** associated with the Children's Peace Statue Project?

When did you first learn about the project? When did you become involved? Do you recall how the project began?

What was your role in the project? What do you recall doing?

Do you recall working closely with any other particular students or adults? Whom?

What kinds of **writing** did you contribute to the project? Did you write for *The Crane* newsletter? Did you contribute to any press releases, flyers, or other kinds of writing?

Did you **speak publicly** about the project at any press conferences, churches, schools, libraries, or other venues?

What do you recall about these occasions?

What were your feelings about the project leading up to the dedication of the statue? After the dedication?

What seemed most important to you about your involvement with the project?

SECTION 2: LATER WRITING EXPERIENCES

Did your involvement with the project influence any of your later academic work, such as your decision about where to go to college or what to study in college?

Did your involvement with the project create any strong associations for you, either positive or negative, related to writing or public speaking? Related to activism or public advocacy?

Do you recall speaking with others about the project in the years after your involvement ended? When, and in what contexts, did you tell others about the project?

Do you see your involvement in the Children's Peace Statue Project playing any role in your schooling, work, hobbies, or other kinds of community involvement?

Do you see yourself now as an activist? As a writer? Did this experience play any role in these developing identities for you?

Individual Interview Questionnaire for Undocumented Activism

REFLECTION QUESTIONS FOR ADULT PARTICIPANTS

For adult participants who first engaged in activism as youth, I hope to learn about what matters to you most about your activist work as you look back on periods of sustained activist involvement, and what significance you identify for your activism within your own life and community.

Change over Time

- How has your participation in activism, or your relationship to your activist community, evolved over time?
- When you reflect back on your earlier experiences with activism, what has surprised you?
- In what ways have your feelings about or motivations for being involved in this activism changed?
- Has your earlier activist work led you to other kinds of activism?

Successes and Setbacks

- What have been your successes and accomplishments, big or small?
- What are you personally proud of in relation to your involvement with your activist community?
- What struggles, challenges, or setbacks have you experienced?

- Have there been any unexpected consequences of your involvement in this activism?

Current Work and Identifications

- What are your current goals for your organization or community? What are you working towards?
- What has been necessary to keep your activist community going over time?
- What is most important to you about your organization or your activist work now?
- Do you identify with the label "activist"? Or with "community organizer"? How about "writer" or "public speaker"? Do you identify with some other label?

Future Plans

- Do you see yourself participating in activism, whether formally or informally, in the future? With different organizations? As a leader or organizer? As a speaker or writer?
- Has anything in your experience as a young activist made you more or less inclined to participate in similar work in the future?

Advice

- What advice do you have for other young activists and organizers?
- What have you learned about activism, advocacy, and organizing that you'd like to pass along to others?
- What strategies do you feel have contributed to your successes?
- What would you say to skeptics who criticize activism among teens and youth?

Closing Thoughts

- What would you like to talk about that hasn't come up yet in our conversation?

Interview Questionnaire for March For Our Lives

What were some reasons you got involved in the March for Our Lives?

When did you first learn about the march? When did you become involved? Do you recall what or who prompted you to get involved?

What was your role in the march? What do you recall doing? Was there a particular structure for the group you were involved with, with tasks assigned to different people?

Do you recall working closely with any other particular students or adults? Whom?

Did you do any **writing** before, during, or after the march? Either personal writing that was meaningful to you, or public writing that you shared with others?

What genres did you write (journaling, letters to the editor, social media posts, posters, press releases, etc.)?

[If you have still have written materials related to your involvement, would you be willing to share any of these with me to include in my study?]

Had you written any of these genres before? In what contexts?

Did you **speak publicly** about the march beforehand? Did you speak during the march? Did you speak in any particular genres (speeches, chants, conversations with classmates, interviews with reporters, etc.)?

[Do you have any notes or recollection of what you said? If you have any recordings or anything written, would you be willing to share any of these with me to include in my study?]

Had you spoken publicly in any of these ways before? In what contexts?

Do you feel like any experiences from your formal schooling (class assignments, projects) or from your extracurricular activities (internships, sports, student council, theatre, etc.) prepared you to do any of this writing or public speaking?

Do you recall how others responded to your involvement in the demonstrations? How did your family respond? How did your friends respond? How did teachers or other adults respond?

Since the march, have you spoken or written publicly or on social media about your involvement? In what ways? What kind of response has this writing or speaking received from others?

What were your feelings leading up to the day of the demonstrations? What were your feelings during the March for Our Lives? Do you recall how you felt after the march was over?

What is the most important outcome for you personally to result from your involvement with the march? Though your involvement surely wasn't motivated by selfish reasons, do you feel you've gained anything especially important through this experience: new connections, new skills, new perspective, new career plans, etc.?

What do you think you'll take with you from this experience going forward?

Focus Group Questionnaire
for March For Our Lives

My initial interviews with MFOL activists focused on preparation: How did you know how to write and speak and organize a march? Now that we're a couple of years past those early events, I'm interested in your reflections about your activism and where you see it going.

As you think about these questions, think about the last couple of years, from the 2018 march itself and beyond.

1. What have you done (personally or collectively) that you're proud of?
2. What goals have you met? What have been your group's accomplishments, big or small?
3. What do you feel has been the most successful work you've done over the past couple of years?
4. What challenges have you experienced (personally or collectively) over the past couple of years of organizing and activism?
5. What difficulties have your group faced? Have there been any unexpected challenges?
6. What's been the hardest thing you've worked on over the past couple of years?
7. What are your current goals for your organization?

8. What are the smaller steps or benchmarks you're working toward?

9. What have you done to keep the organization going?

10. What have you brought to your work with March For Our Lives from your prior experiences with activism, advocacy, or organizing?

11. Have you drawn on prior experiences to do this work? If so, what experiences?

12. Has this work with March For Our Lives led you to other kinds of activism?

13. Do you see yourself participating in activism in the future? With different organizations? As a leader or organizer? As a speaker or writer?

14. Has anything in your experience with March For Our Lives made you more or less inclined to participate in similar advocacy work in the future?

15. What advice do you have for other activists and organizers?

16. What have you learned about activism, advocacy, and organizing that you'd like to pass along to others?

17. What strategies do you feel have led to your successes?

18. Do you identify with the label "activist"? Or with "community organizer"? How about "writer" or "public speaker"? Do you identify with some other label?

19. What would you say to skeptics who criticize activism among teens and youth?

20. What would you like to talk about that hasn't come up yet in our conversation?

BIBLIOGRAPHY

Abrego, Leisy J. "'I Can't Go to College Because I Don't Have Papers': Incorporation Patterns of Latino Undocumented Youth." *Latino Studies*, no. 4 (2006): 212–31.

Abrego, Leisy J., and Genevieve Negrón-Gonzales, eds. *We Are Not Dreamers: Undocumented Scholars Theorize Undocumented Life in the United States.* Duke University Press, 2020.

Anguiano, Claudia A., and Karma R. Chávez. "DREAMers' Discourse: Young Latina/o Immigrants and the Naturalization of the American Dream." In *Latina/o Discourse in Vernacular Spaces: Somos de una Voz?*, edited by Michelle A. Holling and Bernadette M. Calafell, 81–99. Lexington Books, 2011.

Anguiano, Claudia A., and Lourdes Gutiérrez Nájera. "Paradox of Performing Exceptionalism: Complicating the Deserving/Underserving Binary of Undocumented Youth Attending Elite Institutions." *Association of Mexican-American Educators Open Issue* 9, no. 2 (2015): 45–56.

Applegarth, Risa. "News That Isn't New: March for Our Lives and Media Mobilization of Historical Precedent." *Rhetoric Review* 39, no. 2 (March 2020): 159–73.

Ariès, Phillippe. *Centuries of Childhood: A Social History of Family Life.* Vintage, 1965.

Bent, Emily. "This Is Not Another Girl Power Story: Reading Emma González as a Public Feminist Intellectual." *Signs: Journal of Women in Culture and Society* 45, no. 4 (2020): 795–816.

Bergmann, Zoe, and Ringo Ossewaarde. "Youth Climate Activists Meet Environmental Governance: Ageist Depictions of the FFF Movement and Greta Thunberg in German Newspaper Coverage." *Journal of Multicultural Discourses* 15, no. 3 (2020): 267–90.

Bernstein, Mary, Jordan McMillan, and Elizabeth Charash. "Once in Parkland, a Year in Hartford, a Weekend in Chicago: Race and Resistance in the Gun Violence Prevention Movement." *Sociological Forum* 34, no. S1 (2019): 1153–73.

Bernstein, Robin. *Racial Innocence: Performing American Childhood from Slavery to Civil Rights.* New York University Press, 2011.

———. "'You Do It!': Going-to-Bed Books and the Scripts of Children's Literature." *PMLA* 135, no. 5 (2020): 877–94.

Blair, Carole, and Neil Michel. "Reproducing Civil Rights Tactics: The Rhetorical Performances of the Civil Rights Memorial." *Rhetoric Society Quarterly* 30, no. 2 (2000): 31–55.

Blake, Jamilia J., and Rebecca Epstein. *Listening to Black Women and Girls: Lived Experiences of Adultification Bias.* Georgetown Law Center on Poverty and Inequality, 2019.

Bowen, Lauren Marshall. "Age Identity and Literacy." *enculturation*, no. 31 (2020). https://enculturation.net/age_identity_and_literacy.

———. "Composing a Further Life: Introduction to the Special Issue." *Literacy in Composition Studies* 6, no. 2 (2018). https://licsjournal.org/index.php/LiCS/article/view/722/475.

Boyce, Geoffrey A., Sarah Launius, and Adam O. Aguirre. "Drawing the Line: Spatial Strategies of Community and Resistance in Post-SB1070 Arizona." *ACME: An International Journal for Critical Geographers* 18, no. 1 (2019): 187–216.

Boyce, Geoffrey Alan. "The Neoliberal Underpinnings of Prevention through Deterrence and the United States Government's Case against Geographer Scott Warren." *Journal of Latin American Geography* 18, no. 3 (2019): 192–201.

Brandt, Deborah. *Literacy in American Lives.* Cambridge University Press, 2001.

Brandzel, Amy L. *Against Citizenship: The Violence of the Normative.* University of Illinois Press, 2016.

Briggs, Laura. *Taking Children: A History of American Terror.* University of California Press, 2020.

Burman, Erica. "Between Identification and Subjectification: Affective Technologies of Expertise and Temporality in the Contemporary Cultural Representation of Gendered Childhoods." *Pedagogy, Culture, & Society* 20, no. 2 (2012): 295–315.

Butler, Judith. "Rethinking Vulnerability and Resistance." In *Vulnerability in Resistance,* edited by Leticia Sabsay, Zeynep Gambetti, and Judith Butler, 12–27. Duke University Press, 2016.

Chávez, Karma R. "Exploring the Defeat of Arizona's Marriage Amendment and the Specter of the Immigrant as Queer." *Southern Communication Journal* 74, no. 3 (2009): 314–24.

———. *Queer Migration Politics: Activist Rhetoric and Coalitional Possibilities.* University of Illinois Press, 2013.

Chávez, Karma R., and Hana Masri. "The Rhetoric of Family in the US Immigration Movement: A Queer Migration Analysis of the 2014 Central American Child Migrant 'Crisis.'" In *Queer and Trans Migrations: Dynamics of Illegalization, Detention, and Deportation,* edited by Eithne Luibhéid and Karma R. Chávez, 209–25. University of Illinois Press, 2020.

Cisneros, J. David. *The Border Crossed Us: Rhetorics of Borders, Citizenship, and Latina/o Identity.* University of Alabama Press, 2013.

———. "Looking 'Illegal': Affect, Rhetoric, and Performativity in Arizona's Senate Bill 1070." *Border Rhetorics: Citizenship and Identity on the U.S.-Mexico Frontier.* Edited by D. Robert DeChaine, 133–50. University of Alabama Press, 2012.

———. "(Re)Bordering the Civic Imaginary: Rhetoric, Hybridity, and Citizenship in *La Gran Marcha.*" *Quarterly Journal of Speech* 97, no. 1 (2011): 26–49.

Collins, Laura J. "The Second Amendment as Demanding Subject: Figuring the Marginalized Subject in Demands for an Unbridled Second Amendment." *Rhetoric and Public Affairs* 17, no. 4 (2014): 737–56.

Collins, Rebecca. "Great Games and Keeping It Cool: New Political, Social and Cultural Geographies of Young People's Environmental Activism." *Children's Geographies* 19, no. 3 (2021): 332–38.

Condon, Camy. "Kids Invited to Build a Dream." *The Crane* 1, no. 1 (1991): 1.

Conti, Meredith. "The Sound of Silence: A Viewer's Guide to Emma González's March for Our Lives Speech." *Theater Journal* 70, no. 4 (December 2018): E8–E11.

Cooper, Marilyn M. *The Animal Who Writes: A Posthumanist Composition.* University of Pittsburgh Press, 2019.

———. "Rhetorical Agency as Emergent and Enacted." *College Composition and Communication* 62, no. 3 (2011): 420–49.

Cortwright, David. "Los Alamos's Little War with Peace." *The Bulletin of the Atomic Scientists* 51, no. 2 (1995): 5–6.

Costanza-Chock, Sasha. *Out of the Shadows, Into the Streets! Transmedia Organizing and the Immigrant Rights Movement.* MIT Press, 2014.

Cox, Robert, and Christina R. Foust. "Social Movement Rhetoric." In *Sage Handbook of Rhetorical Studies,* edited by Andrea A. Lunsford, Kirt H. Wilson, and Rosa A. Eberly, 605–27. SAGE Publications, 2008.

Cryer, Daniel A. "The Good Man Shooting Well: Authoritarian Submission and Aggression in the 'Gun-Citizen.'" *Rhetoric Society Quarterly* 50, no. 4 (2020): 254–67.

"Dear Friends." Flyer, 1990. In private archive, courtesy of Camy Condon.

De Fina, Anna. "What Is Your Dream? Fashioning the Migrant Self." *Language and Communication,* no. 59 (2018): 42–52.

DeLuca, Kevin Michael. "Unruly Arguments: The Body Rhetoric of Earth First!, Act Up, and Queer Nation." *Argumentation and Advocacy* 36, no. 1 (1999): 9–21.

Diab, Kefaya. "The Rise of the Arab Spring through a Sense of Agency." *Rhetoric Society Quarterly* 51, no. 4 (2021): 261–75.

Edelman, Lee. *No Future: Queer Theory and the Death Drive.* Duke University Press, 2004.

Edgar, Amanda Nell, and Andre E. Johnson. *The Struggle over Black Lives Matter and All Lives Matter.* Lexington, 2018.

Elder, Glen H., Jr. "Time, Human Agency, and Social Change: Perspectives on the Life Course." *Social Psychology Quarterly* 57, no. 1 (1994): 4–15.

Enriquez, Laura E. "Multigenerational Punishment: Shared Experiences of Undocumented Status within Mixed-Status Families." *Journal of Marriage and Family* 77, no. 4 (2015): 939–53.

———. *Of Love and Papers: How Immigration Policy Affects Romance and Family.* University of California Press, 2020.

Enriquez, Laura E., Martha Morales Hernandez, and Annie Ro. "Deconstructing Immigrant Illegality: A Mixed-Methods Investigation of Stress and Health among Undocumented College Students." *Race and Social Problems,* 10, no. 3 (2018): 193–208.

Epstein, Rebecca, Jamilia J. Blake, and Thalia González. *Girlhood Interrupted: The Erasure of Black Girls' Childhood.* Georgetown Law Center on Poverty and Inequality, 2017.

Fahnestock, Jeanne. *Rhetorical Style: The Uses of Language in Persuasion.* Oxford University Press, 2011.

Feldman, Hannah R. "Activists as 'Alternative' Science Communicators: A Rhetorical Perspective on Youth Environmental Activism." *Journal of Science Communication* 19, no. 6 (2020): C07.

Field, Corinne T., and LaKisha Michelle Simmons, eds. *The Global History of Black Girlhood.* University of Illinois Press, 2022.

Fillieule, Olivier, and Erik Neveu. "Activists' Trajectories in Space and Time: An Introduction." In *Activists Forever? Long-Term Impacts of Political Activism,* edited by Olivier Fillieule and Erik Neveu, 1–36. Cambridge University Press, 2019.

Flores, Lisa A. *Deportable and Disposable: Public Rhetoric and the Making of the 'Illegal' Immigrant.* Penn State University Press, 2020.

Frazer-Carroll, Micha. "On Environmentalism, Whiteness and Activist Superstars." *Gal-Dem,* September 25, 2019.

Frost, Alanna. "Literacy Stewardship: Dakelh Women Composing Culture." *College Composition and Communication* 63, no. 1 (2011): 54–74.

Garber, Megan. "The Powerful Silence of March for Our Lives." *The Atlantic,* March 24, 2018.

García, Angela S. "Return to Sender? A Comparative Analysis of Immigrant Communities in 'Attrition through Enforcement' Destinations." *Ethnic and Racial Studies* 36, no. 11 (2013): 1849–70.

Gill-Peterson, Julian. "Implanting Plasticity into Sex and Trans/Gender: Animal and Child Metaphors in the History of Endocrinology." *Angelaki: Journal of the Theoretical Humanities* 22, no. 2 (2017): 47–60.

Gill-Peterson, Julian, Rebekah Sheldon, and Kathryn Bond Stockton. "What Is the Now, Even of Then?" *GLQ: A Journal of Lesbian and Gay Studies* 22, no. 4 (2016): 495–503.

Gonzalez, Roberto G., Kristina Brant, and Benjamin Roth. "DACAmented in the Age of Deportation: Navigating Spaces of Belonging and Vulnerability in Social and Personal Lives." *Ethnic and Racial Studies* 43, no. 1 (2020): 60–79.

González, X. "The Education of X González." *The Cut,* January 3, 2023. https://www.thecut.com/article/x-gonzalez-parkland-shooting-activist-essay.html.

González Ybarra, Mónica. "'Since When Have People Been Illegal?': Latinx Youth Reflections in *Nepantla.*" *Latino Studies* 16, no. 4 (2018): 503–23.

Grant-Davie, Keith. "Rhetorical Situations and Their Constituents." *Rhetoric Review* 15, no. 2 (1997): 264–79.

Gubar, Marah. "The Hermeneutics of Recuperation: What a Kinship-Model Approach to Children's Agency Could Do for Children's Literature and Childhood Studies." *Jeunesse: Young People, Texts, Cultures* 8, no. 1 (2016): 291–310.

———. "Risky Business: Talking about Children in Children's Literature Criticism." *Children's Literature Association Quarterly* 38, no. 4 (2013): 450–57.

Hallenbeck, Sarah. "Toward a Posthuman Perspective: Feminist Rhetorical Methodologies and Everyday Practices." *Advances in the History of Rhetoric* 15, no. 1 (2012): 9–27.

Hartelius, E. Johanna. "'Undocumented and Unafraid'? Challenging the Bureaucratic Paradigm." *Communication and Critical/Cultural Studies* 13, no. 2 (2016): 130–49.

Hawhee, Debra. "Bodily Pedagogies: Rhetoric, Athletics, and the Sophists' Three Rs." *College English* 65, no. 2 (2002): 142–62.

Heilker, Paul, and M. Remi Yergeau. "Autism and Rhetoric." *College English* 73, no. 5 (2011): 485–97.

Herndl, Carl G., and Adela C. Licona. "Shifting Agency: Agency, Kairos, and the Possibilities of Social Action." In *Communicative Practices in Workplaces and the Professions: Cultural Perspectives on the Regulation of Discourse and Organizations.* Edited by Mark Zachry and Charlotte Thralls, 133–54. Amityville: Baywood Press, 2007.

Hesford, Wendy S. *Spectacular Rhetorics: Human Rights Visions, Recognitions, Feminisms.* Duke University Press, 2011.

———. *Violent Exceptions: Children's Human Rights and Humanitarian Rhetorics.* The Ohio State University Press, 2021.

Hogan, J. Michael, and Craig Rood. "Rhetorical Studies and the Gun Debate: A Public Policy Perspective." *Rhetoric and Public Affairs* 18, no. 2 (2015): 359–72.

Hogan, Wesley C. *On the Freedom Side: How Five Decades of Youth Activists Have Remixed American History.* University of North Carolina Press, 2019.

Hogg, Charlotte, and Shari Stenberg. "Gathering Women's Rhetorics for the Twenty-first Century." In *Persuasive Acts: Women's Rhetorics in the Twenty-first Century,* edited by Charlotte Hogg and Shari Stenberg, 3–22. University of Pittsburgh Press, 2020.

Hsu, V. Jo. "Reflection as Relationality: Rhetorical Alliances and Teaching Alternative Rhetorics." *College Composition and Communication* 70, no. 2 (2018): 142–68.

Ingraham, Chris. *Gestures of Concern.* Duke University Press, 2020.

Jackson, Rachel, and Dorothy Whitehorse DeLaune. "Decolonizing Community Writing with Community Listening: Story, Transrhetorical Resistance, and Indigenous Cultural Literacy Activism." *Community Literacy Journal* 13, no. 1 (2019): 37–54.

Johnson, Gavin P. "From Rhetorical Eavesdropping to Rhetorical Foreplay: Orientations, Bodies in Spacetime, and the Emergence of a Queer Embodied Tactic." *Pre/Text* 24, nos. 1–4 (2018): 119–38.

"Judging To Be Held." Flyer. In private archive, courtesy of Camy Condon.

Kafer, Alison. *Feminist, Queer, Crip.* Indiana University Press, 2013.

Keller, Jessalynn. "'This Is Oil Country': Mediated Transnational Girlhood, Greta Thunberg, and Patriarchal Petrocultures." *Feminist Media Studies* 21, no. 4 (2021): 682–86.

"Kim Phuc Interview." *The 700 Club Canada.* YouTube. November 10, 2017.

King, Wilma. *Stolen Childhood: Slave Youth in Nineteenth-Century America.* 2nd ed. Indiana University Press, 2011.

Kynard, Carmen. *Vernacular Insurrections: Race, Black Protest, and the New Century in Composition-Literacies Studies.* State University of New York Press, 2013.

Lathan, Rhea Estelle. *Freedom Writing: African American Civil Rights Literacy Activism, 1955–1967.* National Council of Teachers of English, 2015.

Latour, Bruno. "Technology Is Society Made Durable." *Sociological Review* 38, no. S1 (1990): 103–31.

Lesko, Nancy. *Act Your Age! A Cultural Construction of Adolescence.* Routledge, 2001.

Levander, Caroline F., and Carol J. Singley, eds. *The American Child: A Cultural Studies Reader.* Rutgers University Press, 2003.

Library Board. Letter to Los Alamos County Council. *Council Regular Session Meeting.* 21 November 1994. Meeting Documentation.

López, Gustavo, and Jens Manuel Krogstad. "Key Facts about Unauthorized Immigrants Enrolled in DACA." *Pew Research Center,* September 25, 2017.

Mackin, Glenn. "Black Lives Matter and the Concept of the Counterworld." *Philosophy and Rhetoric* 49, no. 4 (2016): 459–81.

Marback, Richard. "Unclenching the Fist: Embodying Rhetoric and Giving Objects Their Due." *Rhetoric Society Quarterly* 38, no. 1 (2008): 46–65.

Mateo, Lizbeth, Mohammad Abdollahi, Yahaira Carrillo, Tania Unzueta, and Raúl Alcaraz. "The McCain Five: DREAM Act Students Submit to Arrest for the First Time in History." In Wong et al., *Undocumented and Unafraid,* 68–70.

Mayes, Eve, and Michael Everitt Hartup. "News Coverage of the School Strike for Climate Movement in Australia: The Politics of Representing Young Strikers' Emotions." *Journal of Youth Studies* 25, no. 7 (2022): 994–1016.

McKinnon, Sara L., Robert Asen, Karma R. Chávez, and Robert Glenn Howard. "Articulating Text and Field in the Nodes of Rhetorical Scholarship." In *Text + Field: Innovations in Rhetorical Method,* edited by Sara L. McKinnon, Robert Asen, Karma R. Chávez, and Robert Glenn Howard, 1–21. Pennsylvania State University Press, 2016.

McKoy, Temptaous. "Y'All Call It Technical and Professional Communication, We Call It #ForTheCulture: The Use of Amplification Rhetorics in Black Communities and Their Implications for Technical and Professional Communication Studies." PhD diss., East Carolina University, 2019.

Meiners, Erica R. *For the Children? Protecting Innocence in a Carceral State.* University of Minnesota Press, 2016.

Menjívar, Cecelia, and Leisy Abrego. "Legal Violence: Immigration Law and the Lives of Central American Immigrants." *American Journal of Sociology* 117, no. 5 (2012): 1380–421.

Miller, Carolyn R. "What Can Automation Tell Us about Agency?" *Rhetoric Society Quarterly* 37, no. 2 (2007): 137–57.

Moeller, Susan. "A Hierarchy of Innocence: The Media's Use of Children in the Telling of International News." *The International Journal of Press/Politics* 7, no. 1 (2002): 36–56.

Murphy, Patrick D. "Speaking for the Youth, Speaking for the Planet: Greta Thunberg and the Representational Politics of Eco-Celebrity." *Popular Communication* 19, no. 3 (2021): 193–206.

Nakate, Vanessa. *A Bigger Picture: My Fight to Bring a New African Voice to the Climate Crisis.* Harper Collins, 2021.

Nicholls, Walter J. *The DREAMers: How the Undocumented Youth Movement Transformed the Immigrant Rights Debate.* Stanford University Press, 2013.

Nish, Jennifer. *Activist Literacies: Transnational Feminisms and Social Media Rhetorics.* University of South Carolina Press, 2022.

Nolas, Sevasti-Melissa. "Childhood Publics in Search of an Audience: Reflections on the Children's Environmental Movement." *Children's Geographies* 19, no. 3 (2021): 324–31.

Nolas, Sevasti-Melissa, Christos Varvantakis, and Vinnarasan Aruldoss. "(Im)possible Conversations? Activism, Childhood, and Everyday Life." *Journal of Social and Political Psychology* 4, no. 1 (2016): 252–65.

Oleksiak, Timothy. "Queering Rhetorical Listening: An Introduction to a Cluster Conversation." *Peitho: Journal of the Coalition of Feminist Scholars in the History of Rhetoric and Composition* 23, no. 1 (2020). https://cfshrc.org/article/queering-rhetorical-listening-an-introduction-to-a-cluster-conversation/.

On Wings of Peace. Video of Children's Peace Statue Presentation at the Los Alamos County Council Meeting, November 16, 1992. Transcript. In private archive, courtesy of Camy Condon.

Organized Communities Against Deportation. "About Us." 2020. https://www.organizedcommunities.org/about.

"Overview of Undocumented Immigrants." *Immigrants Rising.* Updated September 2022. https://immigrantsrising.org/wp-content/uploads/Immigrants-Rising_Overview-of-Undocumented-Students.pdf.

Pacheco, Gaby. "Trail of Dreams: A Fifteen-Hundred-Mile Journey to the Nation's Capital." In Wong et al., *Undocumented and Unafraid,* 56–58.

Phan Thi, Kim Phuc. *Fire Road: The Napalm Girl's Journey through the Horrors of War to Faith, Forgiveness, and Peace.* Tyndale, 2017.

Plourde, Arienne Thompson, and Amelia Thompson. "The Talk: Surviving Police Encounters While Black." *Notre Dame Magazine,* Winter 2016–17. https://www.utne.com/community/police-racial-discrimination-zm0z17uzcwil/.

Portnoy, Alisse Theodore. "'A Right to Speak on the Subject': The U.S. Women's Antiremoval Petition Campaign, 1829–1831." *Rhetoric and Public Affairs* 5, no. 4 (2002): 601–24.

Prendergast, Catherine. "On the Rhetorics of Mental Disability." In *Embodied Rhetorics: Disability in Language and Culture,* edited by James C. Wilson and Cynthia Lewiecki-Wilson, 45–60. Southern Illinois University Press, 2001.

Preston, Stirling. "David Hogg Claims NRA Would Be OK with Children's Blood on Their Faces." *Minority Report* (blog), March 23, 2018.

Price, Margaret. *Mad At School: Rhetorics of Mental Disability and Academic Life.* University of Michigan Press, 2011.

Pritchard, Eric Darnell. *Fashioning Lives: Black Queers and the Politics of Literacy.* Southern Illinois University Press, 2016.

Puente AZ. "SB1070: Honoring a Decade of Resistance." https://puenteaz.org/sb1070/.

Quinsaat, Sharon. "Competing News Frames and Hegemonic Discourses in the Construction of Contemporary Immigration and Immigrants in the United States." *Mass Communication and Society* 17, no. 4 (2014): 573–96.

Raby, Rebecca. "Children's Participation as Neo-Liberal Governance?" *Discourse: Studies in the Cultural Politics of Education* 35, no. 1 (2014): 77–89.

Raby, Rebecca, and Lindsay C. Sheppard. "Constructs of Childhood, Generation and Heroism in Editorials on Young People's Climate Change Activism: Their Mobilisation and Effects." *Children & Society* 35, no. 3 (2021): 380–94.

Rafaely, Daniella. "'Cropped Out': The Collaborative Production of an Accusation of Racism." *Discourse Studies* 23, no. 3 (2021): 324–38.

Rai, Candice, and Caroline Gottschalk Druschke. "On Being There: An Introduction to Studying Rhetoric in the Field." In *Field Rhetoric: Ethnography, Ecology, and Engagement in the Places of Persuasion,* edited by Candice Rai and Caroline Gottschalk Druschke, 1–21. University of Alabama Press, 2018.

Rand, Erin J. "PROTECTing the Figure of Innocence: Child Pornography Legislation and the Queerness of Childhood." *Quarterly Journal of Speech* 105, no. 3 (2019): 251–72.

Randall, Liam C. "Consent as Rhetorical Ability in 'The Strange Case of Anna Stubblefield.'" *Rhetoric Society Quarterly* 51, no. 5 (2021): 377–91.

Ransby, Barbara. *Making All Black Lives Matter: Reimagining Freedom in the Twenty-First Century.* University of California Press, 2018.

Ratcliffe, Krista. "Eavesdropping as Rhetorical Tactic: History, Whiteness, and Rhetoric." *JAC* 20, no. 1 (2000): 87–119.

———. *Rhetorical Listening: Identification, Gender, Whiteness.* Southern Illinois University Press, 2005.

Ratcliffe, Krista, and Kyle Jensen. *Rhetorical Listening in Action: A Concept-Tactic Approach.* Parlor Press, 2022.

Ribero, Ana Mileno. "'Papá, Mamá, I'm Coming Home': Family, Home, and the Neoliberal Immigrant Nation in the National Immigrant Youth Alliance's 'Bring Them Home' Campaign." *Rhetoric Review* 37, no. 3 (2018): 273–85.

Richardson, Elaine, and Alice Ragland. "#StayWoke: The Language and Literacies of the #BlackLivesMatter Movement." *Community Literacy Journal* 12, no. 2 (2018): 27–56.

Ríos, Gabriela Raquel. "Cultivating Land-Based Literacies and Rhetorics." *Literacy in Composition Studies* 3, no. 1 (2015): 60–70.

Rix Wood, Henrietta. *Praising Girls: The Rhetoric of Young Women, 1895–1930.* Southern Illinois University Press, 2016.

Rodriguez, Jesús A. "The Supreme Court Case That Created the 'Dreamer' Narrative." *Politico Magazine,* October 31, 2021.

Rood, Craig. *After Gun Violence: Deliberation and Memory in an Age of Political Gridlock.* Penn State University Press, 2019.

———. "Protection Narratives and the Problem of Gun Suicide." *Rhetoric and Public Affairs* 25, no. 2 (2022): 29–56.

Roth, Benjamin. "The Double Bind of DACA: Exploring the Legal Violence of Liminal Status for Undocumented Youth." *Ethnic and Racial Studies* 42, no. 15 (2019): 2548–65.

Ryder, Phyllis Mentzell. "Beyond Critique: Global Activism and the Case of Malala Yousafzai." *Literacy in Composition Studies* 3, no. 1 (2015): 175–87.

Samuels, Ellen. "Six Ways of Looking at Crip Time." *Disability Studies Quarterly* 37, no. 3 (2017). https://dsq-sds.org/index.php/dsq/article/view/5824/4684.

Sánchez-Eppler, Karen. *Dependent States: The Child's Part in Nineteenth-Century American Culture.* University of Chicago Press, 2005.

Shalaby, Carla. *Troublemakers: Lessons in Freedom from Young Children at School.* The New Press, 2017.

Sigona, Nando. "'I Have Too Much Baggage': The Impacts of Legal Status on the Social Worlds of Irregular Migrants." *Social Anthropology* 20, no. 1 (2012): 50–65.

Simons, Herbert W. "Requirements, Problems, and Strategies: A Theory of Persuasion for Social Movements." *Quarterly Journal of Speech,* no. 56 (1970): 1–11.

Sirriyeh, Ala. "'Dreamers,' (Un)Deserving Immigrants, and Generational Interdependence." *Population, Space, and Place,* no. 26 (2020): 1–10.

Spyrou, Spyros. "Children as Future-Makers." *Childhood* 27, no. 1 (2020): 3–7.

Squires, Catherine R. Introduction to *Dangerous Discourses: Feminism, Gun Violence, and Civic Life,* xv–xxv. Edited by Catherine R. Squires. Peter Lang, 2016.

Stabile, Carol A., and Bryce Peake. "Coverage That Kills: Misogyny, 'Mass Shootings,' and the Masculine Economy of the U.S. News Cycle." In *Dangerous Discourses: Feminism, Gun Violence, and Civic Life,* edited by Catherine R. Squires, 3–26. Peter Lang, 2016.

Stockton, Kathryn Bond. *The Queer Child, or Growing Sideways in the Twentieth Century.* Duke University Press, 2009.

Swacha, Kathryn Yankura. "Older Adults as Rhetorical Agents: A Rhetorical Critique of Metaphors for Aging in Public Health Discourse." *Rhetoric Review* 36, no. 1 (2017): 60–72.

Taft, Jessica K. "Hopeful, Harmless, and Heroic: Figuring the Girl Activist as Global Savior." *Girlhood Studies* 13, no. 2 (2020): 1–17.

———. "Is It Okay to Critique Youth Activists? Notes on the Power and Danger of Complexity." In *Children and Youth as Subjects, Objects, Agents: Innovative Approaches to Research across Space and Time,* edited by Deborah Levison, Mary Jo Maynes, and Frances Vavrus, 193–207. Palgrave Macmillan, 2021.

———. *The Kids Are In Charge: Activism and Power in Peru's Movement of Working Children.* New York University Press, 2019.

———. "Teenage Girls' Narratives of Becoming Activists." *Contemporary Social Science* 12, no. 1–2 (2017): 27–39.

Teodoro, Renata. "Following the Civil Rights Trail: My Pilgrimage to the South." In Wong et al., *Undocumented and Unafraid,* 59–62.

Thorne, Barrie. "'Childhood': Changing and Dissonant Meanings." *International Journal of Learning and Media 1,* no. 1 (2009): 19–27.

———. "Crafting the Interdisciplinary Field of Childhood Studies." *Childhood* 14, no. 2 (2007): 147–52.

Ticktin, Miriam. "A World Without Innocence." *American Ethnologist* 44, no. 4 (2017): 577–90.

"Tomorrow's Child." Flyer. 1992. In private archive, courtesy of Camy Condon.

Unzueta Carrasco, Ireri. "Coming Out of the Shadows." In Wong et al., *Undocumented and Unafraid,* 65–67.

Unzueta Carrasco, Tania, and Hilda Seif. "Disrupting the Dream: Undocumented Youth Reframe Citizenship and Deportability through Anti-Deportation Activism." *Latino Studies* 12, no. 2 (2014): 279–99.

Uthappa, N. Renuka. "Moving Closer: Speakers with Mental Disabilities, Deep Disclosure, and Agency through Vulnerability." *Rhetoric Review* 36, no. 2 (2017): 164–75.

Valentín-Cortés, Mislael, Quetzabel Benavides, Richard Bryce, Ellen Rabinowitz, Raymond Rion, William D. Lopez, and Paul J. Fleming. "Application of the Minority Stress Theory: Understanding the Mental Health of Undocumented Latinx Immigrants." *American Journal of Community Psychology* 66, nos. 3–4 (2020): 325–36.

Wan, Amy J. *Producing Good Citizens: Literacy Training in Anxious Times.* University of Pittsburgh Press, 2014.

Webster, Crystal Lynn. *Beyond the Boundaries of Childhood: African American Children in the Antebellum North.* University of North Carolina Press, 2021.

———. "The History of Black Girls and the Field of Black Girlhood Studies: At the Forefront of Academic Scholarship." *American Historian* 38 (2020). https://www.oah.org/tah/the-history-of-girlhood/the-history-of-black-girls-and-the-field-of-black-girlhood-studies-at-the-forefront-of-academic/.

Widdicombe, Lizzie. "How Xiye Bastida Became a Leader in the Climate Fight." *Vogue,* December 27, 2021.

Wilkerson, Abby. "Disability, Sex Radicalism, and Political Agency." *NWSA Journal* 14, no. 3 (2002): 33–57.

Wilkes, Lydia, Nate Kreuter, and Ryan Skinnell, eds. *Rhetoric and Guns.* Utah State University Press, 2022.

Williams, Miriam F. "Gun Control and Gun Rights: A Conceptual Framework for Analyzing Public Policy Issues in Technical and Professional Communication." *Technical Communication Quarterly* 31, no. 1 (2022): 33–43.

Winslow, Luke, and Eli Mangold. "Theorizing Rhetorical Children." *Western Journal of Communication* 87, no. 1 (2023): 86–105.

Wong, Kent, Janna Shadduck-Hernández, Fabiola Inzunza, Julie Monroe, Victor Narro, and Abel Valenzuela Jr., eds. *Undocumented and Unafraid: Tam Tran, Cinthya Felix, and the Immigrant Youth Movement.* UCLA Center for Labor Research and Education, 2012.

Yam, Shui-yin Sharon. *Inconvenient Strangers: Transnational Subjects and the Politics of Citizenship.* The Ohio State University Press, 2019.

Yergeau, M. Remi. *Authoring Autism: On Rhetoric and Neurological Queerness.* Duke University Press, 2017.

Zaeske, Susan. "Signatures of Citizenship: The Rhetoric of Women's Antislavery Petitions." *Quarterly Journal of Speech* 88, no. 2 (2002): 147–68.

Zimmerman, Arely. "Transmedia Testimonio: Examining Undocumented Youth's Political Activism in the Digital Age." *International Journal of Communication*, no. 10 (2016): 1886–906.

Zoller, Heather M., and Diana Casteel. "#March for Our Lives: Health Activism, Diagnostic Framing, Gun Control, and the Gun Industry." *Health Communication* 37, no. 7 (2022): 813–23.

Zong, Jie, and Jeanne Batalova. "How Many Unauthorized Immigrants Graduate from U.S. High Schools Annually?" Migration Policy Institute, April 2019. https://www.migrationpolicy.org/research/unauthorized-immigrants-graduate-us-high-schools#:~:text=Using%20this%20dataset%20and%20applying,U.S.%20high%20schools%20every%20year.

INDEX